HIGHER MUSIC EDUCATION AND EMPLOYABILITY IN A NEOLIBERAL WORLD

Also Available from Bloomsbury

A Framework for Teaching Music Online, Carol Johnson

Education, Music, and the Lives of Undergraduates, Roger Mantie and Brent C. Talbot

Activating Diverse Musical Creativities, edited by Pamela Burnard and Elizabeth Haddon

The Bloomsbury Handbook of Popular Music Education, edited by Zack Moir, Bryan Powell and Gareth Dylan Smith

Mastering Primary Music, Ruth Atkinson

Music Education with Digital Technology, edited by John Finney

The Origins and Foundations of Music Education, 2nd edition, edited by Gordon Cox and Robin Stevens

HIGHER MUSIC EDUCATION AND EMPLOYABILITY IN A NEOLIBERAL WORLD

Edited by
Rainer Prokop and Rosa Reitsamer

BLOOMSBURY ACADEMIC
LONDON • NEW YORK • OXFORD • NEW DELHI • SYDNEY

BLOOMSBURY ACADEMIC
Bloomsbury Publishing Plc, 50 Bedford Square, London, WC1B 3DP, UK
Bloomsbury Publishing Inc, 1359 Broadway, New York, NY 10018, USA
Bloomsbury Publishing Ireland, 29 Earlsfort Terrace, Dublin 2, D02 AY28, Ireland

BLOOMSBURY, BLOOMSBURY ACADEMIC and the Diana logo are
trademarks of Bloomsbury Publishing Plc

First published in Great Britain 2024
This paperback edition published in 2026

Copyright © Rainer Prokop and Rosa Reitsamer, 2024

Rainer Prokop and Rosa Reitsamer have asserted their right under the Copyright,
Designs and Patents Act, 1988, to be identified as Editors of this work.

For legal purposes the Acknowledgements on p. xvi constitute an extension of this copyright page.

Cover image © Mauro Rodrigues / Alamy Stock Photo

This work is published open access subject to a Creative Commons Attribution-NonCommercial-NoDerivatives 4.0 International licence (CC BY-NC-ND 4.0, https://creativecommons.org/licenses/by-nc-nd/4.0/). You may re-use, distribute, and reproduce this work in any medium for non-commercial purposes, provided you give attribution to the copyright holder and the publisher and provide a link to the Creative Commons licence.

Bloomsbury Publishing Plc does not have any control over, or responsibility for, any third-party websites referred to or in this book. All internet addresses given in this book were correct at the time of going to press. The author and publisher regret any inconvenience caused if addresses have changed or sites have ceased to exist, but can accept no responsibility for any such changes.

A catalogue record for this book is available from the British Library.

Library of Congress Cataloging-in-Publication Data

Names: Prokop, Rainer, editor. | Reitsamer, Rosa, editor.
Title: Higher music education and employability in a neoliberal world / edited by Rainer Prokop and Rosa Reitsamer.
Description: [1.] | London; New York: Bloomsbury Academic, 2024. | Includes bibliographical references and index. | Summary: "This open access book offers international and interdisciplinary insights into the learning cultures, curricula designs and emancipatory initiatives within higher music education institutions. Drawing together empirical case studies from Austria, France, Germany, Italy, the Netherlands, Portugal, Switzerland, the UK and the USA, the contributors look at the discourses surrounding employability and artistic standards that form the traditional foundation of conservatoire education. They also examine how gender, class and race/ethnicity pervade the creation and performance of music. The ebook editions of this book are available open access under a CC BY-NCND 4.0 licence on bloomsburycollections.com. Open access was funded by University of Music and Performing Arts Vienna"– Provided by publisher.
Identifiers: LCCN 2023051420 (print) | LCCN 2023051421 (ebook) | ISBN 9781350266957 (hardback) | ISBN 9781350266964 (paperback) | ISBN 9781350266988 (epub) | ISBN 9781350266971 (ebook)
Subjects: LCSH: Musicians–Economic conditions. | Employability. | Music–Instruction and study. | Education, Higher. | Neoliberalism.
Classification: LCC ML3795 .H63 2024 (print) | LCC ML3795 (ebook) | DDC 331.11/9178–dc23/eng/20240102
LC record available at https://lccn.loc.gov/2023051420
LC ebook record available at https://lccn.loc.gov/2023051421

ISBN: HB: 978-1-3502-6695-7
PB: 978-1-3502-6696-4
ePDF: 978-1-3502-6697-1
eBook: 978-1-3502-6698-8

Typeset by Deanta Global Publishing Services, Chennai, India

For product safety related questions contact productsafety@bloomsbury.com.

To find out more about our authors and books visit www.bloomsbury.com and
sign up for our newsletters.

Contents

List of Figures	viii
List of Tables	ix
List of Contributors	x
Acknowledgements	xvi

Music Education, Learning Cultures and Employability   1
   Rosa Reitsamer and Rainer Prokop

Part I
The Neoliberal Conservatoire

Chapter 1
Balancing Demand and Supply in Music Labour Markets: The Shifting Role of Italian Music Conservatories   13
   Clementina Casula

Chapter 2
Marketing Conservatoire Education: The Employable White Musicians of European Classical Music   26
   Ann Werner and Cecilia Ferm Almqvist

Chapter 3
From Music Higher Education to the Festival Stage: Questioning the Neoliberal Environments of Scottish Jazz   38
   Sarah Raine and Haftor Medbøe

Chapter 4
Facilitating Dreams, with a Sense of Reality: Employability in Dutch Higher Popular Music Education   50
   Rick Everts, Pauwke Berkers and Erik Hitters

Chapter 5
On the Potential of Niche Markets: The Case of Bluegrass Music   63
   Nate Olson

Chapter 6
From Merit to Engagement: Moving Music Education to the Next Phase   75
   Mina Yang

Part II
Power Relations, Alternative Pedagogies and Activism

Chapter 7
Classical Music After #MeToo: Is Music Higher Education a 'Conducive Context' for Sexual Misconduct?   87
   Anna Bull

Chapter 8
History, Narrative and Equality, Diversity and Inclusion in the Music Conservatoire   101
   Uchenna Ngwe

Chapter 9
Other Acts of Intervention through Hip-Hop Studies: Teaching and Reflecting   115
   Fernando Orejuela

Chapter 10
Access and Technology in Music Education: Negotiating Neoliberalism During a Pandemic Within a Graduate Popular Music Pedagogies Course   129
   Kyle Zavitz, Rhiannon Simpson and Ruth Wright

Chapter 11
The Surge Towards 'Diversity': Interest Convergence and Performative 'Wokeness' in Music Institutions   142
   Juliet Hess

Part III
Transitions and Trajectories of Musicians

Chapter 12
Negotiating Pedagogical Cultures: Adaptive Challenges Facing Music Education Graduates on Their Return to China   159
   Elizabeth Haddon

Chapter 13
Swedish Dance Music Scenes, Female Career Trajectories and the Neoliberal Shift   173
   Anna Gavanas

Chapter 14
The Unstable Lightness of Rock Once Again: Careers, Trajectories and DIY Cultures in Portuguese Indie Rock   185
   Paula Guerra, Ana Oliveira and Andy Bennett

Chapter 15
Music Therapy as Profession and Practice: The Shifting Interrelationship of Precarity and Entrepreneurialism 197
Simon Procter

Epilogue
Neoliberalism's Others: Imperatives of Activism in Portland, Oregon 209
Elizabeth Gould

Index 221

Figures

9.1	The eastern-facing wall of 'Graffiti Bridge'	116
9.2	The western-facing wall of 'Graffiti Bridge'	117

Tables

10.1 Demographic Data of Interview Participants   134
12.1 Demographic Information of Participants   164

Contributors

Cecilia Ferm Almqvist has a PhD in music education and works as Professor of Education at Södertörn University and as Visiting Professor of Education at Gothenburg University, Sweden. Since she defended her thesis *Openness and Awareness*, a phenomenological study of music teaching and learning interaction, her empirical and philosophical research has centred around democracy, equality, inclusion and aesthetic communication in pedagogical situations. Her research is widely spread and published internationally. Currently, she is involved in the research project 'Conservatory Cultures', led by Associate Professor Ann Werner.

Andy Bennett is Professor of Cultural Sociology in the School of Humanities, Languages and Social Science at Griffith University, Australia. He is a Faculty Fellow of the Yale Centre for Cultural Sociology, an International Research Fellow of the Finnish Youth Research Network, a founding member of the Consortium for Youth, Generations and Culture and a founding member of the Regional Music Research Group. He is co-founding editor of the journal *DIY, Alternative Cultures & Society* and co-founder/co-convenor of the biennial KISMIF Conference.

Pauwke Berkers is Professor in Sociology of Popular Music, specifically in relation to inclusion, well-being and resilience in the Department of Arts and Culture Studies, Erasmus University Rotterdam, the Netherlands. Together with Julian Schaap, he co-founded the research group Rotterdam Popular Music Studies (RPMS) as well as the EUR minor MU$IC: The Economy, Sociology and Practice of Popular Music. Pauwke is head of the Department of Arts and Culture Studies, one of the founding members of the Rotterdam Arts and Sciences Lab and a member of the EUR core team Cultuurcampus.

Anna Bull is Senior Lecturer in Education and Social Justice at the University of York, UK, and a former professional pianist and cellist. Her book *Class, Control and Classical Music* was published in 2019 and was the joint winner of the British Sociological Association Philip Abrams Award in 2020. She has also co-edited the volume *Voices for Change in the Classical Music Profession: New Ideas for Tackling Inequalities and Exclusions*. Anna is a co-founder and director of The 1752 Group, a research and campaigning organization working to address staff/faculty sexual misconduct in higher education.

Clementina Casula is Associate Professor in Sociology of Economics and Labour Processes at the Department of Humanities, Languages and Cultural Heritage of the University of Cagliari, Italy, where she teaches sociology of cultural and creative industries; equality, diversity and inclusion in the cultural and creative industries; and sociology of multimedia consumption and production. Her research focuses on the relation between institutions, markets and society with reference to several areas, particularly on cultural and creative industries, higher education, labour markets, territorial developments and ICTs, always paying special attention to the gender dimension of analysis.

Rick Everts obtained his PhD in 2023 from Erasmus University Rotterdam, the Netherlands, specializing in the way early-career musicians aim to establish their careers in the changing music industries in the Netherlands. His research, part of the 'POPLIVE' project, has been featured in publications including *Poetics*, the *Creative Industries Journal* and the *Journal of Cultural Economy*. Prior to his academic pursuits, Rick served as a producer for Sonic Acts at Paradiso in Amsterdam and taught sociology at the University of Amsterdam. Currently, he works as a senior policy advisor in the Department of Culture at the Municipality of Utrecht.

Anna Gavanas is a social anthropologist with a focus on dance music history, working life, migration and family politics. She holds a PhD in social anthropology from Stockholm University (since 2001) and an Associate Professorship from the Department of Ethnology and Gender Studies from Stockholm University (since 2009), Sweden. She has published a number of interview-based and archival studies on Swedish electronic dance music scenes with a focus on technological shifts, gender and cultural politics. Anna has also worked as a DJ and producer since the 1990s.

Elizabeth Gould is Associate Professor Emerita and recently retired from the University of Toronto, Faculty of Music, Canada, where she taught philosophy-based courses in music, music education and sexual diversity studies. She is lead editor of *Exploring Social Justice: How Music Education Might Matter* (2009) and has published in several journals such as *Philosophy of Music Education Review*, *Discourse: Studies in the Cultural Politics of Education*, *Women and Music: A Journal of Gender and Culture* and *Educational Philosophy and Theory*. Her research interests include gender and sexuality in the context of the philosophy of Gilles Deleuze, feminist assemblages and queer theory.

Paula Guerra is Professor of Sociology at the University of Porto, Portugal, and Adjunct Associate Professor at Griffith University, Centre for Social and Cultural Research, Australia. She is the founder/coordinator of the KISMIF Conference and KISMIF Community. Paula is chair of the IASPM-Portugal and a board member of the European Sociological Association's Research Network Sociology of the Arts. She coordinates several research projects subordinated to youth cultures, the sociology of the arts and culture and DIY cultures, among other subjects. She is editor-in-chief (with Andy Bennett) of the journal *DIY, Alternative Cultures & Society*.

Elizabeth Haddon is Senior Lecturer in Music at the University of York, UK. Her pedagogical research has focused on creativity, the music masterclass, hidden learning, empathy and partnership in piano duet playing. Forthcoming publications include an edited volume on instrumental pedagogy (2025), chapters for the *Oxford Handbook of Piano Pedagogy* (2024) and articles on violin duet pedagogy. She created the MA Music Education: Instrumental and Vocal Teaching at the University of York, leads the undergraduate Instrumental Music Education module, holds senior leadership roles and leads new developments in music education at the University of York.

Juliet Hess is Associate Professor of Music Education at Michigan State University, United States, having previously taught public school music in the Greater Toronto Area. Her book *Music Education for Social Change: Constructing an Activist Music Education* (2019) explores activism, critical pedagogy and music education. Juliet received her PhD in sociology of education from the Ontario Institute for Studies in Education at the University of Toronto, Canada. Her research interests include anti-oppression education, trauma-informed pedagogy, activism in music and music education, music education for social justice, disability and mad studies and the question of ethics in world music study.

Erik Hitters is Associate Professor at the Erasmus School of History, Culture and Communication of Erasmus University Rotterdam, the Netherlands, and head of the Department of Media and Communication. He lectures for the MA Programme in Media and Creative Industries and IBCoM, the International Bachelor in Communication and Media. He was principal investigator of the Smart Culture Strategic Research Project 'Staging popular music: Sustainable live music ecologies for artists, music venues and cities (POPLIVE)'. His work on popular music has resulted in multiple conference papers and publications. He co-founded and is board member of the International Music Business Research Association (IMBRA).

Haftor Medbøe is Lecturer and Researcher within the School of Arts and Creative Industries at Edinburgh Napier University, Scotland. His research interests focus primarily on the creative communities of jazz in the European context and in practice-led research, outputs of which have been published and presented at conferences internationally. As a musician, Haftor has to date released fifteen albums and continues, as time allows, to perform his music at festivals in the UK and abroad. He is founding chair of the Scottish Jazz Archive and holds a position on the board of directors of Edinburgh Jazz & Blues Festival.

Uchenna Ngwe is a London-based musician and academic Lecturer at Trinity Laban Conservatoire of Music and Dance and the Royal Academy of Music, UK. Her research interests focus on explorations of Black classical musicians in Britain through the lens of curatorial activism and the curation of *plainsightSOUND* – an online research project promoting historical Black musicians in British classical music. She is also co-founder of the Shared Narratives online conference and network for researchers of colour in the performing arts. Recently, Uchenna has presented several BBC Radio programmes including the Radio 3 Sunday Feature 'Frank Johnson, Queen Victoria and the Black Brass Band', which followed her research into the life of the innovative nineteenth-century African American performer and composer.

Ana Oliveira is a sociologist with a PhD in urban studies. She is Assistant Researcher at DINÂMIA'CET-Iscte and invited Assistant Professor of Urban Sociology at Universidade Aberta, Portugal. Ana is treasurer of the IASPM-Portugal and belongs to the scientific and executive committees of the KISMIF Conference. She is also book review editor (with Robin Kuchar) of the journal *DIY, Alternative Cultures & Society*. Throughout her trajectory, she has participated in several national and international research projects on popular music, do-it-yourself, music careers, underground cultures, cultural policies, urban studies and the sociology of arts and culture.

Nate Olson is Associate Professor and the academic director of the Bluegrass, Old-Time and Roots Music Studies Programme at East Tennessee State University, United States, where he teaches bluegrass and progressive acoustic bands, music theory, career seminars, private lessons and teacher education courses. He earned his doctorate in music education from Teachers College, Columbia University, and his dissertation focuses on the institutionalization of fiddle music in higher education. He has presented at ISME, ASTA, NAfME, CDIME, CMS and other national and international conferences and published in *American String Teacher*, *Strings Magazine* and with Mel Bay Publications.

Fernando Orejuela is Senior Lecturer in the Department of Folklore and Ethnomusicology at Indiana University Bloomington, United States. His research interests centre around hip-hop music and culture, popular music, subculture studies, body art, youth cultures, children's folklore, sports, game and play in culture, popular culture and pedagogy. Fernando's publications include the monograph *Rap and Hip Hop Culture* (2021). Together with Stephanie Shonekan, he co-edited the volume *Black Lives Matter and Music: Protest, Intervention, Reflection* (2018).

Simon Procter is a music therapist and music sociologist based in London, UK, and has worked across both medical and nonmedical mental health services. He leads education and research activities for Nordoff Robbins, UK's leading music therapy charity, specializing in ethnographic engagement with musical experience, interaction and identity. He is a member of the Sociology of the Arts (SocArts) group at Exeter University, a faculty member of the Karol Szymanowski Academy of Music in Katowice, Poland, and a trustee of the UK's National Centre for Early Music.

Rainer Prokop, sociologist, is Senior Scientist at the Department of Music Sociology at the mdw – University of Music and Performing Arts Vienna, Austria.

His research focuses on music labour markets, career trajectories of musicians, study-to-work transitions of classically trained musicians, the sociology of higher music education and valuation practices at higher music education institutions. Rainer's most recent articles, together with Rosa Reitsamer, include *The Role of Music Conservatoires in the Making of Classical Music Careers* (2023) and *The DIY Careers of Young Classical Musicians in Neoliberal Times* (2023).

Sarah Raine is a SFI-IRC Pathway Fellow at University College Dublin, Ireland, and the principal investigator of 'Improvising Across Boundaries: Voicing the Experience of Women and Gender-Minority Improvising Musicians' (2023–7). Sarah's published research considers issues of gender and generation, authenticity and identity and the construction of the past and present in popular music, scene and industry. She is the author of *Authenticity and Belonging in the Northern Soul Scene* (2020) and a co-editor of *Towards Gender Equality in the Music Industry* (2019) and *The Northern Soul Scene* (2019). Sarah is also a co-managing editor of *Riffs* and acts as a book series editor for Equinox Publishing (*Music Industry Studies* and *Icons of Pop Music*) and an editor for *Jazz Research Journal*.

Rosa Reitsamer, sociologist, is Professor at the Department of Music Sociology at the mdw – University of Music and Performing Arts Vienna, Austria. Her research interests include the sociology of higher music education and music labour markets, valuation practices at higher music education institutions and intersectional perspectives on music, gender and social inequalities. Rosa has published numerous articles in journals and co-edited several books, including *Music as Labour: Inequalities and Activism in the Past and Present* (2022). In 2022, she received the Gabriele Possanner Austrian State Award for Gender Studies.

Rhiannon Simpson is Lecturer in Music Education at the University of Melbourne, Australia. She has published book chapters and journal articles in the fields of policy, sociology and music education. She has twice featured as the keynote speaker at the Statewide Instrumental Music Teachers Conference (Victoria, Australia) and has been the recipient of the 'John and Eric Smythe Prestigious Travelling Scholarship' (2019, University of Melbourne), the 'Ontario Graduate Scholarship' (Ontario State Government, 2020, 2021) as well as the David Sell Prize for Outstanding Student Presentation (ANZARME, 2023). When she's not teaching or writing, Rhiannon works as a sought-after blues guitarist across Australia, Europe and the United States.

Ann Werner is Senior Lecturer in Musicology at Uppsala University and Associate Professor in Gender Studies at Södertörn University, Sweden. Her research focuses on gender, popular music and media. She has published widely, for example, on streaming and algorithmic culture and gendered uses of music, drawing on feminist theory. Her latest book is entitled *Feminism and Gender Politics in Mediated Popular Music* (2022). She is principal investigator of the research project 'Conservatory Cultures' (2021–4), examining the construction of nation and gender in classical music higher education.

Ruth Wright is Professor in the Department of Music Education at Western University, Canada. Her research interests are the sociology of music education, popular music in music education and the inclusion and empowerment of marginalized students in and through music education. She is passionate about the rights of all young people to a rewarding and culturally relevant experience of music in education. Ruth publishes regularly in books and refereed journals on the subject of music education and is a speaker at national and international conferences.

Mina Yang is a musicologist, pianist and educational consultant who currently works as a senior academic programme manager for Minerva Project and teaches at the Colburn School of Music in Los Angeles, United States. She is the author of *California Polyphony: Ethnic Voices, Musical Crossroads* (2008) and *Planet Beethoven: Classical Music at the Turn of the Millennium* (2014) as well as of numerous articles in journals and edited collections. She has been on the faculty of the University of California, San Diego, University of Southern California, Minerva University and San Francisco Conservatory.

Kyle Zavitz is Postdoctoral Researcher at the Schulich School of Music in McGill University, Canada. Previously, he studied at Western University, the University of Manitoba, the University of Music and Performing Arts Graz and Carleton University. He has worked as a sessional instructor for courses in jazz, theory, musicianship and acoustics of music. He has studied and taught in the fields of music and music education, with a particular focus on popular music and jazz pedagogies. His research explores the ways identity and experience are regulated through knowledge production and recontextualization within higher music education.

Acknowledgements

The editors and authors of this publication acknowledge the financial support by the Open Access Fund of the mdw – University of Music and Performing Arts Vienna.

Music Education, Learning Cultures and Employability

Rosa Reitsamer and Rainer Prokop

In recent years, a growing body of research has been reassessing the role of higher music education institutions in light of the challenges posed by neoliberalism and the debates over the reproduction of social inequalities in access to education and the music and cultural industries. This edited collection contributes to this scholarship by providing insights into the learning cultures, curricula design and emancipatory initiatives within higher music education as well as the various ways of transitioning from education to work and the world of uncertainty and job insecurity currently being experienced by a younger generation of musicians. In order to provide insights into these processes and practices, the book brings together empirical studies, activist voices, theoretical considerations and (auto-) ethnographic studies from various disciplines, work contexts and geographical regions, including Italy, Portugal, the Netherlands, Sweden, Estonia, Hungary, Finland, the United Kingdom, the United States, Canada and China. In their respective contributions, the authors examine the reactions of higher music education institutions to the neoliberal restructuring of the educational field and the music labour markets and take a critical look at the discourses surrounding employability. They also shed light on dominant power structures at music conservatoires that create the context for the reproduction of social inequalities. Finally, they specifically examine how race/ethnicity, gender and class pervade the creation and performance of music and highlight alternative pedagogical approaches and strategies for moving forward in the era of Black Lives Matter, #StopAsianHate and #MeToo.

We have organized the contributions around the themes of the neoliberal conservatoire (Part I); power relations, alternative pedagogies and activism (Part II); and transitions and trajectories of musicians (Part III). These three themes, as well as the contributing authors' focus on a variety of different musical worlds, including Western art music, jazz, indie rock, hip-hop and electronic dance music (EDM), resulted in part from our own research into higher music education, the career pathways of musicians and music, cultural labour and activism in Austria. This work includes the curation of this volume, the organization of the international conference *Creative Identities in Transition: Higher Music Education and Employability in the 21st Century* at the mdw – University of Music and Performing Arts Vienna (2020), the online lecture series *Music, Sexual Harassment, Racism: Continuities & Change* (ongoing; together with Katharina

Alexi in 2022) and the showcase *Popular Music, Equity, Diversity: The Struggle for Creative Justice* at Waves Vienna Festival & Conference (2022), as well as the publication of several journal articles and book chapters (e.g. Prokop and Reitsamer, 2023a,b).

Before we provide a brief overview of the key issues addressed in each thematic section and introduce the chapters, we would like to express our sincere gratitude to Vice Rector Gerda Müller and the Department of Music Sociology at the mdw – University of Music and Performing Arts Vienna for the financial support of our research and the realization of this book as well as to the authors. We hope this book contributes to a better understanding of the relationship between higher music education, work and activism in neoliberal times for those who are new to this research while at the same time offers new insights for those who are already well immersed in these fields.

Part I: The Neoliberal Conservatoire

Neoliberalism is a contested concept that has been examined and theorized differently across disciplinary contexts, times and places. Most scholars agree that neoliberalism has established new political, economic and social arrangements that emphasize the extension of competitive markets into all areas of life, the withdrawal of the state from many forms of social provision and the self-responsibility of individuals (e.g. Bourdieu, 1999; Brown, 2015; Dardot and Laval, 2013; Harvey, 2005; Springer, Birch and MacLeavy, 2016). Consequently, neoliberalism has also affected public and higher education and transformed its institutions into 'entrepreneurial universities' (Clark, 1998) by installing corporate management schemes; reinforcing an audit culture based on metrics, control and the display of performance; and imitating the organizational structure of the market economy. According to Henry Giroux (2014) the new corporate university defines 'faculty as entrepreneurs, students as customers, and education as a mode of training' (p. 30) and regards critical thought, knowledge and dialogue with suspicion, thus hindering education from its purpose of teaching young people to become reflective, critical and socially engaged actors. This neoliberal transformation of public and higher education, which has spread from the United States and Britain to other countries to varying degrees, has also affected music conservatoires.

In Europe, the Bologna declaration played a central role in this process. As a response to the requirements of New Public Management and cuts in spending for higher education (e.g. Štech, 2011), this declaration placed music conservatoires and other arts academies on the university level and enabled the instrumental logic of marketization and commodification of higher music and arts education institutions while at the same time fostering global competition between universities. Clementina Casula's chapter examines the situation of music conservatoires in Italy through a before-and-after comparison of the 1999 Bologna reform. Drawing on interviews with teachers and students, she shows that the implementation of this law has led to a number of shortcomings and conflicts.

These include, for example, the introduction of courses on popular music genres taught by a younger generation of teachers who are kept in precarious working conditions or the heightened expectations of students to obtain a degree that grants them access to the music labour market.

In many countries, the state, through the introduction of laws such as the Bologna declaration, has created an institutional framework that is characterized by 'strong private property rights, free markets, and free trade' (Harvey, 2005: 2) and supports the intrusion of neoliberal principles into higher education. One of these principles refers to employability, which has become 'a performative function of universities, shaped and directed by the state' (Boden and Nedeva, 2010: 37). Higher music education institutions increasingly embrace this function by shifting their focus away from a general employability of students towards entrepreneurship courses and curricula that teach students how to develop an entrepreneurial career identity and create their own artistic employment to meet the realities of the shrinking labour market (e.g. Essig, 2017). However, this new employability agenda is closely intertwined with the spread of conditions of precariousness for a significant proportion of teachers working at universities, including the neoliberal conservatoire, as well as for students who are habituated to the uncertainty and insecurity of the labour market through the promotion of entrepreneurship and portfolio careers (Giroux, Neut-Aguayo and Rivera-Vargas, 2022; Moore, 2016; Casula and Yang, this volume).

Several authors discuss the effects of this new employability agenda for higher music education institutions, curricula design and faculty and students. Ann Werner and Cecilia Ferm Almqvist show in their study of the representation of teachers, students and Western art music on the websites of music conservatoires in Estonia, Hungary and Finland that white students are constructed as 'employable' classical musicians, while images of East Asian students are exclusively included on pages labelled 'international' or 'exchange programmes'. Resonating with studies on the pervasiveness of anti-Asian racism in the classical music world (e.g. Kawabata, 2023; Yang, 2007), their study demonstrates that the neoliberal marketing of classical music education programmes reproduces globally circulating prejudices about classically trained East Asian musicians by presenting them as happy 'diversity tokens' (Ahmed, 2009) or by making them invisible through omission.

Racialized and gendered constructions of employability are not limited to the world of Western art music but are also produced in other music cultures under neoliberal conditions. As Sarah Raine and Haftor Medbøe's chapter demonstrates, jazz higher education and the jazz scene in Scotland remain white, male-dominated and middle class, which crucially informs notions of 'employable' students and musicians. In this context, as teachers themselves, Raine and Medbøe have developed their own pedagogical approach to create a critical space for student music-making and discussions about the realities of the jazz music labour market and the students' diverse expectations about their employability and careers. While Raine and Medbøe present their own pedagogical toolbox for challenging neoliberal ideologies, Rick Everts, Pauwke Berkers and Erik Hitters examine the strategies employed by teachers at higher popular music education programmes in the Netherlands to prepare students for a precarious, unstable and insecure music career and working life and to increase their employability. On the one hand, the authors argue, these strategies promote entrepreneurship and self-responsibility, which often trigger feelings of stress and anxiety in students; on the other hand, they seem to be 'pragmatic', in that they introduce students to a 'mixed professional practice' that goes beyond performance and supports their artistic ambitions, rather than pushing them towards an economically profitable career or music genre. Nate Olson explores the issue of employability through the example of the Bluegrass, Old-Time and Roots Music Studies Programme at East Tennessee State University, United States. He describes the lengthy process to establish this music study programme, which is predominantly attended by white male students and consequently resonates with the social demographics of bluegrass performers and audiences in the United States. However, as the programme's academic director, Olson rejects a neoliberal employability agenda, arguing that there is an inherent and multifaceted value in providing rich study opportunities to understand the history, culture and aesthetics of bluegrass music, which, in turn, responds to the students' desire to invest in deepening their passion for this music and to forge a career in the niche of the bluegrass music market.

Regardless of the music programmes examined by the authors, they all stress the significance of meritocracy underlying the new agenda of employability in higher music education. Jo Littler (2013) has reminded us of two key problems in the neoliberal language of meritocracy, which disseminate 'the idea that whatever our social position at birth, society ought to offer enough opportunity and mobility for "talent" to combine with "effort" in order to "rise to the top"' (Littler, 2013: 52). Thus, the first problem of meritocracy refers to the essentialized conception of 'talent' or 'intelligence' as innate abilities that give the chance to succeed or not and that, at their logical conclusion, share the logics of eugenics, as some must inevitably be left behind (p. 54). The second closely aligned problem is that meritocracy 'offers a "ladder" system of social mobility, promoting a socially corrosive ethic of competitive self-interest which both legitimises inequality and damages community' (p. 54). Mina Yang draws upon the concept of meritocracy to examine the phases of change in music curricula in US higher education over the past few decades. According to Yang, the vast majority of these changes, such as the inclusion of courses on popular and non-Western music as well as entrepreneurship training in the existing curriculum, does little more to prepare students for meaningful and sustainable professional careers. Moreover, only recently have a few institutions expanded the representation of marginalized Black, Indigenous and People of Colour (BIPOC) and other excluded music traditions into part of their own raison d'être, rather than as a 'token' in existing curricula. However, there are changes proposed by Yang that have yet to be implemented by higher music education institutions, with courses and curricula that teach students how neoliberalism shapes the relationship between music, power and society and support students in acquiring the tools to engage politically and push back against the effects of neoliberal policies. This call for comprehensive and sustainable changes clearly challenges the neoliberal discussions about employability, most of which 'focus on the functional aspects of becoming employed, that is, a solid curriculum vitae, proficiency in interviews and auditions, and perhaps a website containing examples of work' (Bennett, 2016: 391), and brings us to the second thematic section of the book.

Part II: Power Relations, Alternative Pedagogies and Activism

At the beginning of the twenty-first century, music conservatoires can look back at a long history of alternative pedagogies that challenge institutional hierarchies and dominant learning environments and seek to dismantle social inequalities. The articles grouped together in this section provide insights into the dominant power relations at higher music education institutions and explore the initiatives and strategies aiming to bring about change. However, as several authors point out, it is important to study the longer histories of music learning cultures rather than focusing solely on the effects of neoliberalism on universities in order to understand the historical formations of colonial and patriarchal power structures and the resistance to them. Anna Bull in her chapter draws on Liz Kelly's (2016) theorization of the 'conducive context' to describe the historically established factors that enable sexual harassment to occur in classical music higher education, most notably institutionalized power and authority, power dynamics between teachers and students and limited external challenges of institutional authority. Against this background, and given that survivors of sexual violence rarely report their experiences to their institutions, Bull argues that 'raising awareness' is certainly not enough to bring about change. She suggests several measures to challenge the existing gendered, sexualized and racialized power structures, including the development of a strong student voice and a change to the master-apprentice model of one-to-one teaching, which is characterized by imbalanced power dynamics between teachers and students (e.g. Gaunt, 2009) and focuses primarily on teaching technical skills and the interpretation of works by white male composers of past eras.

Besides feminist and queer considerations of music education (e.g. Gould, 2013; Koza, 1994), historical analyses are important for deepening our understanding of the impact of colonialism and the resulting ideologies of racism on music education. Deborah Bradley (2016), Juliet Hess (2021), Uchenna Ngwe (this volume) and others have shown how music education was employed as a civilizing force within the colonial project to deliberately cultivate the values of the white middle class. From the early 1830s onwards, these values were conveyed by teaching songs in schools, which encouraged patriotic sentiments and imposed strict notions of physical comportment and compliance onto children, while Black and Indigenous musics were omitted in music curricula and deemed inferior to Western art music (Gustafson, 2009). This cultivation of white middle-class values 'served to elevate Whiteness and further participate in the minoritizing process [of Black, Indigenous and People of Colour] inherent in internal colonialism' (Hess, 2021: 28). Until today, a characteristic of whiteness – as a privileged position in society – is the 'luxury of ignorance' (Howard, 2006), which manifests as much in the belief in a post-race society as in music pedagogies that reinforce colonialist epistemologies, such as the myth of music as universal language (Bradley, 2016). As Uchenna Ngwe argues in her chapter, the diversity initiatives that emerged at higher music education institutions after the murder of George Floyd in 2020 and the subsequent rise in awareness of the Black Lives Matter movement have hardly changed this situation, since they often serve the neoliberal marketization of higher music education institutions that lack the 'institutional will' to change (see also Ahmed, 2012; Hess, this volume). Building on the findings of the *Black Curriculum Report* (Arday, 2021) and Deborah Gabriel's (2020) understanding of 3D Pedagogy, Ngwe suggests counter-telling and online art music activism as methodologies to restore the Black and Indigenous narratives that have been erased from the history of music conservatoires through 'strategic silencing' (Gilroy, 2002). As scholar-performer-activist herself, Ngwe has delved into these practice-based methodologies of curatorial activism in her project *plainsightSOUND*, which is concerned with the rediscovery of the long history of contributions that composers and performers of African descent have made to the performance and study of classical music in Britain before the 1970s. Fernando Orejuela's chapter describes a pedagogy of anti-racism that he developed in his courses on hip-hop music and culture at a predominantly white institution in the United States and seeks to help students to understand the symbolic expressions and narrative conventions used in hip-hop lyrics that continue to be part of African American and African diasporic cultural life. Essential to this pedagogy, which he situates in the context of the Black Lives Matter movement and the racist hostility towards BIPOC faculty and students, is the social positionality of students and teachers inside and outside the classroom following Black feminist thought, the basic tenets of Critical Race Theory and an investment in the students' listening practices. Kyle Zavitz, Rhiannon Simpson and Ruth Wright explore the potential of online teaching formats to support alternative pedagogies based on technology and popular music, consequently shifting the focus away from the hegemonic pedagogic model of band, orchestra and chorus and its Western art music repertoire and towards online popular music education experiences and an engagement with issues of social justice, inclusion and access to technology. The authors outline the design of the online popular music pedagogies course they developed during the Covid-19 pandemic and provide insights into the students' reactions to the course that show a tension between their view of the liberatory potential of the course material and experiences and their internalization of neoliberal discourses. Finally, Juliet Hess takes a critical look at diversity initiatives at higher music education institutions across the United States and Canada that have become a means to perform 'wokeness' for these institutions, aiming to present themselves as 'good' and supportive of their minoritized groups. However, Hess's analysis goes beyond a critique of these initiatives. She puts forward Derrick Bell's (1995) principle of interest convergence to explore a possible convergence of interests in 'diversity work' between white and BIPOC groups in higher music education institutions that goes far beyond conversations about recruitment and demographics and looks critically at music conservatoires as historically and contemporary 'white spaces', which are often violent places for minoritized communities. Institutions must therefore follow up their purported commitments to increasing equity, inclusion and diversity with action and give space to anti-racist, decolonial, feminist and queer music pedagogics and curricula, including the music traditions and cultures of BIPOC communities, in order to bring about change.

Part III: Transitions and Trajectories of Musicians

The book's final section comprises chapters concerned with different professions such as musician, music therapist and music pedagogue as well as other creative occupations that play a central role in the worlds of music, including event organization, journalism or graphic and fashion design. The authors examine the non-linear transitional pathways from study to professional working life, encompassing multiple entry attempts, spells of unemployment, self-employment, short-term contracts and part-time work within and outside the music and creative industries (e.g. Haukka, 2011), and present the strategies used by musicians to manage the increasing precariousness, insecurity and entrepreneurialism that underpin music labour markets in neoliberal times. Thus, they revisit the notion of employability from the perspective of creative workers and highlight the significance of the concept of precarity, which refers to experiences of 'precarious, unstable, insecure forms of living, and, simultaneously, new forms of political struggle and solidarity that reach beyond the traditional models of the political party or trade union' (Gill and Pratt, 2008: 3). Elizabeth Haddon looks at the strategies of a small group of students returning to their country of origin, China, after completing a master's in music education at a British university. Haddon draws attention to the situation of Chinese students in British higher music education institutions, which is shaped by positive learning outcomes but also by anti-Asian racism, exploitation due to their high fee status and the lack of investment by the institutions and teachers in collaborative work to support cross-cultural music pedagogies, which, in turn, complicates the transition into professional working life in China. The main focus of Haddon's analysis is on the challenges faced by instrumental and vocal teachers working in different employment contexts in China that partly mirror the neoliberal developments in the country and restrict their agency and the strategies they have developed without any institutional support to reconcile their pedagogical ideals and the realities of working in the country. As Haddon's study illustrates, today many young people who aspire to the creative professions are forced to adopt a do-it-yourself (DIY) approach to the transition from higher education to work, as neoliberalism has restructured labour markets according to post-Fordist economic models and encourages individuals to manage their careers and lives themselves without relying on the state by becoming an 'entrepreneur of the self' (Bröckling, 2016). Anna Gavanas considers the career trajectories of female pioneers in EDM scenes in Sweden in the 1990s, which were situated outside the 'official' youth transition spaces of universities and the conventional labour market. These women were not primarily DJs but decorators, promoters, clubwear importers, shop owners, dancers, costume and outfit designers, journalists, photographers and door staff and carried out other low-status but indispensable activities. Gavanas sheds light on the significance of the gendered division of labour in youth-oriented music scenes and shows how some of these women who studied art, design or journalism were able to advance a DIY career as they grew older and how Sweden, like many welfare states in Europe, restructured its cultural policy and subsequently pushed cultural producers to adopt an entrepreneurial position. Paula Guerra, Ana Oliveira and Andy Bennett's chapter on the indie rock scene in Portugal explores how the DIY careers of musicians have been shaped by neoliberalism. Their analysis begins with a discussion of the social positions of the protagonists within the Portuguese indie rock scene in terms of gender and class and the sociopolitical and economic changes that took place between 2010 and 2020. The authors then present a typology of DIY careers based on more than 270 interviews with people involved in the production and mediation of indie rock in Portugal, illustrating how the overwhelming majority of musicians combine performance with a variety of other activities within and outside the indie rock scene in order to make a living. Simon Procter examines the changing relationship between precarity and entrepreneurship that the music therapy profession in the UK has undergone since the early 1990s. He describes three phases of change, with the development of a new music therapy industry marking the third and current phase, in which entrepreneurship has been economically enforced by neoliberal policies, leading to various 'privatizing effects' for music therapy and a precarization of the profession. This, as Procter vividly demonstrates, has far-reaching implications, including a discouraging of potential entrants into the profession, a restriction of the kinds of work that music therapists do and the profession becoming dominated by 'entrepreneuralists'. However, as in other music professions, alternative models of higher education and employment for music therapists as well as activism are now emerging. The book therefore concludes with a philosophical essay by Elizabeth Gould on the tactics – especially singing – that were used by protesters in Portland, Oregon, to demonstrate against the killing of George Floyd by a white police officer. Building on this, she conceptualizes this anthology and music education in general as a Deleuzian collective assemblage of enunciation and discusses the potentialities for music education's plural performativity to articulate anti-racist activism. The collection of approaches, suggestions and ideas put forward by the authors in this volume is intended to provide inspiration for action towards this goal.

References

Ahmed, S. (2009), 'Embodying Diversity: Problems and Paradoxes for Black Feminists', *Race, Ethnicity and Education*, 12 (1): 41–52.
Ahmed, S. (2012), *On Being Included: Racism and Diversity in Institutional Life*, London: Duke University Press.

Arday, J. (2021), *The Black Curriculum: Black British History in the National Curriculum*, The Black Curriculum. Available online: https://static1.squarespace.com/static/5f5507a 237cea057c5f57741/t/5fc10c7abc819f1cf4fd0eeb/1606487169011/TBC+2021++Report .pdf (accessed 17 April 2023).

Bell, D. (1995), 'Brown v. Board of Education and the Interest Convergence Dilemma', in K. Crenshaw, N. Gotanda, G. Peller and K. Thomas (eds), *Critical Race Theory: The Key Writings that Formed the Movement*, 20–9, New York: The New Press.

Bennett, D. (2016), 'Developing Employability in Higher Education Music', *Arts & Humanities in Higher Education*, 15 (3–4): 386–413.

Boden, R. and M. Nedeva (2010), 'Employing Discourse: Universities and Graduate "Employability"', *Journal of Education Policy*, 25 (1): 37–54.

Bourdieu, P. (1999), *The Weight of the World: Social Suffering in Contemporary Society*, Oxford: Polity.

Bradley, D. (2016), 'Hidden in Plain Sight: Race and Racism in Music Education', in C. Benedict, P. K. Schmidt, G. Spruce and P. Woodford (eds), *The Oxford Handbook of Social Justice in Music Education*, 190–203, New York: Oxford University Press.

Bröckling, U. (2016), *The Entrepreneurial Self*. Los Angeles, London: Sage.

Brown, W. (2015), *Undoing the Demos: Neoliberalism's Stealth Revolution*, New York: Zone Books.

Clark, B. R. (1998), *Creating Entrepreneurial Universities: Organizational Pathways of Transformation*, Oxford: Pergamon Press.

Dardot, P. and C. Laval (2013), *The New Way of the World: On Neoliberal Society*, London, New York: Verso.

Essig, L. (2017), 'Same or Different? The "Cultural Entrepreneurship" and "Arts Entrepreneurship" Constructs in European and US Higher Education', *Cultural Trends*, 26 (2): 125–37.

Gabriel, D. (2020), 'Teaching to Transgress through 3D Pedagogy: Decolonizing, Democratizing and Diversifying the Higher Education Curriculum', in D. Gabriel (ed.), *Transforming the Ivory Tower: Models for Gender Equality and Social Justice*, 5–17, London: Trentham Books.

Gaunt, H. (2009), 'One-to-One Tuition in a Conservatoire: The Perspectives of Instrumental and Vocal Students', *Psychology of Music*, 38 (2): 178–208.

Gill, R. and A. Pratt (2008), 'In the Social Factory? Immaterial Labour, Precariousness and Cultural Work', *Theory, Culture & Society*, 25 (7–8): 1–30.

Gilroy, P. (2002), *There Ain't No Black in the Union Jack: The Cultural Politics of Race and Nation*, 2nd edn, London: Routledge.

Giroux, H. A. (2014), *Neoliberalism's War on Higher Education*, Chicago: Haymarket Books.

Giroux, H. A., P. Neut-Aguayo and P. Rivera-Vargas (2022), 'Pedagogies of Precariousness in the Neoliberal Educational Order: Insecurity and Recomposition of Possibilities in the Current Political-pedagogical Context', *Foro de Educación*, 20 (2): 39–60.

Gould, E. (2013), 'Companion-able Species: A Queer Pedagogy for Music Education', *Bulletin of the Council for Research in Music Education*, 197: 63–75.

Gustafson, R. I. (2009), *Race and Curriculum: Music in Childhood Education*. New York: Palgrave Macmillan.

Harvey, D. (2005), *A Brief History of Neoliberalism*, Oxford, New York: Oxford University Press.

Haukka, S. (2011), 'Education-to-Work Transitions of Aspiring Creatives', *Cultural Trends*, 21 (1): 41–63.

Hess, J. (2021), 'Music Education and the Colonial Project: Stumbling toward Anti-colonial Music Education', in R. Wright, G. Johansen, P. A. Kanellopoulus and P. Schmidt (eds), *The Routledge Handbook of Sociology of Music Education*, 23–39, New York: Routledge.

Howard, G. R. (2006), *We Can't Teach What We Don't Know: White Teachers, Multiracial Schools*, 2nd edn, New York: Teachers College Press.

Kawabata, M. (2023), 'The New "Yellow Peril" in "Western" European Symphony Orchestras', in A. Bull, C. Scharff and L. Nooshin (eds), *Voices for Change in the Classical Music Profession: New Ideas for Tackling Inequalities and Exclusions*, 159–71, New York: Oxford University Press.

Kelly, L. (2016), 'The Conducive Context of Violence against Women and Girls', Discover Society, 1 March. https://archive.discoversociety.org/2016/03/01/theorising-violence-against-women-and-girls (accessed 17 April 2023).

Koza, J. E. (1994), 'Music Education Revisited: Discourses of Exclusion and Oppression', *Philosophy of Music Education Review*, 2 (2): 75–91.

Littler, J. (2013), 'Meritocracy as Plutocracy: The Marketising of Equality under Neoliberalism', *New Formations*, 80: 52–72.

Moore, A. (2016), 'Neoliberalism and the Musical Entrepreneur', *Journal of the Society for American Music*, 10 (1): 33–53.

Prokop, R. and R. Reitsamer (2023a), 'The DIY Careers of Young Classical Musicians in Neoliberal Times', *DIY, Alternative Cultures & Society*, 1 (2): 1–14.

Prokop, R. and R. Reitsamer (2023b), 'The Role of Music Conservatoires in the Making of Classical Music Careers', in A. Bull, C. Scharff and L. Nooshin (eds), *Voices for Change in the Classical Music Profession: New Ideas for Tackling Inequalities and Exclusions*, 31–41, New York: Oxford University Press.

Springer, S., K. Birch and J. MacLeavy, eds (2016), *The Handbook of Neoliberalism*, New York: Routledge.

Štech, S. (2011), 'The Bologna Process as a New Public Management Tool in Higher Education', *Journal of Pedagogy*, 2 (2): 263–82.

Yang, M. (2007), 'East Meets West in the Concert Hall: Asians and Classical Music in the Century of Imperialism, Post-Colonialism, and Multiculturalism', *Asian Music*, 38 (1): 1–30.

Part I

The Neoliberal Conservatoire

Chapter 1

Balancing Demand and Supply in Music Labour Markets

The Shifting Role of Italian Music Conservatories

Clementina Casula

Introduction

Only twenty years ago in Italy, after a lengthy parliamentary process, a national law (n. 509/1999) established the system of Higher Education in Arts and Music (*Alta Formazione Artistica e Musicale* or AFAM) on the tertiary level of education.[1] Music conservatories and other state-recognized academies for applied arts – historically assigned a marginal position within the national education system – were suddenly elevated to its most prestigious rung, until then exclusive dominion of Italian universities. As a consequence, higher art and music education institutions were adapted to the general rules governing universities, recently revised to comply with the Bologna declaration. Signed in Bologna in June 1999, this declaration defined a set of measures to be adopted to harmonize national higher education systems and establish a European Higher Education Area.

Several researchers (e.g. Štech, 2012) have noted how, behind the flag of European integration, the Bologna declaration shares common traits with neoliberal ideology. While an extensive debate has developed in Italy about the impact of neoliberal ideology in the restructuring of the university system (De Feo and Pitzalis, 2017), little attention has been paid to higher art and music education institutions.

In this chapter, I will address the latter issue, drawing on my research on Italian music conservatories (Casula, 2018a).[2] Following a neo-institutional approach (Powell and DiMaggio, 1991; Scott, 2008), I consider conservatories not as neutral and autonomous educational organizations but as social constructions embedded in wider organizational fields, shaped in turn by historical paths and social processes. Organizations belonging to the same field are prompted to comply with the rules, norms and beliefs prevalent within the field: Although change is usually urged as aimed at reaching a greater quality and efficiency of organizations, more often it responds to institutional reasons such as legitimacy, conformity and self-reproduction (Meyer and Rowan, 1991). That is why scholars refer to those types of processes producing organizational homogeneity with the expression 'institutional isomorphism' (DiMaggio and Powell, 1991).

This chapter begins by offering a brief account of the historical path of Italian music conservatories and then focusses, through a before/after comparison, on the main changes following the implementation of the 1999 reform, also pointing to some of the issues it has ignored, such as gender inequalities. This account will be illustrated with excerpts from the semi-structured interviews with nearly 100 conservatory students, teachers and professional musicians trained in Italy, conducted between 2013 and 2017 and updated more recently.[3] Conclusions note how the critical points identified in the reorganization of Italian music conservatories may find an adequate policy answer only from a strong political engagement that considers music a strategic asset for the country.

A Brief History of Italian Music Conservatories

The origin of Italian music conservatories dates back to charities founded around the sixteenth century to preserve ('*conservare*') foundlings and orphans by offering them vocational training in a series of activities that would allow them to make a living as adults (Colarizi, 1971). With the growing demand for musicians, conservatories served as a sort of recruitment agency supplying pupils to the thriving market of music production; they specialized in music training, appointing renowned musicians as *maestri* and also accepting paying scholars (Delfrati, 2017). Their name, having become a synonym for an organization for vocational music training, was adopted by the Paris conservatoire, founded in 1795. The French conservatoire, however, followed the more ambitious project to socially upgrade the music occupation, hiding its humble origins to achieve bourgeois respectability: The construction by its teachers of a specialized body of theoretical knowledge and techniques, taught through standardized state-legitimized training, was functional to this aim (Pierre, 1990).

This process, converting the know-how of qualified craftsmanship into expert knowledge associated with 'high culture' to turn vocational occupations into respectable bourgeois careers, had already proved to be successful in the process of professionalizing liberal occupations, such as medicine or law (Freidson, 1986). In the case of the music profession, this was further supported by the diffusion of the romantic aesthetics of 'absolute music', the celebrating of the *virtuoso* artist and the establishment of a canon of selected works by the (male) masters of the past (Weber, 1999; Frederickson and Rooney, 1990). The Paris conservatoire served as a model for the institutions for music education that were founded during the nineteenth century in the Western world (Kingsbury, 1988; DiMaggio, 1982).

In Italy, though, the process of including classical music into the realm of 'high culture' was met with resistance. The national education system, introduced after the political unification of the country in 1861, was based on an elitist ideology prioritizing theoretical over practical knowledge (Grimaldi and Serpieri, 2012). Conservatories, still associated with craftsmanship work and humble social classes (Aversano, 2021), were assigned a marginal position, which also meant greater autonomy in defining the boundaries of the field of professional music training and exerting monopolistic control within it. During the fascist regime, a series of laws sets the norms that ruled Italian conservatories for nearly a century.

Actually, the decades following the foundation of the Italian Republic in 1946 saw the launching of a parliamentary debate over the proposal to introduce music education horizontally in all school levels, while reserving a vertical curriculum for vocational music training. However, in the face of parliament's inability to reach an agreement, in the last decades of the century, the government found a stopgap solution in the founding of new music conservatories scattered throughout the country. This led to the creation of positions for music teachers and to an exponential growth in the number of students pursing music training for recreational, rather than vocational aims. The radical change in the scope and type of educational demand, however, was not accompanied by a revision of the curricular offerings. Conservatory teachers who advocated for increased staffing resisted pressures for change and continued to reproduce the canonical classical music model to which they had been socialized but which, in the meantime, had become increasingly outdated.

Since the last quarter of the twentieth century, Italy and other Western states have started to adopt neoliberal prescriptions in response to global recession and the crises of the welfare state by cutting public spending and promoting deregulation and flexibilization of the labour force. In the 1990s, Italian opera houses were transformed from public to semiprivate institutions,[4] increasingly relying on short-term contracts to recruit new orchestra members, while three of the four orchestras of the RAI (National Radio and Television Company) were closed. As a result of these transformations, the demand for classically trained musicians declined, while the growing number of conservatories offered an oversupply of graduates.[5]

The increasingly urgent need to reorganize Italian music conservatories found an answer in the approval of the national law n. 508/1999, which introduced a system of Higher Education in Arts and Music (AFAM) at the tertiary level of the national education system. The law, however, only outlined the general framework of the reform but left to the national parliament and the Ministry for University and Research the difficult job of laying down the operational guidelines needed to implement it. Over the past twenty years, conservatories and arts academies have adapted at a slow and uncertain pace to the rules of the national university system, seen as the legitimate model for regulating higher education in light of the Bologna declaration.

In what follows, drawing on the interviews collected for my research, I shall discuss from a comparative perspective the shifting role of Italian music conservatories in balancing the professional training and employability of their students before and after the 1999 reform.

Education and Employability Before the 1999 Reform

Before the 1999 reform, Italian conservatories followed the norms established at the beginning of the twentieth century for the canonical training of professional classical musicians. The educational programme provided a limited number of courses reproducing the main practices, repertoires and hierarchies of the canon. The length of studies varied between five and ten years, depending on the course of study, and was supplemented by a few complementary subjects in theoretical and practical music.

To ensure early training, students were admitted at the end of primary school after passing a selection process in which musical and vocational attributes were evaluated by an internal committee of teachers who assigned students to courses according to supposedly 'objective' criteria that in reality were often guided by social factors (Prokop and Reitsamer, 2023). A particularly influential factor was gender: Although since the beginning of the twentieth century the number of girls and young women within conservatories was almost as high as that that of boys and young men, the training of female students was limited to instruments associated with conventional feminine stereotypes and roles such as harp, piano and voice, which, in turn, limited their access to professional careers in music (Casula, 2023).

A prominent occupational opening for graduates from instrumental courses was offered by the concert scene. Students of the so-called 'noble' instruments, especially piano and violin, associated with upper-class education and the prestige of the romantic *virtuoso* artist, were encouraged to consider careers as soloists. Teachers' adherence to the ideal of *virtuoso* training could easily result in an explicit banning of their pupils to engage in any kind of activity (from school study to sports to dating) they considered a potential distraction from the ascetic concentration required to construct the solid technique and habitus of the *virtuoso*, reinforced by practices of distinction adopted to mark superiority over other musical careers. The latter aspect is well illustrated in the following quote from a conservatory teacher who studied with a famous violinist:

> There was a conflict with my *maestro* who just wanted me to study, and when he heard about the orchestra, he raged [. . .] because he was a great soloist and so whoever studied with him only had to think of becoming a great soloist, no? Nice thing, but let's come out of the clouds. (Violin teacher, female, 55)

Orchestral positions, on the other hand, were particularly sought after by students of the so-called 'agricultural' instruments, such as wind instruments associated with the rural or lowbrow classes and with a limited soloist repertoire. Teachers often managed to introduce their best students to national orchestras, because they were either acquainted with orchestra members or members themselves (a double public duty that was allowed until the end of the 1980s). Students' introduction as orchestra members often took the form of an apprenticeship reminiscent of the craft workshop model, as nicely illustrated in the following quote, describing how a young bassoon player was trained on the job under the careful supervision of his *maestro*:

> My *maestro* managed to place five or six pupils within [symphonic] orchestras. Today this would be impossible [. . .] but in the past, there was this workshop

relationship where [conservatory] teachers formed the first rows in orchestras and those who followed in the row came from their school; [...] I still remember my *maestro* would let me play the solo part whenever he could and would check [...] if everything was all right; if he heard problems with the reed [...] he would come and give me a little flick without being noticed and put me in a position to play well. (Bassoon teacher, male, 55)

Another favoured occupational route for young classically trained musicians was teaching, a 'pool profession' offering economic resources, reputation and sufficient free time to launch and pursue an artistic career. Once more, the *maestro* served as a recruiting agent, introducing older students to families of beginners or suggesting graduates as substitute teachers to fill vacancies easily converted into permanent positions at the newly opened conservatories. As these examples show, teachers had a significant influence on their students' careers. This influence and the associated power could easily degenerate into various forms of abuse – from corporal punishment to psychological and sexual harassment – affecting female students more often and more severely than male students (Casula, 2018a, 2019).

Since the end of the twentieth century, the mismatch between the decreasing demand for classical musicians and the increasing numbers of conservatory graduates has intensified, exposing young musicians entering the labour market to persistent precarity forcing them to take multiple poorly paid jobs with no clear prospects for occupational stability. Those working in the classical field – trained to aspire to the most prestigious and protected segments of the labour market – recall this experience as quite traumatic, while their colleagues active in other musical fields normalize occupational uncertainty as a standard feature of artistic careers or even as a source of independence that nurtures creativity.

The latter interpretation of occupational insecurity prevails, regardless of the different musical specializations, among the younger generations of musicians interviewed, who seem ready to adapt to an increasingly flexible and uncertain labour market through different strategies, including the development of diversified 'portfolio careers' and the skilful use of social media for self-promotion (Casula, 2018b). The young age at which Italian conservatory students usually graduated before the 1999 reform (early twenties for instrumentalists, a few years later for other subjects), in addition to the high level of musical training received, has helped them in their gradual adjustment to the changing demands of the labour market. This, however, has often required them to move abroad to gain access to highly specialized training or more dynamic working environments.

Throughout the twentieth century, Italian conservatories managed to offer a solid grounding in music education to large numbers of future musicians recruited all over the country. In the past decades of the century, however, their inability to exit from the self-referential ivory tower in which they had entrenched themselves (Roselli, 2015), still structured according to an increasingly outdated model of music production, had become evident: A deep reorganization allowing them to take into account ongoing changes at the cultural, social and economic levels was widely recognized as a necessary and urgent step.

Education and Employability After the 1999 Reform

The original draft of law n.508/1999 foresaw the inclusion of only a selection of the nearly eighty conservatories within the AFAM system, while the others should have offered pre-academic training. However, as a result of a long-lasting corporatist battle won by the artists' trade unions, the final version of the law placed all conservatories on the level of higher education, leaving unsolved the crucial issue of the lack of public offerings for pre-academic music training.[6]

Once the law was approved, music conservatories and other higher art education organizations were asked to gradually conform to the general rules governing universities, as revised to comply with the Bologna declaration. One of the main objectives set by the declaration was the organization of higher education systems according to a degree-cycle structure, encompassing a first cycle of undergraduate programmes and a second cycle of graduate and doctoral programmes.[7] In the case of Italian conservatories, innovation was not limited to the adoption of the degree structure but also included a significant widening of the curricular offerings, entrenched throughout the twentieth century in the canonical model of classical musicians' training: New curricula included classical music courses going beyond the strict canon or the *virtuoso* ideal, such as baroque or ensemble music – or courses on a variety of musical genres or styles, such as jazz, pop, rock or electronic music. Age restrictions – quite strict in the previous curricular offerings – were formally abolished: To audition for entry at an Italian conservatory, candidates need a secondary school certificate and preliminary music skills, which vary according to the course chosen.

The significant changes following the introduction of Italian music conservatories into the field of higher education, however, were realized without additional state funding. In the case of new courses, each conservatory decided for itself which one to activate according to its budget, bearing the costs of the teachers hired on temporary contracts. The result is a paradoxical situation: Younger generations of teachers, artistically active and usually more innovative in teaching, are kept in precarious and underpaid employment conditions, while occupational stability is granted to their tenured colleagues who are often ill-equipped to meet the demands of the newly reformed institutions. A voice student sums up this paradox:

> Even here [in this conservatory] we have amazing, very good teachers. Most of them, strangely [with an ironic tone], are precarious, and unfortunately there are those others who have the posts instead, who do nothing to improve themselves, to teach in English, to better service their students who work their asses off. [. . .] There are [European] students who come to an [Italian] conservatory for an Erasmus [programme] and choose a teacher who is like a guru, and then in November they find out that no one knows yet where he will work the next year. (Student in the postgraduate classical voice course, male, 30)

Due to the artists unions' obstructions, the regulations for the flexible hiring of new teachers envisaged by the 1999 reform law have not yet been adopted. Currently, the only possibility for new teachers to seek tenure is to replace tenured colleagues from the classical music department, whose course may be cancelled after retirement. This mechanism results in a zero-sum game between different departments, in which one side's gain is offset by the other's loss, enhancing conflictual relationships between professional groups (Abbott, 1988). Older generations of teachers in particular, whose professional identity is rooted in teaching and performing the classic musical canon, view the introduction of other music genres into conservatories as suicide for the classical music tradition. Some of them believe that it would have been better to create new institutions for jazz and popular music education, which would allow for richer music education offerings while preserving the classical music tradition. This kind of solution, as noted by other interviewees, sounds unrealistic at a time when public funding is being cut and the marketization of public education is on the rise. In the words of the teacher quoted below, the reform overtly follows a market logic that adapts the educational offerings to the demands of the 'students-clients' rather than to the autonomous logic of the music field:

> Like the audience for television, now we have a share: 'How many students do you have? Then your course is activated!' It's madness, because if one teaches a discipline that is elitist but finds its own necessity within an artistic field. (Piano teacher, male, 50)

The tensions between the classical music and popular music departments are also evident in the different understandings of the musical competence and technical proficiency demanded from students, both in the selection and the training processes. This, in turn, reveals different aesthetic, cultural and even socio-economic values underlying the respective 'art worlds' (Becker, 1982). As the following quote suggests, classical music teachers reward students who demonstrate technical and performative proficiency framed within specific bodies of theoretical knowledge, while their colleagues in popular music departments legitimize self-taught learning and 'spontaneous authenticity' (Hunter, 2019: 45). In the context of market logic, however, the increased demands placed on classical music degree programmes mean that their attractiveness among the 'students-clients' continues to decline.

> I'm a little critical on those new jazz music classes. I told you that I believe it's fundamental, very important to include them. But the recruitment of their students: They do two chords, two motives [and they're in], while we butcher our candidates [of the classical department] before selecting them. That's why I say: I understand, it's jazz, but it can't be that you can't read two chords [. . .]. But you know, in our conservatory, 70 to 80 percent are enrolled in these [new] courses, so it's a kind of market: 'Sell, sell!' But if you don't have clients, what do you sell? (Clarinet teacher, male, 50)

The differentiation in the criteria guiding selection and training processes in the classical and popular music departments also reveals a gender dimension: Quantitative and qualitative data on female students after the reform show their increased and legitimized presence in a greater variety of courses on the classical canon (still limited to the lower levels of its traditional hierarchy) but their limited and often discouraged participation in non-classical music courses, with the exception of voice classes (Casula, 2019).

Another innovation introduced by the reform following the Bologna declaration is the introduction of external indicators and procedures for the certification and continuous improvement of the quality of higher education institutions. These new tasks are assumed by the teachers who are asked to formally monitor the teaching and production activities of the institutions, usually without technical or administrative support, in order to assess their consistency with the adopted strategic planning documents. As one pianist explains in the following quote, these burdensome activities, along with growing expectations of instantaneous responses to the hyperconnected communication via digital devices, are difficult to reconcile with the daily time required to practice an instrument and, indirectly, with maintaining the professional level and *ethos* of the teachers:

> Since the reform [of conservatories] my printer has no rest . . . But: Was I a musician? What have I become? It is a continuous: 'Fill in the form, the model, the declaration, the evaluation and the report . . .!' [. . .] With these emails, certainly great but, frankly, I can't take it anymore, because I'm afraid to check what has arrived [. . .] always problems in sight, it's not easy . . . and that's also work [to manage emails]; it steals your time. For me, who I'm a pianist, let's be realistic: If I have to practice a piece, I'm not able to reply [to emails] every half an hour. (Piano teacher, female, 55)

The reform also introduces the European Credit Transfer and Accumulation System (ECTS), a key objective of the Bologna declaration. This tool, intended to facilitate the transition of students' educational careers from one national system of higher education to another, was welcomed by conservatories, given the long and established tradition of transnational vocational music education.[8] Its etymology, however, reveals its closeness with the neoliberal approach, applying business management criteria to public administration in order to improve efficiency (Osborne and Gaebler, 1992). The logic underlying this tool encourages students to adopt a calculative approach to the accumulation of ECTS credits, which they tend to conceive as a certification of the knowledge achieved rather than an approximate assessment of course load. In the following quote, a teacher explains why this approach, weakening the teachers' role in terms of both control and responsibility over pupils' actual achievements, ultimately leads to the decline in the average proficiency level reached by conservatory students:

> [After the reform] I became a vending machine of hours, teaching hours. I mean, students came and said: 'I must prepare this, this and this . . .' When they reached a certain amount of teaching hours: '*Maestro*, I have finished, I have to take the exam'; 'You cannot do the exam, because you are not in the condition to take the exam: I know you've done all the hours and that you can do it, but you won't do it, because you're not ready!'; 'I don't care: I'll take the exam anyway,

because I have finished the hours and I have no intention to continue attending the course'. (String quartet teacher, male, 55)

As noted by the interviewee in the following quote, teachers feel frustrated and 'blackmailed' by the new system, as it forces them to obey to a market logic linking the survival of courses to the economic contribution of the enrolled students who – even when not adequately committed to their studies – are still paying their fees:

> The problem, for instance, is how to dismiss students if they don't study: We [teachers] are also under blackmail [. . .] because if I know that the student has to be kept in [the conservatory], because he pays the fees, even if he only gets barely sufficient marks, this doesn't allow me to dedicate myself with the right commitment. (Electronic music teacher, male, 50)

Students' adherence to the logic of credentialism – privileging formal educational credentials over more practical assessments of competence or experience (Collins, 2011) – also emerges in the motivations for different categories of students mainly enrolled in Italian conservatories to achieve a qualification that is expendable in the Italian labour market. There are those, often mature, students who already have a career in music but are self-taught, or lack an academic degree, or are concerned about the validity of their pre-reform conservatory degrees, or aim to add a further qualification to their *curriculum vitae*; but there are also those young and talented students who are studying either privately or in foreign music institutes with internationally renowned teachers but who wish to easily obtain a degree from an Italian conservatory to widen their employability in the Italian labour market. Students' motivations seem to match with the type of demand mostly encountered by conservatory graduates in the national labour market. A recent report on the employability of students with an AFAM degree (the majority of whom graduated from conservatories) shows that more than half of the respondents reported being employed within one or two years after graduation (respectively, in 2013 and 2014), but only one-fifth in artistic occupations, while the majority is employed as teachers of artistic or other disciplines (AlmaLaurea, 2016), a job usually obtained through rankings defined on the basis of formal certifications.

In sum, although the 1999 reform law has undoubtedly contributed to a new visibility and prestige to higher music and artistic education within the national educational system, in the case of music conservatories its implementation has produced significant shortcomings that do not seem sustainable in the long term without affecting the quality of the training and of the employment chances granted to their students.

Conclusion

The implementation of the law upgrading Italian music conservatories to the tertiary level of education, welcomed by many as a departure from the self-referential ivory tower in which they had entrenched themselves during the twentieth century, has met with mixed results. The process of institutional isomorphism that followed this change – prompting conservatories to conform with the rules, norms and beliefs regulating the university system according to the Bologna declaration – has produced a series of shortcomings. As discussed in the chapter, some of these shortcomings seem to have been created by resistance to change (as in the case of the powerful obstruction of trade unions, taking advantage of the government's disinterest in the field to defend teachers' vested interests regardless of the consequences to the overall system). Others, in contrast, seem related to the wider global pressures to regulate national education systems according to neoliberal models, privileging the quantity of 'students-clients' over the quality of their training and shifting the role of higher education institutions from recruitment to certification agencies.

The complex picture that emerges calls for a thorough policy intervention that reconsiders the organization of Italian conservatories in terms of efficiency and equity, both at the internal level and in relationship to the wider national system of education. This policy, in my view, should primarily focus on the following objectives: Regarding internal reorganization, a meritocratic system for the recruitment of staff and students needs to be adopted that critically addresses issues of implicit biases and other forms of direct or indirect discrimination. With reference to external reorganization, music education needs to be horizontally integrated into all segments of compulsory schooling in order to offer all citizens the basic knowledge necessary to appreciate and practice musical culture. At the same time, the music curricula should be vertically integrated following a pyramidal rather than the actual funnel-shaped model, granting access to advanced training in music only to a selection of students aiming to pursue a professional career, countering the market logic prompted by neoliberal ideology. Obviously, none of this can be achieved in the absence of a political will to recognize music as a fundamental cultural, social and economic value for the country.

Notes

1 Law n. 508 of 21 December 1999 (entered into force on 19 January 2000): Reform of Fine Arts Academies, National Dance Academy, National Academy of Drama, Higher Institutes for Artistic Industries, of Conservatories of Music and state-recognized Musical Institutes.
2 I refer here to state-recognized music conservatories and musical institutes, funded either by the state or local authorities (the 1999 reform defines them as Higher Institutes for Musical Studies, but the term did not come into use).
3 Interviews reconstructed the educational and professional paths of musicians and were analysed following an inductive and comparative approach (Brinkmann and Kvale, 2015). Excerpts cited here from the interviews, conducted in Italian, were translated into English by the author. In addition to interviews, the study included the analysis of official statistics, parliamentary records, newspapers and a questionnaire for conservatory teachers. The research complied with the rules and ethical codes concerning the collection, analysis and protection of data for social research.

4 Italian Opera Houses are institutions organizing opera and concert activities, considered by the state of relevant public interest as intended to promote the musical, cultural and social education of the national community. Originally set as public bodies (Enti lirico-sinfonici, Law n. 800, 14 August 1967), they have been later qualified as private law foundations (Fondazioni lirico-sinfoniche, Decree Law n. 367, 29 June 1996), although they still obtain significant state funding.
5 To give an idea of the scale of change, in the school year 1966–7, there were thirty-five music conservatories, encompassing 6,026 students and 1,279 teachers; twenty years later, the number of conservatories rose to sixty-nine, with 33,884 students and 5,352 teachers. In the academic year 2019–20 there were seventy-eight institutes, with 43,713 students (72 per cent of whom registered in academic courses) and 6,363 teachers (38 per cent on temporary contracts) (source: Statistics on education collected by the National Institute of Statistics (ISTAT) and by the statistical office of the Ministry of Education, University and Research – Department for Higher Artistic and Musical Education (MIUR-AFAM), various years).
6 A stopgap was found allowing conservatories to temporarily activate pre-academic courses and with the creation of musical lyceums, whose scarce distribution in the territory and limited curricular offerings do not solve the issue.
7 Doctoral programmes were to be added later in a third cycle.
8 Wagner (2015). In the academic year 2019–20, the percentage of foreign students enrolled in Italian conservatories was nearly 12 per cent of the total student population, while for state universities, it was nearly 6 per cent in the following academic year.

References

Abbott, A. (1988), *The System of Professions. An Essay on the Division of Expert Labor*, Chicago: Chicago University Press.
AlmaLaurea (2016), 'Esiti occupazionali dei diplomati accademici delle Istituzioni di Alta Formazione Artistica, Musicale e Coreutica (AFAM)', Report. Available online: https://www.almalaurea.it/sites/almalaurea.it/files/docs/universita/altro/afam-occupazione-2016/report_occupazione_afam_finale.pdf (accessed 11 December 2021).
Aversano, L. (2021), 'La musica nella formazione scolastica degli italiani', in A. Estero (ed.), *La cultura musicale degli italiani*, 3–35, Milano: Guerini.
Becker, H. S. (1982), *Art Worlds*, Berkeley: University of California Press.
Brinkmann, S. and S. Kvale (2015), *InterViews. Learning the Craft of Qualitative Research Interviewing*, Los Angeles: Sage.
Casula, C. (2018a), *Diventare musicista. Indagine sociologica sui Conservatori di musica in Italia*, Mantua: Universitas Studiorum.
Casula, C. (2018b), 'Torn between Neoliberal and Postmodern Trends, Corporatist Defence and Creative Age Prospects: The Ongoing Reshaping of the Classical Music Profession in Italy', *Cambio. Rivista sulle Trasformazioni Sociali*, 8 (16): 71–82.
Casula, C. (2019), 'Gender and the Classical Music World: The Unaccomplished Professionalization of Women in Italy', *Per Musi Journal*, 39: 1–24.
Casula, C. (2023), 'Class and Gender Inequalities in the Recruitment of Classical Musicians: Reflections on the Case of Italian Music Conservatoires', in A. Bull, C. Scharff and L. Nooshin (eds), *Voices for Change in the Classical Music Profession: New*

Ideas for Tackling Inequalities and Exclusions, 19–30, New York: Oxford University Press.

Colarizi, G. (1971), *L'insegnamento della musica in Italia*, Roma: Armando.

Collins, R. (2011), 'Credential Inflation and the Future of Universities', *Italian Journal of Sociology of Education*, 3 (2): 228–51.

De Feo, A. and M. Pitzalis (2017), 'Service or Market Logic? The Restructuring of the Tertiary Education System in Italy', *Rassegna Italiana di Sociologia*, 2 (LVIII): 219–50.

Delfrati, C. (2017), *Storia critica dell'insegnamento della musica in Italia*, ebook, Ancona: Antonio Tombolini.

DiMaggio, P. (1982), 'Cultural Entrepreneurship in Nineteenth-Century Boston: The Creation of an Organizational Base for High Culture in America', *Media, Culture & Society*, 4 (1): 33–55.

DiMaggio, P. and W. W. Powell (1991), 'The Iron Cage Revisited: Institutional Isomorphism and Collective Rationality in Organizational Fields', in W. W. Powell and P. DiMaggio, *The New Institutionalism in Organizational Analysis*, 63–82, Chicago: University of Chicago Press.

Frederickson, J. and J. F. Rooney (1990), 'How the Music Occupation failed to become a Profession', *International Review of the Aesthetics and Sociology of Music*, 21 (2): 189–206.

Freidson, E. (1986), 'Les professions artistiques comme défi à l'analyse sociologique', *Revue française de sociologie*, 27 (3): 431–43.

Grimaldi, E. and R. Serpieri (2012), 'The Transformation of the Education State in Italy: A Critical Policy Historiography from 1944 to 2011', *Italian Journal of Sociology of Education*, 4 (1): 146–80.

Hunter, M. (2019), 'Considering Techne in Popular Music Education: Value Systems in Popular Music Curricula', in Z. Moir, B. Powell and G. Dylan (eds), *The Bloomsbury Handbook of Popular Music Education: Perspectives and Practices*, 45–58, London: Bloomsbury Academic.

Kingsbury, H. (1988), *Music, Talent and Performance. A Conservatory Cultural System*, Philadelphia: Temple University Press.

Meyer, J. W. and B. Rowan (1991), 'Institutionalized Organizations: Formal Structure as Myth and Ceremony', in W. W. Powell and P. DiMaggio (eds), *The New Institutionalism in Organizational Analysis*, 41–62, Chicago: University of Chicago Press.

Osborne, D. and T. Gaebler (1992), *Reinventing Government: How the Entrepreneurial Spirit is Transforming the Public Sector*, Reading: Addison-Wesley.

Pierre, C. (1990), *Le Conservatorie national de musique et de declamation*, Paris: Imprimerie Nationale.

Powell, W. W. and P. DiMaggio, eds (1991), *The New Institutionalism in Organizational Analysis*, Chicago: University of Chicago Press.

Prokop, R. and R. Reitsamer (2023), 'The Role of Music Conservatoires in the Making of Classical Music Careers', in A. Bull, C. Scharff and L. Nooshin (eds), *Voices for Change in the Classical Music Profession: New Ideas for Tackling Inequalities and Exclusions*, 31–41, New York: Oxford University Press.

Roselli, E. (2015), *Uscire dal ghetto. Riflessioni sulla riforma dei Conservatori di musica a 15 anni dall'approvazione della legge 508*, Roma: Armando.

Scott, W. R. (2008), 'Lords of the Dance: Professionals as Institutional Agents', *Organization Studies*, 29 (2): 219–38.

Štech, S. (2012), 'The Bologna Process as a New Public Management Tool in Higher Education', *Journal of Pedagogy / Pedagogický casopis*, 2 (2): 123–42.
Wagner, I. (2015), *Producing Excellence: The Making of Virtuosos*, New Brunswick: Rutgers University Press.
Weber, W. (1999), 'The History of the Musical Canon', in N. Cook and M. Everist (eds), *Rethinking Music*, 336–55, Oxford: Oxford University Press.

Chapter 2

Marketing Conservatoire Education

The Employable White Musicians of European Classical Music

Ann Werner and Cecilia Ferm Almqvist

Introduction

Neoliberalism as a discourse, and as a method of measuring the quality of education in accordance with New Public Management (NPM) ideas, has had an effect on higher music education (HME) institutions. This can be seen, for example, in the increasing competition by HME institutions for the 'best' students, teachers and rankings. Neoliberal ideas also shape the websites and other media produced by HME institutions by portraying students and teachers as excellent and employable. Consequently, website representations of HME institutions illustrate how general discourses in neoliberal capitalism affect musicians' work in a job market where self-optimization has become important (Scharff, 2015). The impact of neoliberal capitalist policies within HME and the university system in general has been comprehensively discussed in research on internal evaluation and monitoring systems as well as on how students are turned into consumers of education (Giroux, 2014). Nevertheless, the marketization of HME deserves more attention.

This chapter considers the websites of the Estonian Academy of Music and Theatre (Tallinn, Estonia), the Sibelius Academy of the University of the Arts (Helsinki, Finland) and the Liszt Ferenc Academy of Music (Budapest, Hungary)[1] and critically investigates the following questions: How do these conservatoires market their classical music[2] education programmes? How, through this marketing, is the employable musician constructed in terms of European whiteness? How is 'otherness' represented on the websites of these conservatoires that are considered as the top HME institutions in their respective countries?

We understand websites as performative, as doing something by showing some students and not others and by suggesting some careers and not others. Representations on websites are not reflections of the world; they do not present the actual racial or ethnic composition of students at the institutions. Rather, the websites show a certain image of classical music education and, by doing so, promote a certain image of the classical musician. The consequences of these constructions are not discussed here, but by comparing our analysis of the web pages with other research, it becomes clear that an ideal of whiteness translates into difficulties for non-white students of classical music (Wang, 2015).

Our study is based on the analysis of the opening pages of each conservatoire's website; the pages for piano, strings, voice and percussion study programmes; and pages labelled 'international/exchange/guest studies'. The opening pages were chosen because they are the 'face' of the conservatoires and the first marketing interface that website visitors encounter. The four classical music programme pages were selected in order to analyse how classical music education programmes are presented, and the 'international/exchange/guest studies' pages were chosen in order to explore the limits of a European white tradition. We mapped the visual and textual content of these pages in the spring of 2021 and documented our work with screenshots and field notes. These were then synthesized using content analysis, where *what* was represented and *how* it was represented provided a structure in the form of a table for our analysis (Schreier, 2012). After this initial phase, a discourse-analytical approach (Laclau and Mouffe, 1985) was employed in order to examine how representations of careers, work and whiteness function as signs and determine meanings in discourses about classical music.

Our analysis is divided into four parts: After a brief discussion of recent research on neoliberalism, HME and whiteness (part one), we analyse how classical music education and the classical musicians (teachers and students) are constructed in relation to whiteness and how non-white students are represented on the websites (parts two and three). In the fourth part, we examine how the three conservatoires relate their educational goals and the content of their courses to the working world of classical musicians and how students and teachers are visually represented in work contexts. In the conclusion, we make a few suggestions intended to overcome tokenistic representations of non-white students and to present a nuanced picture of the careers of classical musicians in the twenty-first century.

Neoliberalism and Whiteness in HME

Neoliberal capitalism has affected the higher education sector through NPM. NPM consists of processes whereby market economic ideas about how an organization should be run become dominant through budget processes, evaluation processes and the professionalization of leadership. The impact of self-monitoring, the commodification of education and market ideas (ideas about how best to market education) as applied to the university sector have been critically discussed and seen as an obstacle to quality and as at odds with democratic and critical practice (Giroux, 2014). Marketization is a central aspect of neoliberal capitalism, whereby institutions incorporate market-focused thinking. In accordance with neoliberal discourse, higher education institutions act as if the 'product' (education) must be marketed to the 'consumers' (students). The neoliberal marketing of higher education brings the norms and ideals of institutions to the forefront, for example, on web pages. Ideals include the whiteness assumed in HME institutions.

Patterns of whiteness and the conservation of European cultural heritage have been observed in both participation and curricula within HME institutions (Shim, 2021). Dyer (1997) argues that whiteness is signified by invisibility – there is no white race defined as such – and being white is seen as not having a colour. This invisibility is a prerequisite for white power. White people are seen only as 'people', while people otherwise raced are linked to racial stereotypes. The lack of racialized stereotypes and ideas about white people as a group constitutes whiteness as normative and powerful. It is because it is normative that white culture can be perceived as 'culture' per se. In line with Dyer's theorization of the invisibility of whiteness as a racialized position, classical music often includes representations of whiteness as pervasive but invisible.

Thurman (2012) has investigated whiteness as an integral part of the sound and representation of classical music culture through the German tradition. Her case study of the reception of Grace Bumbry, a Black singer, performing work by Richard Wagner in 1961, highlights the racialized ideas that equate classical voices with white voices and regard roles in stage performances of opera as white roles. Thurman argues that these racialized ideas exclude Black singers from the classical music repertoire. The significance of whiteness in classical music performance has also been studied from the perspective of Asian American performers. Wang (2015) argues that while there are large numbers of Asian Americans in HME institutions in the United States, racism and the association of classical music practice with whiteness present challenges for their full participation in the classical music labour market (cf. Yoshihara, 2007). Leppänen (2015) shows that media discourses around the Sibelius violin competition in Finland were shaped by everyday racism directed against East Asian performers, while simultaneously reproducing the discourse about classical music as untouched by gender, race, class and nation. On a symbolic level, Ware and Back (2002) discuss how whiteness ideals are central to music culture in both popular and classical music. From the composer Richard Wagner to White Power music and online music culture, they all interact with race and racism in terms of whiteness. According to Hess (2018), whiteness dominates the narratives of children's music education and is being challenged by practices of anti-racist pedagogies in teaching. Anti-racist pedagogies and diversity work have found a place in European conservatoire education in recent years (Guerra et al., 2020).

Parkinson and Gardner's (2021) analysis of mission and vision statements on the websites of seventy-one conservatoires and music departments in Turkey found that classical music culture was portrayed as national and shaped by a white European canon. At the same time, an advocacy of pluralism was expressed. Such contradictions were also identified by Moberg and Georgii-Hemming (2021) in their study of websites of HME institutions in Sweden, where boundary transgression, openness and diversity were portrayed in writing, while the images constructed a white Swedish ideal through pictures of young, healthy people embodying white Swedish ethnicities. They also found that the websites of HME institutions in Sweden referred to male composers more than 200 times, while female composers were mentioned only ten times. Most of the composers, male and female, were born in Europe. However, Moberg and Georgii-Hemming did not investigate the association of whiteness with Europeanness. HME institutions in the United States have also been found to have a system that privileges white male European and American composers (Kajikawa, 2019: 156–7). Kajikawa (2019) argues that the privileging of whiteness in HME in the United States is accepted as the norm, and the status quo of the white male classical music canon permeates daily routines and habits of thought. The colour-blind language often used to describe music avoids questioning whiteness, but there are also instances where US classical music is directly linked to the ideology of white supremacy (Kajikawa, 2019: 158–9).

The Multiple Whiteness of Classical Musicians

We will now turn to the visual and textual representations of students and teachers on the websites of the Estonian Academy of Music and Theatre, the Sibelius Academy and the Liszt Ferenc Academy of Music.

On the opening page of the Estonian Academy of Music and Theatre, we found a photo of two young white men playing the piano and clarinet on a stage; of five additional photos on the opening page, all except one show white people in practice rooms or on a stage. These photos portray student life when performing and practising. The Sibelius Academy and the Liszt Ferenc Academy of Music also display photos on their opening pages and the pages marketing the music performance programmes for piano, strings, voice and percussion, which almost exclusively show white students and white male teachers in leadership positions. This confirms the white European tradition of classical music and the symbolic connection between white (male) European heritage and classical music (Thurman, 2012).

A detailed analysis of the photos makes clear that there are differences in the representation of whiteness. For example, next to the image of two young white male cellists on the opening page of the Sibelius Academy, we found a link to the Orchestra Academy of the Music Centre with the caption 'When future musicians are educated in the same building as the best experts in the orchestra world, a unique educational concept is created'.[3] The young man in the foreground is blond, the one in the background has sand-coloured hair. They look pale, slim and serious and wear blue button-down shirts. Their whiteness is boreal, Nordic.

In contrast, the opening page of the Liszt Ferenc Academy of Music shows a photo with the caption 'student life', featuring four young white female students with instruments and musical scores.[4] The woman in the middle of the picture has dark brown curls, red lipstick and olive skin. She is smiling and holding up a violin case with colourful stickers representing places she may have travelled to. Here, whiteness is portrayed as youthful and cheerful but in a slightly darker colour scale compared to the images on the opening page of the Sibelius Academy discussed earlier. Another example of the portrayal of whiteness on the website of the Liszt Ferenc Academy of Music is a photo with the caption 'university studies', showing three male percussionists in black shirts with black or dark brown hair, looking serious and focused. Compared to the cellists from Finland studying at the Sibelius Academy, they too represent a darker shade of whiteness.[5]

The youthful and playful attitude of the girls on the opening page of the Liszt Ferenc Academy of Music is also reflected in photos on the opening page of the Sibelius Academy: a group of students laughing and practising, apparently sitting on the floor with their instruments.[6] Like the pale cellists on the same opening page, these students have lighter hair and skin tones than the students at the Liszt Ferenc Academy of Music page. On the website of the Estonian Academy of Music and Theatre, the portrayal of whiteness is more in line with the Finnish version. For example, on the string department page, most of the performers in the photos are blonde or have sand-coloured hair and pale skin. On the piano department page, one photo shows a young female and blonde pianist in an evening gown and her three young female violinists who are all blonde and pale.[7]

While students are sometimes portrayed playfully, the white teachers and professors are not. These are mostly male; one exception is Andrea Vigh, the president of the Liszt Ferenc Academy of Music, who as a woman holds power and control over the entire institution. She is a blonde, white woman.

The conclusion to be drawn from the earlier analysis is that the visual representations reproduce the association of classical music with whiteness by depicting only white people on the opening pages and, as a result, whiteness becomes an unquestioned norm. Furthermore, the different forms of whiteness in representations of classical music in the European context highlight that European whiteness is multiple and hierarchized through its connections with different regions of Europe.

Non-white Subjects and Internationalization

Since the websites of the HME institutions predominantly show photos of white students and teachers, we specifically looked for representations of non-white people. On the international/exchange web pages of the three HME institutions we found photos of non-white students and artists. The 'international' web page of the Estonian Academy of Music and Theatre contains six photos.[8] Three photos show performances, one photo shows a group of people walking outside (possibly on a field trip) and the remaining two are group photos of students of whom two appear to be East Asian. The nationality of the students is not indicated; they could be Estonian nationals or visiting students from Finland or another country. However, the placement under the heading 'international' associates them with 'otherness' because they are 'international' and not from 'here'. Leppänen (2015: 23) argues in a study of representations of the Sibelius violin competition that East Asian classical musicians are portrayed by the media as peaceful people and technically skilled performers. While these are positive qualities, they serve to distinguish East Asian musicians from 'true' classical musical geniuses, whose musicality and sensitive interpretations are emphasized rather than technical skill (Leppänen, 2015: 30). Work ethic and discipline are further qualities that make up the stereotype of Asians in classical music (Wang, 2015).

Photos of East Asian students and artists are rarely shown on the websites of HME institutions, and if they are included, it is often as nameless smiling young faces. This representation underlines Ahmed's (2009) claim that non-white people are expected to be happy and grateful to be included and to represent 'diversity'. At the same time, these photos tend to reproduce globally circulated prejudices and racist stereotypes of East Asian classically trained musicians as above all 'friendly'.

On the 'student exchange' page of the website of the Sibelius Academy, the photos of named white students are accompanied by stories about their student exchange. On the 'international' page of the website of the Estonian Academy of Music and Theatre we also found videos of white students talking about their experiences of exchange in Europe and a photo of two international students, a young woman with an East Asian appearance and a young white man with dark brown hair and beard, being hugged by the Estonian composer Arvo Pärt. The caption reads 'international students with Arvo Pärt', and in the background we see a concert stage, instruments and chairs. The woman is small, a smiling nameless face with glasses. Other images of short and young East Asian-looking students can be found on the 'student exchange' page of the website of the Sibelius Academy and on the 'exchange studies & mobility'[9] page of the website of the Liszt Ferenc Academy of Music, the latter showing a young white woman with a violin and a young East Asian woman at a piano. Their photo is captioned 'guest studies'.

The 'international visitor programme' page of the website of the Sibelius Academy features photos of high-profile musicians visiting the Academy. Here, seven white male 'artists who represent the highest talent level of their respective fields'[10] are introduced with photos and biographies (in spring 2021 it was Emmanuel Ceysson, David Dolan, Neil Heyde, Robert Levin, Andreas Schmidt, Lars Ulrik Mortensen and Franco Bianchini), accompanied by links to their websites and, further down, a longer list of visitors without photos. The only non-white artist presented in this showcase is the Chinese cellist Jian Wang.[11]

East Asian musicians appear mostly under the 'international', 'exchange' or 'mobility' headings on the three websites. Exceptions include female East Asian students shown in group photos representing strings and voice on the website of the Estonian Academy of Music and Theatre.

Musicians, students and teachers who are not white are portrayed as 'not-from-here' by their placement on the websites and by the way they are shown as happy diversity tokens (Ahmed, 2009) or made invisible by omission. There are many famous East Asian performers in classical music today, performing in all parts of the world. Still, persons of East Asian appearance are marginalized on the websites of the HME institutions. Other non-white students are totally missing. The image of the 'Asian other' enhances the white norm of the institution by its marginal presence, adding 'good' values of diversity (Ahmed, 2009) to the institutional marketing.

Employability of Future Musicians

Entrepreneurial skills are increasingly included in HME courses, a change that illustrates how neoliberal discourse permeates higher education. Learning skills such as writing a CV or creating a YouTube channel is assumed to increase HME students' employability and make them more attractive as musicians in the job market. In recent years, different arguments have been put forward by researchers in relation to the education of music students. On the one hand, it is argued that it is necessary to train students to become skilled instrumentalists (Stepniak and Serotonin, 2020); on the other hand, it is argued that the jobs of musicians might include a number of different tasks (López-Íñiguez and Bennett, 2021; Bennett, 2013). Despite these discussions, researchers have shown that musical performance is presented as the most important aspect of the education of conservatoire students on the websites of HME institutions in Sweden (Moberg and Georgii-Hemming, 2021) and the United States (Turner, 2004). Blackstone (2019: 33) argues that the prospectuses and websites of British HME institutions also include elements of career preparation such as self-promotion, financial management, CV preparation and networking.

On the websites analysed here, the institutions present their study programmes by describing the course content and the educational goals. Students and teachers are portrayed in working contexts as performing and practising, and – as shown earlier – whiteness dominates these portrayals.

The website of the Liszt Ferenc Academy of Music states that students in classical piano training 'learn a significant number of important compositions which belong to the heart of the piano repertoire and to practice performing them at an artistically high level'[12] and refers to one possible career: that of musician. The MA programme in violin aims to enable students 'to function as members of various orchestras, or in chamber ensembles, or perform as soloists in a national or international setting'.[13] Here, three career options are highlighted: orchestra musician, soloist and chamber musician. Very similar expressions are used to describe the future career paths of voice students. The website of the Estonian Academy of Music and Theatre states that voice studies offer students 'comprehensive preparation for their future work on concert stages and in professional opera theatres',[14] pointing to performance as the only option after graduation. The piano programme at the Sibelius Academy is presented as preparation 'for a professional life as a soloist, chamber musician or a pedagogue',[15] while the strings programme enables students to 'play together with top professionals in a symphony orchestra'. In addition, it is stated that 'our graduates work as competent pedagogues and orchestra musicians, chamber musicians and soloists'.[16] These descriptions of future careers for classical music students support the findings of previous research that musical performance is presented as the preferred career for students, since it is often mentioned first and most frequently. However, there are usually no indications of how to achieve these career goals and there is no reflection of the discussion about providing HME students with generic skills to meet the demands of the employment market. The classical musician is thus, in neoliberal terms, presented as already embodying the generic skills required, implying that these musicians hail from musical families of the middle and upper classes and possess the required cultural and social capital.

The following analysis will demonstrate how the websites of HME institutions also address the changing nature of the labour market for classical musicians and construct 'new' subjectivities. The BA performance programme in piano at the Estonian Academy of Music and Theatre is said to include 'a variety of creative events – concerts and competitions – that support the professional ambitions of the students, help develop their personal styles as musical interpreters, and encourage self-sufficiency which is essential in our rapidly changing world'.[17] On the same website, in the context of the programme for strings, students are said to 'learn a wide range of skills enabling them to succeed and adapt in today's rapidly changing professional environment'.[18] In both of these quotes, the world and the profession are described as changing and students are portrayed as being in need of skills to meet these changes. The description of these changes and of the skills needed to meet the demands of a neoliberal classical music labour market remains vague, but unlike in the examples given in the previous paragraph, it is implied that instrument proficiency is not enough to advance a career in classical music. The website of the Sibelius Academy includes statements describing the skills students need in order to face the contemporary situation for classical musicians: 'In addition to mastering their instrument, we want to develop students' artistic and informational skills and provide them with the ability to apply skills in a variety of contexts in the workplace.'[19] While this variety of contexts where students can find themselves working after graduating is not described in any detail, the multiplicity of work contexts and the need for 'informational' skills suggest that there is more to being a musician than playing and teaching. This is in line with the idea that musicians' work contains a plurality of tasks (López-Íñiguez and Bennett, 2021; Bennett, 2013). The idea that the skills needed for many tasks should be taught in HME programmes fits in with neoliberal discourse, in which skills are seen as something that individuals acquire, possess and use to meet the challenges of the labour market.

There is also a specific course offered by the Sibelius Academy, entitled 'career and study skills', that aims to achieve the following learning outcomes: 'be able to apply his/her skills in new situations and environments' and 'be able to network and to find new ways of being employed as a musician in a changing society'.[20] As in the earlier examples, 'change' and 'new situations' are presented as challenges for the profession but then countered by the course helping students to 'find new ways to be employed'. Networking, as a method for finding work in the classical music profession, is both central in a precarious job market and coloured by gendered and classed dimensions of power, where some can network better than others (Scharff, 2018). Scharff (2018) argues that (new) subjectivities are created when female classical musicians successfully network and promote themselves. Networking is mentioned again in the presentation of the classical music performance programme in voice on the website of the Sibelius Academy: it is said to give students 'the chance to cooperate with international partners and build global networks already during your studies'.[21]

For musicians who graduate from the three conservatoires, their future employment options are suggested to be as orchestral, ensemble or solo players or as teachers, with fewer mentions of the teaching option. However, at the same time, the role of the musician is described as changing and challenged by a job market that requires new skills. The HME institutions suggest that to face this job market, musicians will require informational skills, networking skills and the ability to find new types of work.

Based on our study of these websites, we argue that 'new' subjectivities are suggested for future musicians, which include skills in presenting themselves, networking and so on. However, these indications of 'new' subjectivities are placed on web pages that mainly show images of white performers and that do not discuss race or ethnicity, thus making this an invisible dimension. Therefore, the 'new' subjectivities of classical music performers in Europe are still presented as white.

Conclusion

This chapter has considered how the websites of the Estonian Academy of Music and Theatre, the Sibelius Academy and the Liszt Ferenc Academy of Music market their classical music education programmes; how, through this marketing, the employable musician is constructed in terms of European whiteness; and how 'otherness' is represented. When the HME institutions portray their education programmes, they show white musicians practising and performing, and performance is often highlighted in descriptions of careers. At the same time, it is argued that the classical music profession, and the world, is changing (Bennett, 2013). However, the whiteness of the students and teachers is central to the portrayal of the performance tradition of classical music in Europe – and to the value ascribed to it. Thus, the whiteness of the websites reinforces the traditional representation of the career paths of classically trained musicians. By not addressing diversity in careers, or routes to diverse careers, the way the neoliberal job market works becomes a mystery. By the omission of musicians who are not white or East Asian, these become completely invisible and the unspoken whiteness of the institutions of classical music education in Central and Eastern Europe and the Nordics is confirmed (Blackstone, 2019)[22]. Employment and studies in classical music are symbolized by a strong, albeit diverse, European whiteness.

How could marketing efforts avoid the obvious risk that musicianship and the employable classical musician are portrayed as white and that job market challenges are obscured? As Hess (2021) suggests, the key is to avoid a totalizing discourse and instead encourage diversity. The message of whiteness and European classical music that the web pages mediate could be viewed as examples of how music education perpetuates colonialism and contributes to cultural hegemony (Hess, 2021). How could marketing mediated through websites that confirm a totalizing discourse of European whiteness connected to employability be changed towards a more anti-colonialist approach? Anti-colonialism aims to resist and change colonialism and to contribute to something new, for example, through emphasis on agency and the analysis of power structures. Hence, to use web pages to challenge the totalizing discourse that this chapter has highlighted, a variety of voices should be heard and multiple images seen. Webmasters should cooperate with conservatoire students, teachers and leaders to do so. Such cooperation must include discussions regarding potential conservatoire students, teachers and possible future employment as well as critical discussions about classical music's whiteness. To mediate a broad and open vision of the future HME institution, including diversity in race and ethnicity, diverse genders and power relations, as well as a variety of future possible employments, would be an example of an action-oriented approach to anti-colonialism (Hess, 2021). In addition, such a change has to be accompanied by a reformulation of broader goals and visions for classical music programmes in HME.

Notes

1. The empirical material drawn upon here is part of the research project Conservatory Cultures (2021–4), funded by the Foundation for Baltic and East European Studies and concerned with how nation and gender are shaped in contemporary conservatoire music education in Estonia, Finland and Hungary.
2. In the context of Central and Eastern Europe, the concept of 'Western classical music' (or indeed 'Western art music') becomes a dilemma. The classical music canon from Central and Eastern Europe is not 'Western' in origin if 'Western' signifies the United States and Western Europe. 'Western' may also imply a division between Europe and Asia, where Asia is the 'East'. Such a division is also problematic, given the importance of 'Asian' performers in classical music today. In this chapter, we settle for 'classical music' due to these conceptual problems.
3. In all cases, the reference is to the English version of the websites; https://www.uniarts.fi/en/units/sibelius-academy (accessed 10 February 2022).
4. https://lfze.hu/en (accessed 10 February 2022).
5. https://lfze.hu/university-studies (accessed 10 February 2022).
6. https://www.uniarts.fi/en/units/sibelius-academy (accessed 10 February 2022).
7. https://eamt.ee/en/departments/classical-music-performance/keyboard (accessed 16 February 2022).
8. https://eamt.ee/en/international/international-cooperation (accessed 11 February 2022).
9. https://lfze.hu/exchange-mobility (accessed 11 February 2022).
10. https://www.uniarts.fi/en/projects/international-visitor-programme (accessed 24 March 2022).
11. Dana Hall, African American jazz drummer, was added to the page in autumn of 2021; this was after we conducted the material collection.
12. https://lfze.hu/university-studies/ma-classical-piano-course-description-116729 (accessed 14 December 2021).
13. https://lfze.hu/university-studies/ma-violin-course-description-116713 (accessed 14 December 2021).

14 https://eamt.ee/en/departments/classical-music-performance/voice (accessed 14 December 2021).
15 https://www.uniarts.fi/en/study-programmes/piano-main-instrument (accessed 14 December 2021).
16 https://www.uniarts.fi/en/study-programmes/strings-main-instrument (accessed 14 December 2021).
17 https://eamt.ee/en/departments/classical-music-performance/keyboard (accessed 14 December 2021).
18 https://eamt.ee/en/departments/classical-music-performance/strings (accessed 14 December 2021).
19 https://www.uniarts.fi/en/units/sibelius-academy (accessed 14 December 2021).
20 https://opinto-opas.uniarts.fi/en/study-module/S-IP009/4428 (accessed 14 December 2021).
21 https://www.uniarts.fi/en/units/sibelius-academy (accessed 14 December 2021).
22 Whiteness may be debated in other practices within the institutions. The websites are in focus here.

References

Ahmed, S. (2009), 'Embodying Diversity: Problems and Paradoxes for Black Feminists', *Race, Ethnicity and Education*, 12 (1): 41–52.

Bennett, D. (2013), *Understanding the Classical Music Profession: The Past, the Present and Strategies for the Future*, Aldershot: Ashgate.

Blackstone, K. L. (2019), 'How do Conservatoire Graduates Manage their Transition into the Music Profession? Exploring the Career-building Process', PhD diss., Leeds: University of Leeds, School of Music.

Dyer, R. (1997), *White: Essays on Race and Culture*, London: Routledge.

Giroux, H. A. (2014), *Neoliberalism's War on Higher Education*, Chicago: Haymarket.

Guerra, A., G. Baptiste, C. Barbera, D.-E. Wickström, K. Thomson, M. Pison, and S. Heckael (2020), 'How Are Diverse Cultures Integrated in the Education of Musicians across Europe? An Introduction'. Available online: https://sms.aec-music.eu/diversity-identity-inclusiveness/how-are-diverse-cultures-integrated-in-the-education-of-musicians-across-europe-introduction (accessed 28 December 2021).

Hess, J. (2018), 'Troubling Whiteness: Music Education and the "Messiness" of Equity Work', *International Journal of Music Education*, 36 (2): 128–44.

Hess, J. (2021), 'Music Education and the Colonial Project. Stumbling toward Anti-colonial Music Education', in R. Wright, G. Johansen, P. Kanellopoulos and P. Schmidt (eds), *The Routledge Handbook to Sociology of Music Education*, 23–39, New York: Routledge.

Kajikawa, L. (2019), 'The Possessive Investment in Classical Music: Confronting Legacies of White Supremacy in U.S. Schools and Departments of Music', in K. Crenshaw, L. C. Harris, D. M. HoSang and G. Lipsitz (eds), *Seeing Race Again: Countering Colorblindness across the Disciplines*, 155–74, Oakland: University of California Press.

Laclau, E. and C. Mouffe (1985), *Hegemony & Socialist Strategy*, London: Verso.

Leppänen, T. (2015), 'The West and the Rest of Classical Music: Asian Musicians in the Finnish Media Coverage of the 1995 Jean Sibelius Violin Competition', *European Journal of Cultural Studies*, 18 (1): 19–34.

López-Íñiguez, G. and D. Bennett (2021), 'Broadening Student Musicians' Career Horizons: The Importance of Being and Becoming a Learner in Higher Education', *International Journal of Music Education*, 39 (2): 1–17.

Moberg, N. and E. Georgii-Hemming (2021), 'Institutional Personas – Dis/harmonic Representations of Higher Music Education', *Högre Utbildning*, 11 (1): 27–40.

Parkinson, T. and O. M. Gardner (2021), 'Protectionism and Rapprochement in Turkish Higher Music Education: An Analysis of the Mission and Vision Statements of Conservatoires and University Music Departments in the Republic of Turkey', *Arts and Humanities in Higher Education*, 20 (4): 365–85.

Scharff, C. (2015), 'Blowing Your Own Trumpet: Exploring the Gendered Dynamics of Self-Promotion in the Classical Music Profession', *The Sociological Review*, 63 (1): 97–112.

Scharff, C. (2018), 'Inequalities in the Classical Music Industry: The Role of Subjectivity in Constructions of the "Ideal" Classical Musician', in D. Dromey and J. Haferkorn (eds), *The Classical Music Industry*, 96–111, London: Routledge.

Schreier, M. (2012), *Qualitative Content Analysis in Practice*, Los Angeles: Sage.

Shim, J. (2021), 'Token Fatigue: Tolls of Marginalization in White Male Spaces', *Ethnic and Racial Studies*, 44 (7): 1115–34.

Stepniak, M. and P. Serotonin (2020), *Beyond the Conservatory Model: Reimagining Classical Music Performance Training in Higher Education*, New York: Routledge.

Thurman, K. (2012), 'Black Venus, White Bayreuth: Race, Sexuality, and the Depoliticization of Wagner in Postwar West Germany', *German Studies Review*, 35 (3): 607–26.

Turner, M. E. (2004), 'A Descriptive Analysis of the Images Observed on Music Department Web Sites', *Journal of Music Teacher Education*, 13 (2): 41–8.

Wang, G. (2015), *Soundtracks of Asian America: Navigating Race through Musical Performance*, Durham: Duke University Press.

Ware, V. and L. Back (2002), *Out of Whiteness: Color, Politics, and Culture*, Chicago: University of Chicago Press.

Yoshihara, M. (2007), *Musicians from a Different Shore: Asians and Asian Americans in Classical Music*, Philadelphia: Temple University Press.

Chapter 3

From Music Higher Education to the Festival Stage
Questioning the Neoliberal Environments of Scottish Jazz

Sarah Raine and Haftor Medbøe

Introduction

Jazz has occupied a defined space within Scotland's cultural landscape since the 1930s, performed in dance halls, pubs and clubs, and later at urban and rural festivals, while providing the background for dinner dances, wedding celebrations and corporate entertainment. As elsewhere in the UK, jazz has over the years enjoyed peaks and endured troughs in popularity and in present times is facing considerable existential challenges. Chief amongst these challenges are musician wages that have not kept step with rising living costs, a fragile and precarious working environment that has little to no institutional safety net in place and an oversupply of (often academy trained) musicians for a shrinking marketplace (Medbøe et al., 2023). It is tragically ironic that musicianship and creativity have arguably never been of a higher standard, while the delicate ecology that supports jazz in the UK is under severe threat on most fronts.

Musician engagement with jazz in Scotland has evolved from the emulatory import of the American artform to a glocalized expression of personal and collective identities.[1] Scottish musicians have long attempted to establish their own identity within a music of African American heritage, welding recognized symbols of Scottishness to the urban iconography of jazz to give meaning to the domestic scene and imbue distinctiveness within the global marketplace. However, with dwindling opportunities for live performance, the financial devaluation of both live and recorded music, continual erosion of the efficacy (and therefore relevance) of the Musicians' Union and an increasingly politically driven funding environment, Scotland's jazz musicians must navigate a competitive and deregulated domestic marketplace. Despite a progressively diverse population and society, Scotland's jazz scene remains predominantly white, male and middle class, and jazz has struggled to attract significant numbers of musicians – or fans – from Scotland's non-white ethnic groups, musicians with disabilities and from the LGBTQIA+ community. And while gender balance amongst school-age musicians is generally observed as equitable according to the music educators we interviewed as part of our 2019–22

PLACE study, barriers continue to hamper the progress of women and gender non-conforming instrumentalists, with very few going on to study in the academy or to perform professionally on the scene. The lack of women, gender minority and students of colour on jazz and improvisation courses in higher education (HE) is evidenced in our engagement with music conservatoires in the UK, and this legacy is clear on the festival stage (see Raine, 2020).

Within this chapter, we are interested in issues concerning jazz in HE, particularly in relation to developing a sustainable and diverse future scene. For us, sustainability – economic, cultural and environmental – is impossible without a complementary focus on diversity, bringing new people from across society, new experiences and new ideas, which in turn speak to an expanding audience.

In this chapter, we consider the entanglement of neoliberalism and dominant jazz practices, processes and politics in the jazz scene and in HE as well as the barriers to access and scene development that these entanglements engender. Although a 'loose signifier' (Brown, 2015: 20), in this work, we consider neoliberalism as a form of political rationality (Brown, 2015) within which 'everything is understood through the metaphor of capital' (Phipps, 2020: 229). As a core institution (Lynch, 2013; Rudd and Goodson, 2017) within the neoliberal mission, we build upon the work of McCaig (2018) in framing the neoliberal university as a business driven by market incentives and structured through a 'regulatory regime'. And in discussing issues of access and providing examples of exclusionary and entangled neoliberal and jazz scene ideology, we further problematize the neoliberal assumption that social good will be ensured through the neutrality of market forces (McNay, 2009) in the face of a weaking collective (state) welfare offering.

This chapter builds on insights developed through a PLACE (Scottish Government, City of Edinburgh Council)-funded research project (2019–22), through which we aimed to map the current state of the Scottish jazz scene. The project captured (in-person and virtually) stakeholder experiences and reflections during the pre-pandemic, Covid-19 and emerging post-pandemic periods. This chapter is therefore grounded in data gathered through semi-structured interviews, questionnaires and virtual focus groups with jazz musicians, educators and festival professionals in Scotland and, in recognition of the interconnected touring and musician circuit of the UK, additional interviews with jazz musicians and festival promoters undertaken across the UK by the authors beyond this funded project.[2]

In the sections that follow, we firstly consider the ways in which neoliberalism has shaped the contrasting views of jazz musicians and promoters and discuss the impact of notions of the free market and neoliberal public funding models. Secondly, we explore the convergences of jazz and neoliberal ideologies and highlight the problems these conditions pose for developing and maintaining an inclusive, diverse and sustainable jazz scene. In the third section, we reflect upon how this ideological entanglement plays out in jazz in Scottish HE and offer strategies for the conscious disruption and subversion of exclusionary ideologies and practices. We conclude by considering the potential futures of music HE in Scotland and beyond.

Neoliberal Jazz: Musicians and Sector

As Chapman (2018) notes, the contemporary neoliberal musician is expected to be a master of 'dexterous, virtuosic self-reliance' (p. 453) and 'self-sufficiency, economic thrift and multi-competence' (p. 467). This neoliberal view is held by many Scottish jazz promoters, festival teams and funders about musicians: 'Professional' musicians should be multi-competent and able to demonstrate their value (or promotability) through not only their creative work but also their social media following, industry connections and/or previous successes in gaining funding or gigs. In essence, contemporary Scottish jazz musicians are expected to create a coherent and oven-ready product for promoters that encompasses high-quality video material, press release copy, polished and impactful promotional photography and expansive and well-maintained social media networks, all produced or paid for by the artist as a self-employed worker, as these music professionals describe:

> The problem comes when musicians don't have official press photos, a social media presence, or a professional website. It's a lack of professionalism. (Steve, jazz promoter, focus group, October 2019)

> Promoters rely too heavily on musicians to promote the gigs, or booking musicians on their perceived promotability, their online audience, so who they can bring to a gig. Promoters are not promoting but just booking and expecting musicians to do the promotional work themselves. (David, musician in his thirties, interview, March 2020)

From statements like these, it is clear that contemporary Scottish jazz musicians feel the pressure of this neoliberal understanding of the musician as a multi-competent entrepreneur. The weight of these expectations is particularly felt by those who lack the training for creating marketing materials (Medbøe et al., 2023) or those without significant support systems and networks, such as women, who consciously occupy a peripheral place on the scene (Buscatto, 2021; Raine, 2020).

Fair pay within the jazz scene in Scotland (and, arguably, beyond: Umney and Kretsos, 2015; Umney, 2016) has been eroded by the neoliberal notion of the free market, with musicians further stretched – both financially and in terms of their perceived self-worth and cultural identity – through the expanding expectations placed on musicians by festival programmers, promoters and media professionals. The stagnation of fees and the proliferation of an exploitative free gig scene (Medbøe et al., 2023) are further compounded by the competitive nature of Scotland's small, city-based jazz scenes, poor national touring circuits, ageing and shrinking audience and (for minority groups especially) discriminatory and exclusionary scene politics (Raine, 2019, 2020, 2021). The precarious position of Scottish jazz musicians was particularly exposed during the Covid-19 pandemic, captured through the PLACE project (Raine, Medbøe and Dias, 2022; Taylor, Raine and Hamilton, 2023). This imposed breathing space provided an opportunity for reflections on the jazz scene's neoliberal practices and issues relating to inequality and access. In Scotland, as elsewhere, musicians convened online to vent about perceived and real issues, to stimulate momentum for change and to lay the groundwork for musician incorporation and activism for change. Yet throughout our engagement with Scottish and international musician communities, it became clear that these aspirations were short-lived. As noted by Briggs et al. (2020), the activism and desire for change expressed by individuals during the Covid-19 lockdown period was not supported by the 'structures and mechanisms holding up neoliberalism' (p. 831), with governments and small organizations (such as jazz festivals) alike determined to get back to business as usual at the earliest opportunity.

Bearing in mind the economic context noted earlier, our research found unsurprisingly that the Scottish jazz scene is significantly reliant upon public cultural funding for the creation of original work. This is particularly true of Creative Scotland[3] where successful applications – and therefore musician narratives – articulate cultural and community values rather than economic returns or even economic sustainability. Musicians are thereby expected to demonstrate both commercial and cultural value while enduring diminishing status and financial recompense and perceiving their creative autonomy as being challenged by the demands made by both industry gatekeepers and funders. Developing a fundable project and writing a successful bid represents yet another key skill (the development of which lies primarily with the individual and their network in the face of limited central support) required for the contemporary multifaceted jazz musician. Furthermore, the partnership approach of Creative Scotland also clearly exposes neoliberal expectations on the part of the national funders, who request match-funding or in-kind contributions as part of the application process. As Abilgaard and Jørgensen (2021) note, public-private innovation represents yet another form of marketization, which encourages individuals to 'model and transform themselves into the entrepreneur' (2) as market principles permeate the public sectors of the neoliberal system (McNay, 2009: 60). Equally, through an expectation of creatives to fulfil (and provide evidence for) funding criteria that are politically driven, the government increasingly exercises control over publicly funded artistic outcomes. As we look towards a period of likely austerity in the UK (following the costs of national pandemic relief, the economic failings of government and the fuel and cost of living crises), it is also likely that arts funding will once again be used to make up for a lack of funding in other areas (such as mental health provision, education and community outreach) as happened during the last austerity period in the country (Rimmer, 2018), with a move away from the welfare state to individual responsibility – in this case, of creatives (Clarke, 2007; Lazzarato, 2009).

As we will now explore, these financial limitations of the jazz sector in Scotland are further compounded at an ideological level through the entanglement of both dominant jazz mythologies and neoliberalism. Furthermore, through the dominant jazz myth of talent, the individualized neoliberal self is further emphasized and the complex reasons for differences in access are reduced by key gatekeepers to being 'good enough'.

Exclusionary Jazz Myths in Scene and Education

Previous research has shown how neoliberalism has reinforced hegemonic and patriarchal practices, processes and politics, as well as racism, in music-focused contexts (Macarthur, 2014; Scharff, 2017) and in the university (Tomlinson and Lipsitz, 2013; Hamer and Lang, 2015) and, more generally, exposed levels of racism within the neoliberal world view (Barlow, 2003; Brown et al., 2003; Kundnani, 2021). Such research highlights how the comparative lack of success in engaging minority groups is either neutralized through meritocratic discourses of hard work – and 'talent' within the jazz scene – or co-opted through neoliberal organizational attempts to 'address' inclusion issues. An example of the latter is the ATHENA SWAN initiative in UK HE institutions. This initiative aims to support women and gender minority workers but attempts to do so through the additional unpaid labour of workers who are already struggling within male-dominated, high-pressure organizations that are run on a business model advocating and actively perpetuating precarity.

In a detailed ethnographic study of the jazz scene in France, Buscatto (2021) documents the pervasive and continuing jazz myth of talent, which is used by gatekeepers and musicians who are opposed to providing support for underrepresented groups within the scene by questioning the standard of their music. As differently positioned researchers, educators and individuals within jazz scenes, it has become clear to us that this discourse of talent has become a key way for individuals active in jazz – most significantly, those in gatekeeper roles – to excuse or neutralize (Griange, 2020) a lack of diversity in the jazz scene, classroom, festival stage or specialist media. Such gatekeepers argue that those given the opportunity represent the most hard-working and talented musicians, relying on discourses of 'quality' as a means to sidestep discussions of gender-imbalanced line-ups or predominantly white jazz HE cohorts. In one interview, a jazz promoter claimed that he was not discriminatory as 'it does not matter whether they are women or men, just as long as they are any good' (Patrick, jazz promoter, interview, March 2022). Through such actions and declarations, gatekeepers define their role as that of genre experts and tastemakers – selecting the best – rather than accepting and actively engaging in their roles as instigators of change (Raine, 2021).

Other common approaches to engaging with issues of underrepresentation within jazz includes the 'Women in Jazz' brand, used by promoters and agents to market all-woman bands and all-woman festivals. As Zola (2022) notes, rather than galvanizing feminist activism, this approach further frames successful jazz women as the exception, ultimately doing 'little to change the gender dynamics in jazz at large, favouring the neoliberal model of individual success in its capitalist system' (p. 413). Again, the neutrality of market forces – talented musicians succeeding in gaining opportunities – is assumed to ensure social good (McNay, 2009), yet has limited and unsustainable impact beyond the individual.

In terms of jazz-specific HE courses, the pattern of the white, male, middle-class jazz musician continues for both student cohorts and teaching staff (Raine,

2020). This male-dominant environment was cited by women-identifying jazz musicians in our PLACE-funded study in Scotland (Medbøe et al., 2023) and other UK-wide research (Raine, 2019, 2020) as a key barrier to engagement for women (particularly those of colour) as both students and, later, HE educators. This homogenous cohort identity – reflecting the dominant all-male, white bands on jazz festival stages – is likely the product of continuing exclusionary HE practices, in addition to issues earlier in the music education pipeline. For example, blind entry auditions have not yet been implemented for places on jazz courses, even though these have been common in orchestra auditions for many decades. Equally, prospective students are expected to pay an application fee to Conservatoire UK for each application, adding incremental financial barriers to accessing higher music education (this is not the case for other HE courses in the UK). Alongside these exclusionary entry practices and processes, musicians have also reported in interviews their experiences of the competitive and (white) male-dominated spaces of jazz courses and a lack of staff support for minority groups. This is particularly prevalent amongst musicians of colour from working-class backgrounds who do not identify as heterosexual men. As Abi, a musician in her early twenties, notes on her experience as a Black British instrumentalist on a jazz course at a UK conservatoire:

> Until I was 18, my identity had not been politicized as far as I was concerned. ... [At the conservatoire] I felt like I was under a telescope. It was horrible. I was suddenly very highly aware that I was a woman and that I was black. . . . What people don't understand about the whole going to college thing, as a minority – regardless of what that minority is – you've probably had to fight your way into that space. By asking why so few minorities are at universities studying music, you're already ten years too late. I already feel like I've got the weight of the world on my shoulders because my entire presence is just completely politicized.

Abi, and many other students like her, arrived at music HE courses having already experienced significant barriers to access. In her first year at university, Abi felt the pressures of being a highly visible minority person within a homogenous cohort, compounded by the lack of support she received from her tutors (as she detailed further in the interview). As with the dominant approaches undertaken by industry professionals briefly discussed earlier, the approaches taken by HE gatekeepers take a similar individualistic attitude. Davies and Saltmarsh (2007: 3) note that in neoliberalism, 'populations are administered and managed through the production of a belief in each individual in his or her own freedom and autonomy'. By focusing on the success and talent of the individual in gaining a place at an HE institution and performing well on the course, rather than addressing the key intersectional barriers to access faced by minority pupils (as they apply for and undertake HE courses), UK music schools emphasize 'individualism and the "privatization" of responsibility', framing the individual as 'solely responsible for their own outcomes' (Tomlinson and Lipsitz, 2013: 7–8). While this points to a wider issue within the neoliberal university – beyond jazz (see Scharff, 2017, and

Bull, 2019, on classical music) and indeed beyond music or the arts (see, e.g. Hamer and Lang, 2015, on HE in America) – the focus on individual success through hard work is further compounded by the dominant myth of talent within the jazz world, leading to a wider scene culture of competition rather than understanding. In order to support those students who have yet to fully access, benefit from or feel welcome in the jazz scenes and in formal jazz education, we must proactively and reflexively develop pedagogical and outreach strategies.

Jazz and Scottish Higher Education

Within the HE sector, a disconnect between senior management and teaching staff, underpinned by conflicting political and philosophical positions, can be readily observed. Post-1992 UK universities are essentially products of neoliberal ideology, coming into being during the eighteen-year Conservative government under the premierships of Margaret Thatcher and John Major and furthered under Tony Blair and Gordon Brown's New Labour after 1997. Pedagogical quality frameworks have been devised to encourage and promote 'entrepreneurialism and a competitive spirit, to reproduce neoliberal capitalist relations of production and an ideological agenda for and in education' (Maisuria and Cole, 2017: 605), which is often at odds with the more radical or egalitarian perspectives held by teaching staff. This ideological shift can also be observed in the 'ancient' or 'red-brick' universities as they keep step with developments in the wider HE sector. Across all UK HE institutions, there is a palpable friction between aspirations to provide a safer space for 'broadening horizons' (Maisuria and Cole, 2017: 607) and feeding the neoliberal agenda by preparing students for the free market economy. Through our own multiple roles within and outside of the Scottish jazz scene, this balancing act is one that we know well, as we aim to prepare our students not only to knowledgeably engage with the world beyond the academy's walls but also to subvert and contest this reality in order to protect themselves and safeguard others.

In our own pedagogical approaches, we address the clash between the realities of a jazz sector driven by a neoliberal world view and the diverse expectations of music graduates (whether ideologically, practically or economically rooted – inherited, assumed or informed) and attempt to disrupt the neutralizing nature of neoliberal and jazz ideologies by creating a safer, critical space for student discussion and music-making. In so doing, we draw upon a range of work which offers research-led pedagogical approaches and aims to resist or circumnavigate problematic neoliberal culture (Griange, 2020; Karlsen, 2019; Maisuria and Cole, 2017). As Karlsen (2019: 193) invocates, '[t]his time, we imagine and aim for no less than societal change.'

Our pedagogical toolbox draws typically on practice-as-research and academic engagement with grassroots community music and industry. Again, there is a tension between employing music-making as an agency for societal change while simultaneously operating within the commercial paradigm. At the heart of community music are utopian aspirations of access, inclusion and empowerment that sit somewhat uncomfortably alongside the competitive self-promotion demanded within the commercial arena. It is typical to observe fellow jazz educators within HE drawing more on ideals of 'art for art's sake' and the personal and artistic growth of students through critical reflection, viewing university education as taking place somehow separate from, or beyond, the commercial realities of the music industries. The 'business' of music often appears to be grudgingly included within curricula – again an embodiment of the discomfort experienced by many practitioner-educators in balancing their own artistic integrity against the commercial pressures of industry. The activist elements embedded across our pedagogy are thereby concerted acts of subversion in the hope of a brighter future, rather than simply continuing to service the 'demands' of what we perceive, in common with many musicians, to be a broken economic model. Through encouraging responsible and contextually informed freedom of thought and action we attempt to encourage and enable our students to lead this change, as we go on to illustrate later in this section.

Where universities typically give equal if not greater focus to contextual studies, music conservatoires offer a syllabus more grounded in practice (see https://conservatoiresuk.ac.uk). Scotland has just one dedicated undergraduate programme in jazz, offered by the Royal Conservatoire of Scotland. Elsewhere across the country's university sector, jazz studies constitute strands or electives within broader programmes of music education, either as a part of or an adjunct to popular music. Beyond the HE sector, jazz education in Scotland takes place across a range of formal and informal spaces, from individual music tuition and school-based group activities led by jazz-enthusiast teachers to courses and summer schools run in association with festivals, laying the groundwork for pathways to higher-level education. The informal sector is built largely on supply and demand and not least on the dogged enthusiasm of its animators. Equally, it is also often dependent on the shifting sands of public funding (Medbøe et al., 2023).

Jazz as a topic of practical, and latterly contextual, study has been part of the suite of module options in music at Edinburgh Napier University since 1998. Available to students of classical and popular music, the nature of its delivery and content has undergone significant transformations in the intervening years. Originally titled Jazz Improvisation 1, 2 and 3, the modules were offered as a practice-led strand of study and delivered through established, conservatoire-derived pedagogies with a fundamental focus on the music's American heritage.

In 2013, these modules were revised and rewritten to reflect a more global perspective: Jazz 1: America, Jazz 2: Europe and Jazz 3: Glocal. These changes represented a conscious effort to provide a pathway that, while not underplaying the cultural and historical importance of the music's African American roots, could lead students to a more geographically situated and inclusive relationship with jazz, one in which students were less likely to feel like cultural tourists or, worse, appropriators. In doing so, a significant degree of theory-led critical thinking was introduced into the curriculum to encourage students to challenge received or accepted tropes and lay the groundwork for the development of new knowledge and understanding around the social and political complexities of jazz history and practice. Through these changes, we have increasingly challenged the neoliberal model of entrepreneurship through engagement with theory and embedded practice that focuses on the imperative value of culture to society, the decolonization of the curriculum and pedagogy and mutual respect and sensitivity towards others. This approach has been furthered through instruments of assessment in which we have moved away from subjective notions of performance-related value and towards the foregrounding of critical thinking behind creative action.

This pedagogical toolkit that encompasses the flattening of pedagogical hierarchy and the questioning of canon, placing greater value on freedom of thought through critical understanding of theory, has encouraged students to explore beyond simply the acquisition of received practical and professional acumen in discovering that jazz represents a unique and useful lens through which to view wider thinking around identity, equality, gender, ethnicity, (dis)ability and inclusion. The aim, rather than simply preparing the student for a notional marketplace, is to enable students to use their education to their own ends in forming their musical *and* philosophical identities. In doing so, we (the authors) have also aimed to create a safer space in which students who have been excluded from jazz – whether by race, gender, social or musical backgrounds – are able to claim knowledge and practice as their own.

In using jazz as a frame through which to explore persisting social issues such as racism, gender and social inequalities, we aim to challenge the free market, neoliberal world view and embed a social and political awakening across our provision. Academics can often be heard asking where the political activism – of, for example, the Civil Rights Movement – has gone in popular music and, more specifically, amongst those of typical student age. But perhaps we have simply asked the wrong questions or provided the wrong platforms. In creating safer and more open spaces for discussion, led by haphazard learning pathways rather than by dogmatic pedagogic agenda, we have sought to challenge hierarchies of authority. In doing so, we have found the students to be both willing and equipped to grapple with the prevalent and pervasive issues affecting the society for which we are charged with preparing them.

Conclusion

A cursory scratch at the surface of the pre-pandemic music sector, for which many continue to purport to equip our students, reveals an underbelly of discrimination and inequalities. Might we, in response, aspire to a radical reimagining of the music world by giving a stronger voice to the underrepresented and taking greater direction from those we teach? Many educators have spent the past decades in HE constructing narratives around a commodified and professionalized conception of the music industry, plotting its histories, qualifying its canons and quantifying its structures, employment pathways and value to the economy. Perhaps unkindly, this has been done in part to justify the place of popular music within HE as a 'worthwhile' path of study regarding graduate employment opportunities. In doing so, we have tacitly tied our pedagogies to the neoliberal environments in which we work and learn. The 'industry' of music is in itself a problematic construction to delineate or unpack, even if as parsed by, amongst others, Williamson and Cloonan (2007) as 'music industries' representing a notion which most musicians find to be a highly precarious, fragmented and intangible ecosystem through which to navigate their art. Allowing ourselves a moment of honesty, and putting to one side the constraints of institutional bondage, are such constructions of industry the most appropriate lens through which to seek socially and politically conscious progress in and through the arts?

As activists advocating for social change *and* mindful of the realities of the neoliberal music labour market, we are tasked to develop approaches for preparing emerging artists to equally engage with *and* disrupt damaging elements of the neoliberal world view applied to both creative practice and pedagogy. In negotiating multiple inherent ideologies, we aim through our own practice as creatives, music educators, researchers and writers to cultivate experientially informed and research-supported pathways towards more diverse and sustainable music scenes. At the same time, we acknowledge our privilege and work hard to present a decolonized curriculum that meaningfully reflects a post Western-centric world view and promotes a more level societal playing field.

Notes

1 The form and key social processes of creating a Scottish jazz diaspora is considered in Medbøe, MacLean and Raine (forthcoming) in relation to the creation and scene use of the Scottish Jazz Archive.
2 All names used within this chapter are pseudonyms, and identifying elements have been removed to protect the identity of the interviewee. Due to the sensitive topics under discussion (such as gender and racial discrimination, for example) and the intimate nature of the scene, anonymity was essential. All research was undertaken in accordance with Edinburgh Napier University Research Ethics guidelines.
3 Creative Scotland is the public body that distributes funding from the Scottish government and the National Lottery Fund to creatives and organizations in the arts, screen and creative industries.

References

Abilgaard, A. and K. M. Jørgensen (2021), 'Enacting the Entrepreneurial Self: Public-private Innovation as an Actualization of a Neoliberal Market Dispositive', *Scandinavian Journal of Management*, 37: 1–10.

Barlow, A. L. (2003), *Between Fear and Hope. Globalization and Race in the United States*, Lanham: Rowman & Littlefield.

Briggs, D., A. Ellis, A. Lloyd and L. Telford (2020), 'New Hope or Old Futures? Neoliberalism, the Covid-19 Pandemic and the Possibility for Social Change', *International Journal of Sociology and Social Policy*, 4 (9–10): 831–48.

Brown, M. K., M. Carnoy, E. Currie, T. Duster, D. B. Oppenheimer, M. M. Shultz and D. Wellman (2003), *Whitewashing Race. The Myth of a Color-blind Society*, Berkeley: University of California Press.

Brown, W. (2015), *Undoing the Demos: Neoliberalism's Stealth Revolution*, New York: Zone Books.

Bull, A. (2019), *Class, Control and Classical Music*, Oxford: Oxford University Press.

Buscatto, M. (2021), *Women in Jazz*, New York, London: Routledge.

Chapman, D. (2018), *The Jazz Bubble: Neoclassical Jazz in Neoliberal Culture*, Oakland: University of California Press.

Clarke, J. (2007), 'Subordinating the Social? Neo-liberalism and the Remaking of Welfare Capitalism', *Cultural Studies*, 21 (6): 974–87.

Davies, B. and S. Saltmarsh (2007), 'Gender Economies: Literacy and the Gendered Production of Neo-liberal Subjectivities', *Gender and Education*, 19 (1): 1–20.

Griange, J. (2020), 'Singing and Dancing for Diversity: Neoliberal Multiculturalism and White Epistemological Ignorance in Teacher Professional Development', *Curriculum Inquiry*, 50 (1): 7–27.

Hamer, J. F. and C. Lang (2015), 'Race, Structural Violence, and the Neoliberal University: The Challenges of Inhabitation', *Critical Sociology*, 41 (6): 897–912.

Karlsen, S. (2019), 'Competency Nomads, Resilience and Agency: Music Education (Activism) in a Time of Neoliberalism', *Music Education Research*, 21 (2): 185–96.

Kundnani, A. (2021), 'The Racial Constitution of Neoliberalism', *Race & Class*, 63 (1): 51–69.

Lazzarato, M. (2009), 'Neoliberalism in Action: Inequality, Insecurity and the Reconstitution of the Social', *Theory, Culture & Society*, 26 (6): 109–33.

Lynch, K. (2013), 'New Managerialism, Neoliberalism and Ranking', *Ethics in Science and Environmental Politics*, 13 (2): 141–53.

Macarthur, S. (2014), 'The Woman Composer, New Music and Neoliberalism', *Musicology Australia*, 36 (1): 36–52.

Maisuria, A. and M. Cole (2017), 'The Neoliberalism of Higher Education in England: An Alternative is Possible', *Policy Futures in Education*, 15 (5): 602–19.

McCaig, C. (2018), *The Marketisation of English Higher Education*, Bingley: Emerald Publishing Limited.

McNay, N. (2009), 'Self as Enterprise: Dilemmas of Control and Resistance in Foucault's "The Birth of Biopolitics"', *Theory, Culture & Society*, 26 (6): 55–77.

Medbøe, H., D. MacLean and S. Raine (forthcoming), 'Vivid Stories: Oral Histories, Collective Memory, and the Scottish Jazz Archive', in B. Johnson, A. Havas and D. Horn (eds), *Routledge Companion to Diasporic Jazz*, New York, London: Routledge.

Medbøe, H., S. Raine, J. Ali-Knight and D. K. Bhachu (2023), *Researching the Scottish Jazz and Blues Scene (2019–2022): Challenges for Stakeholders and Ways Forward for Post-pandemic Growth and Sustainability of the Sector*, Open Access Report.

Phipps, A. (2020), 'Reckoning Up: Sexual Harassment and Violence in the Neoliberal University', *Gender and Education*, 21 (2): 227–43.

Raine, S. (2019), 'Keychanges at Cheltenham Jazz Festival: Issues of Gender in the UK Jazz Scene', in S. Raine and C. Strong (eds), *Towards Gender Equality in the Music Industry: Education, Activism and Practice*, 187–200, New York: Bloomsbury Academic.

Raine, S. (2020), *Keychanges at Cheltenham Jazz Festival. Challenges for Women in Jazz and Ways Forward for Equal Gender Representation at Jazz Festivals: Findings and Recommendations*, Open Access Report. Available online: https://www.academia.edu/44565803/Keychanges_at_Cheltenham_Jazz_Festival_Challenges_for_women_musicians_in_jazz_and_ways_forward_for_equal_representation_at_jazz_festivals (accessed 21 February 2023).

Raine, S. (2021), 'Gender Politics, UK Jazz Festivals and COVID-19: Maintaining the Momentum of Social Change during a Time of Crisis', *Jazz Research Journal*, 14 (2): 183–204.

Raine, S., H. Medbøe and J. Dias (2022), 'Jazz Festivals in the Time of Covid-19: Exploring Exposed Fragilities, Community Resilience, and Industry Recovery from the Festival Stage', in G. Morrow, D. Nordgård and P. Tschmuck (eds), *Rethinking the Music Business: Music Contexts, Rights, Data and COVID-19*, 109–27, New York: Springer.

Rimmer, M. (2018), 'The Art Survival: Community-based Arts Organisations in Times of Austerity', *Community Development Journal*, 55 (2): 295–312.

Rudd, T. and I. F. Goodson (2017), 'Negotiating Neoliberal Education', in T. Rudd and I. F. Goodson (eds), *Negotiating Neoliberalism: Developing Alternative Educational Visions*, 1–11, Rotterdam: Sense Publishers.

Scharff, C. (2017), *Gender, Subjectivity and Cultural Work*, London, New York: Routledge.

Scottish Jazz Archive. Available online: http://scottishjazzarchive.org/interviews (accessed 11 November 2022).

Taylor, I. A., S. Raine and C. Hamilton (2023), 'Reconceiving Spatiality and Value in the Live Music Industries in Response to COVID-19', in I. Woodward, J. Haynes, P. Berkers, A. Dillane and K. Golemo (eds), *Remaking Culture and Music Spaces: Affects, Infrastructures, Futures*, 75–87, New York: Routledge.

Tomlinson, B. and G. Lipsitz (2013), 'Insubordinate Places for Intemperate Times: Countering the Pedagogies of Neoliberalism', *Review of Education, Pedagogy, and Cultural Studies*, 35: 3–26.

Umney, C. (2016), 'The Labour Market for Jazz Musicians in Paris and London: Formal Regulations and Informal Norms', *Human Relations*, 69 (3): 711–29.

Umney, C. and L. Kretsos (2015), '"That's the Experience": Passion, Work Precarity and Life Transitions among London Jazz Musicians', *Work and Occupations*, 42 (3): 313–34.

Williamson, J. and M. Cloonan (2007), 'Rethinking the Music Industry', *Popular Music*, 26 (2): 305–22.

Zola, R. (2022), 'Women in Jazz: A Failed Brand', in J. Reddan, M. Herzig and M. Kahr (eds), *Routledge Companion to Jazz and Gender*, 412–22, New York: Routledge.

Chapter 4

Facilitating Dreams, with a Sense of Reality

Employability in Dutch Higher Popular Music Education

Rick Everts, Pauwke Berkers and Erik Hitters

Introduction

The music industries represent a precarious labour market for musicians. Just like in other sectors of the creative industries, the supply of labour tends to exceed its demand (Hesmondhalgh and Baker, 2013; Menger, 1999). As a result, careers in music are insecure: Most musicians struggle to earn a decent living, they have to combine multiple unstable sources of income and work is often sporadic with little long-term career prospects (Bridgstock, 2005; Hennekam and Bennett, 2016; Von der Fuhr, 2015). At the same time, neoliberal policies have increasingly framed this market in terms of 'competition and commerce' (McRobbie, 2016: 42), and notions of entrepreneurship and individual responsibility have been promoted to reconcile musicians with these market conditions (McRobbie, 2016). Yet only a small number of musicians will become (financially) successful (Von der Fuhr, 2015), and as result, it is difficult for starting musicians to assess their chances of a sustainable career (Menger, 1999).

The insecure nature of work in the music industries has consequences for the role music education can or should play in musicians' career building. In general, enrolling in arts education does not necessarily guarantee an economically successful career in the arts. As career paths are often 'fuzzy or even nonexistent' (Fine, 2017: 1464), art schools like pop academies cannot provide a recipe that guarantees success in the music industries (Frith, 2007). For that reason, the way higher popular music education, and arts education in general, addresses issues of employability and possible career paths is an important consideration and a 'moral imperative' for administrators and teachers (Beckman, 2007: 93). Here, Dutch higher popular music education programmes make an interesting case, because compared to traditional music education, where teachers tend to focus on students' artistic training in one-on-one teaching lessons, these programmes are characterized by a strong emphasis on cultural entrepreneurship and establishing a connection with the labour market (HBO-Raad, 2011), reflecting broader cultural policy trends in the Netherlands (Essig, 2017). Yet while these programmes may be more successful at preparing students for the labour market, a neoliberal focus on employability might also contain a risk of devaluating the importance of devoting time to one's artistic practice and might not increase the *'economically viable opportunities for graduates overall'* (Kenning, 2019: 127; emphasis in original) due to the insecure nature of art markets. Therefore, in this chapter, we critically explore how Dutch higher popular music education programmes prepare students to cope with the uncertainty of building a career in the popular music industries.

Earlier research has identified at least three (interrelated) strategies that higher popular music education could use to increase the employability of their students. First, art students tend to be generally unsatisfied with the career advice received in the course of their education (Fine, 2017). This lack of information creates difficulties for students in becoming aware of their chances of achieving their goals and adjusting their career plans and study trajectory accordingly (Bennett, 2007). Subsequently, research has suggested that music education programmes should provide detailed information about possible careers, chances for success and the market as a whole (Hall, 2019), thus increasing the students' 'career preparation and industry awareness' (Bennett, 2007: 10).

Secondly, musicians can increase their chances for a career in the music industries by engaging in 'occupational risk diversification' (Menger, 1999: 562) – that is, by taking on different kinds of work in the music industry to improve their financial position. By doing so, musicians build a 'career portfolio' that can help them to gain a better position in the market and guarantee the continuity of their careers (Menger, 1999). While a lot of musicians aim to make a living from creating and selling their own music, research has shown that musical careers frequently require performing multiple roles within (and outside of) the music industry, which most often include teaching (Bennett, 2007; Menger, 1999; Von der Fuhr, 2015). As such, careers in music have been described as 'protean, boundaryless, or portfolio careers' (Bridgstock, 2005: 40), because they are characterized by a combination of multiple occupational roles. Therefore, music education programmes can improve the career prospects of their students by preparing them to perform multiple roles in the music industry (Bridgstock, 2005).

Thirdly, higher popular music education programmes can increase students' employability by helping them to acquire work experience, for example, in the form of internships (Hennekam and Bennett, 2016). By gaining experiences in the industry, students identify whether they are suited for the work and learn how to assess their chances of success (Menger, 1999) and what skills are required in order to perform various industry roles well (Bennett, 2007). Because of these benefits, music students consider such practical experiences to be more important than the diploma, as they assume that graduating does not hold a lot of value for future employers (Hall, 2019). Moreover, researchers have found that having a 'music degree with experience' (Comunian, Faggian and Jewell, 2014: 185), rather than just a degree, might signal an exceptional development to employers and thus increase the reputation of students (Comunian, Faggian and Jewell, 2014; Menger, 1999).

In this chapter, we will investigate whether these risk management strategies are embedded in Dutch higher popular music education programmes. To answer this question, we conducted in-depth interviews with ten teachers and five focus groups with students studying at three different pop programmes in the Netherlands in 2020. These programmes are part of three universities of applied sciences and offer four-year bachelor programmes and two-year master programmes focusing on pop music (and subgenres such as pop, rock, hip-hop, electronic music, metal, funk, singer-songwriter) on the level of higher vocational education. Each bachelor programme, which we are focusing on here, has an admission exam and attracts around 40–140 new students per year. Within these programmes, students choose a main track based on their instrument of choice, and they can also follow tracks on entrepreneurship, music education and recording/producing. In the interviews and focus groups, the perspectives on future employment and the various ways in which these programmes prepare students for work in music were addressed.[1] Based on an inductive thematic analysis (Braun and Clarke, 2006) of the collected data, we will first show how these programmes provide a *reality check* for their students. Second, we discuss the role that a *mixed professional practice* plays in preparing students for a career in music. Third, we highlight the perceived importance for students to gain *work experience* throughout the course of their programmes.

Reality Check

Both students and teachers mention that students enter higher popular music education programmes with big dreams. Most students hope to have their own band and earn money with their own music, as this quote from one student illustrates:

> When I entered the programme, I wanted to play as much as possible, and that is still partly the case for me. I still want to make and produce my own music and let the world hear it. (15, voice student, female)

Similarly, a teacher notes:

> The percentage of students that enter with the dream like 'I'm going to make my own music, I'm going to record it myself and play it live and I'm going to make a living from that' [. . .] that percentage would be around 75 percent upon arrival. (6, keyboard teacher, male)

A minority of the students had a more general ambition of just to 'make as much music as possible' (14, drum student, male) and was pragmatic about the form this could take. Yet for most students who want to earn a living with their own music, in practice, this dream might be very difficult to reach. From the teachers' perspective, most students overestimate their chances (see also Menger, 1999), as the number of students who will reach this level of success is small:

So, if you're going to look at bands that just got out of school, I think that that is very difficult. (12, audio production teacher, male)

Teachers understand the market for live acts to be a superstar or winner-takes-all economy (Ordanini and Nunes, 2016) and argue that even if musicians have the right strategy for their act and take the right steps when it comes to building a career in this market, they will have to accept the considerable risk that they will not become successful. This might be especially the case in the Netherlands as the Dutch popular music industries remain relatively small compared to, for example, the UK (Everts and Haynes, 2021), which makes it difficult to earn a living from touring or selling recorded music.

Therefore, the goals that students pursue upon entering the programme pose a dilemma for the teachers. On the one hand, teachers want to cater to the students' dreams by helping in their attempt to become successful with their own music. On the other hand, teachers realize that they have to prepare students for a different career in order for them to make a living. For example, one teacher explained that even though they can instruct students on how to build a career, there is no guarantee of success:

And then of course you also have to be realistic. This is a very hard job. Everyone has a dream, but it is not for everyone to eventually play in the major leagues. [...] On the other hand, we do try to explain how to get into the major leagues. [...] Because you cannot [...] reduce that to: 'Yes, but this person has a unique quality'. [...] There is no recipe for that success. (1, business teacher, male)

Pop academies account for this dilemma between dream and reality in their programmes by facilitating what students and teachers have called a 'reality check' that aims to give students a realistic understanding of the popular music industries and their chances of achieving careers in music. Several teachers expressed that they rarely advise students against a certain career due to the small chance to become a (economically) successful artist. However, they do invite students to investigate the viability of such career paths:

I'm not going to say to them [the students]: 'No, you shouldn't do that. You don't earn anything from that.' It is not for me to say that. What I do say is: 'Okay. Can you find out for me where the world is, where you want to end up. Do your research. Also look at the money flows in that industry. Then draw your own conclusion.' And often people find out themselves: 'Shit ... that is actually a very difficult world to get into or succeed in.' So, I am never going to take that dream away from them. I am going to try to wake them up on their own. (9, guitar teacher, male)

In this way, these programmes facilitate an orientation around the consequences of students' career choices in various ways: For example, students are asked to interview established musicians early in their studies to learn more about their perspective on the industry and their financial situation. They also attend courses where they acquire knowledge about the industry and revenue streams. Towards the end of their studies, they develop a career plan where teachers work with students to develop an assessment of which level of success is required to become financially sustainable and what strategy should be employed to increase their chances of success. Furthermore, students are advised by teachers throughout the programme on how to organize the business side of things, and they help to evaluate contracts that labels (and other parties) offer to students.

Students are not discouraged from pursuing artistic projects with less economic potential. Yet several students did mention that they changed directions during their studies because of this *reality check* and are now aiming for a different kind of work in the music industries after graduation, such as this student:

> In the first year, everyone wants to make as much music as possible. Which makes perfect sense, because you come here because you are a musician. Eventually, you will think again: 'Of course I want to make music, but I can still do other things and [. . .] still work in the music industry.' (15, bass student, male)

For example, one student decided to learn how to work in a studio, while others considered (part-time) work as music teachers. Another student focused on a career in the music industries away from his own music-making and acquired a more widely applicable skill set in the course of his studies:

> Setting up your own act is very difficult. It didn't really come out of myself and I also thought it was better to broaden myself more. So, I'd rather focus on the business side now. That feels good and I really learn new things that I can apply a bit more broadly. (8, voice student, male)

The students' feelings about the *reality check* were twofold: Some, like the student quoted earlier, discovered that there is more to a career in music than just having an act and that other work can be enjoyable as well. At the same time, the pessimistic prognosis for a career in music also caused stress and feelings of anxiety and depression for some students: 'There isn't a single person here in our programme who didn't suffer from a form of depression for a while' (15, voice student, female). Students therefore called for more attention to their mental health, as these feelings were widespread: 'There are more people who suffer from a kind of burnout here at school than the school knows' (13, songwriting student, female).

All in all, on the one hand, the *reality check* provided by these programmes is an important strategy for increasing student awareness of ways to find employment. As a result, it helps students to decide for themselves whether they want to focus on achieving their dreams or adjust their plans to build a more realistic career in music. At the same time, it also indicates an inability of these programmes to aid students in reaching their initial career goals, and it mirrors neoliberal policies as it attempts to coalesce students' goals with the nature of the music industry market

(Kenning, 2019). Moreover, it transfers the responsibility for the outcomes of these choices onto the students, causing feelings of stress.

Mixed Professional Practice

Due to the small chance that students will have a successful career with their own music, several teachers mentioned that the majority of graduates turn to other kinds of musical work to remain active and earn a living in the music industries and pursue what they call a *mixed professional practice*. In this mixed professional practice, graduates earn an income by combining different work activities in music. These findings reflect the general trend that musicians and creative workers pursue a 'protean career' by combining a diverse range of jobs (Hennekam and Bennett, 2016; Von der Fuhr, 2015). Teachers indicate that graduates engage in a wide range of industry roles. Most prominently, graduates play in their own acts and in cover bands, work as session musicians and as music teachers. Teaching is especially important, as it provides an indispensable source of steady revenue (see also Bennett, 2007; Menger, 1999). In addition, other mentioned sources of income included being a songwriter, arranger or composer for others, working as a band coach, producer or studio engineer, making music for advertisements or movies and performing non-musical tasks such as working for labels, bookers and festivals (e.g. in marketing or production), or as a manager.

By turning students into versatile musicians who are able to perform multiple roles in the industries, pop programmes aim at preparing them for a *mixed professional practice*. This training can be understood as the second strategy for how pop programmes seek to increase students' employability. Preparing student to take on different jobs in the music industries in order to earn a sustainable income is a form of occupational risk diversification (Menger, 1999). It also promotes the students' flexibility to take on different job opportunities and to adapt to changes in the music labour markets, thus increasing their chances of staying in the music industries in the long term. Even students who strive for a career with an act are encouraged to prepare for a mixed professional practice because teachers believe that the chances of such a career are low and may be short-lived. For this reason, one teacher explained that they even try to keep students in the programme who want to leave because their career is starting to take off:

> What we want is for them to become very good at many things. And suppose they have a breakthrough with that one little thing, because they have a hit or excel in The Voice [a television talent show]. [. . .] Suppose that one little thing doesn't turn out what they had hoped for, then we'll keep them in the programme to also teach them the rest. And that can be teaching, but also songwriting, or producing, or more studio work. (10, keyboard teacher, male)

To train versatile musicians, pop programmes expand the students' musical toolboxes. They do this not only by introducing students to different genres, for example, by teaching about music histories, but also by giving assignments in which students have to write, perform and record music in certain genres. In addition, teachers invite students to experiment and increase their technical skills and knowledge; they teach them to read sheet music and help them to perform on stage well with little preparation. As one teacher summarizes how 'they have received all the necessary resources from our programme so that they can actually master that repertoire in no time, with a scrap sheet, if necessary' (4, drum teacher, male). Moreover, pop programmes train students for non-performing work in music. Here, most prominently, students learn didactic skills and how to develop training material to prepare them to be music teachers. Due to the reality check, all students feel that preparing for multiple industry roles is important, because to make a living, 'it is especially necessary that you do different things' (13, vocal student, female). Consequently, students argued that the main benefit of attending a pop higher education programme is the versatility – rather than specialization – in the skills they acquire.

This mixed professional practice helps students to align the commercial and artistic interests in their careers in music, as they can pursue less economically promising artistic endeavours while earning enough on the side to remain active in the music industries. Yet, at the same time, participants also realize that this focus on a generalist skill set and approach to work might also lower their chances for commercial success with an artistic act, because they then have to divide their time and resources between different projects. The same teacher addresses this issue as such:

> I also strongly believe that you need to focus on something. You have to believe in something. And then do it. I also don't believe in teaching four days a week and then trying to build your career one day a week. That doesn't work. I think that the focus is very important. (9, guitar teacher, male)

This quote highlights a contradiction in these programmes, as students are prepared for a mixed professional practice to widen their career prospects while at the same time needing to focus on a certain career path (e.g. building their own act). While teachers feel it is their duty to train students in different professional activities, again they leave it to the students' responsibility to choose between a mixed professional practice and other approaches to work. As a result, students are forced to self-govern in this regard as each student must individually figure out how to navigate the music industries, again manifesting a neoliberal logic that has been increasingly promoted in education policy (Kenning, 2019).

Work Experience

The third way higher popular music education programmes aim to increase the employability of their students is by encouraging them to start their career already during the programme. The teachers share the view that if students wait until after graduation to plan and work on their careers in music, they are too late:

> It has to start at school. It is very common that students who are in their third year are already registered with the Chamber of Commerce. (6, keyboard teacher, male)

Therefore, these programmes motivate students to take advantage of the relatively convenient circumstances of having a four-year period, including coaching and resources, by already starting to work in the industry: 'Yes, they stimulate that you already start working in the industry and already develop yourself' (13, vocal student, female). The teachers and the students cite various reasons why it is important for students to gain work experience during their study. First, they believe that graduating from a pop academy alone does not convince employers to hire graduates:

> I always ask: 'Have you seen that placard at Paradiso [a big venue] right next to the door that says that only higher vocational education certified musicians are allowed to perform here?' It's not there. (1, business teacher, male)

As such, the value of the diploma is low for future employers in the music industries and does not automatically guarantee work. For this reason, it is important that students collect a record of achievements during their studies that helps to increase the value of this diploma. They do so by already starting to work and building a 'career portfolio'. This shows that students are able to meet professional standards, and in this way, they improve their employability. Furthermore, the work they do during their study might then generate more work (Comunian, Faggian and Jewell, 2014; Menger, 1999).

A second reason for starting a career during their study is that students learn what their chances of success are in certain career paths and identify other career options they might want to pursue. Pop programmes facilitate acquiring experiences in the music industries: Students go to songwriting camps, get gigs as session musicians and learn how to record music in studios. Furthermore, programmes offer teaching internships, and one programme offered internships to experience other non-musical industry roles (Hennekam and Bennett, 2016). In this way, gaining work experience functions – again – as a form of *reality check*, which helps students to adjust their goals. As a result, one student pointed out: 'I also found out that I like having control over management things, over production things, so also to actually do things like that in the music industry' (15, vocal student, female).

Thirdly, by letting students gain these experiences, pop programmes help students to realize what competencies are expected from them in the market and which quality level they need to achieve – and they get the opportunity to develop themselves in that regard. In this way, starting to work and supplementing courses with hands-on industry knowledge present an opportunity for artistic and professional development (Comunian, Faggian and Jewell, 2014). Most importantly, by offering this industry experience, these programmes try to cultivate an entrepreneurial approach to work, consisting of competencies such as self-reliance, self-reflexivity, perseverance, discipline and the ability to create and find job opportunities. By starting to work on their careers during their training and reflecting on how they can achieve their dreams, students are confronted with the importance of these competencies. Teachers emphasize that students need to take responsibility for their career early during their studies because if they do not do so, no one else will do this on their behalf. For example, one teacher mentioned that a willingness to work hard might increase a student's chances for success more than being an exceptionally competent musician:

> There are also students of whom I think: 'You think it will all come naturally.' Sometimes there are also students of whom I think: 'You might be able to play a little less than him. But I rather believe in you because you believe 'I just know what I want. And if I have to study until four in the morning, I will.' (12, audio production teacher, male)

This entrepreneurial attitude is also important for students who (continue to) dream of a career with their own act:

> So, when people think in their second year, 'wow it's very hard to become the next Kensington [a well-known Dutch band]', never mind. Yes, then you don't have it in you. (12, audio production teacher, male)

At the same time, this expectation of an entrepreneurial attitude brings with it a lot of pressure, and the question remains whether this attitude will offset the precariousness of the labour market for all students. This then might be a second reason why students report high levels of stress:

> I feel like I have said 'yes' to a lot of various projects [. . .] in order to be working in the music industry. At some point, your calendar is just completely full. [. . .] There is little balance. I also have the feeling that people work very hard towards their EP release, they work very hard towards their final exams, they work very hard towards a certain thing which is the next step in their career. After that, they fall into a black hole. I hear from so many people how tough it is. Mentally and physically. (13, voice student, female)

Again, the analysis reveals a dilemma: On the one hand, by encouraging students to gain work experiences, pop programmes aim to provide students with the best starting position for establishing a career in the risky market of the music industries. At the same time, the promotion of notions of self-reliance and entrepreneurship demands that students take control of their own careers in a precarious market marked by little job security. This creates pressure for students to take advantage of the opportunities the programmes offer and to successfully start their careers, which can also feel like a burden, causing feelings of stress and anxiety. As such, this emphasis on being enterprising seems like an attempt to positively frame the students' future experiences and reveals a neoliberal understanding of the music industries in which workers are expected to self-organize and compete with each other (McRobbie, 2016).

Conclusion

The investigated higher pop music education programmes aim to increase the employability of their students. However, they experience a tension because, on the one hand, these programmes want to help students to achieve their dream careers (with little chance for economic success), but on the other hand, they aim to prepare students for careers in music that are more realistic in terms of success – to which fewer students initially aspire. Our analysis reveals that the programmes do not push students towards the career and the music that is economically the most viable, but that they also support artistic ambitions which may result in a more marginalized career. At the same time, these programmes aim to counter the insecurity of the market and increase their students' employability. They do this by facilitating a realistic perspective on career prospects, by encouraging students to prepare for a mixed professional practice and by encouraging students to gain work experiences throughout their studies. In this way, pop programmes are, as stressed by a teacher, 'facilitating dreams, with a sense of reality' (1, business teacher, male).

As a result, one of the functions that higher pop music education programmes have in the careers of their students is to burst the romantic myths about how to build a career in music that students might have upon entering and to propose a more realistic approach to work in the field. One teacher explicitly mentioned that distorted ideas about careers in the music industries exist:

> It is the monkey on top of the rock who will say in interviews: 'Yes, nobody believed in me and I still managed to get this successful.' But yes, that is easy for them to say. (9, entrepreneurship teacher, male)

Therefore, he intends to fight such misconceptions by functioning as a 'catalyst' and by ensuring a more 'realist' view. This finding is reflected in other research that has suggested that one of the functions of art education is to help students to envision 'occupational imaginaries' (Fine, 2017: 1463) and to visualize their place in the arts market and develop their artistic and professional identities in line with that imagined future.

Considering the precarity of the labour markets for musicians, these strategies to ensure employability might be understood as an example of neoliberal policies at play, as it burdens individual musicians with the obligation of coping with these working conditions and contains the risk of promoting self-exploitation in a precarious market (McRobbie, 2016). Overall, the idea is communicated that students are solely responsible for achieving their goals while chances for success are small, and most students can only partially pursue the career for which they entered these programmes in the first place. At the same time, this approach is pragmatic as it provides students with the tools necessary to find employment in the market and leaves them the freedom to choose a career model of their liking, although it transfers the responsibility of the outcomes of these choices upon the students. Even though the interviewed students and teachers expressed that even more could be done to help students in this regard, and the market students are active in remains precarious, the students in these programmes acquire various strategies for occupational risk management. In any case, these strategies reveal a specific understanding of the work of musicians in changing music industries perceived to have a winner-take-all labour market in which most musicians struggle to earn a modest income (Von der Fuhr, 2015), in which the holding of multiple jobs is the rule rather than the exception (Bridgstock, 2005; Comunian, Faggian and Jewell, 2014) and in which strong portfolios 'with an accumulation of hiring records' function 'as a reputational signal' (Menger, 1999: 550) and, in this way, generate more work.

Implications and Recommendations

First, students' employability should be an ongoing consideration within higher pop music education – at the start, during and after the programme. Hence, higher education institutions should on the one hand carefully monitor what the sector expects of graduates; on the other hand, they should critically address and help solve the precarious nature of the music industries as a system instead of seeing it as an individual problem (Newsinger and Serafini, 2021). Second, the sooner aspiring musicians are made aware of the nature of work in the music industries and the corresponding likelihood of success, the more informed and conscientious their choices for a career in music can be. Therefore, to the extent they are not doing this already, such programmes could even consider informing students upon application about the nature of work in the music industries. This could take the form of a more formalized 'reality check'. Third, it remains that this chapter only mapped the perceptions of students and teachers on how students are successfully prepared for a career in music. Future research might investigate to which extent these career strategies actually increase chances of success in the market. In this way, we can gain a deeper understanding of whether these apparent advantages genuinely yield positive outcomes or merely perpetuate established industry norms, thereby perpetuating existing disparities and instability in the music sector while encouraging self-exploitation. Moreover, some risk management strategies may benefit some students and not others. For example, entrepreneurship education is often rather gendered and catered towards men in terms of how success is defined (Jones, 2015). In conclusion, by proactively addressing the challenges faced by aspiring musicians, higher pop music education institutions can play a role in the employability of their graduates: They can inform students about their prospects but should also aim to contribute to reshaping the dynamics of the music industries, ultimately striving for a more equitable and sustainable future for their students.

Note

1   For privacy reasons, the higher popular music education programmes, teachers and students have been anonymized. In this chapter, we will refer to the interviews and focus groups with an individual case number, after which we specify the gender, role and instrument or specialization they teach or study, for example: (3, entrepreneurship teacher, male).

References

Beckman, G. D. (2007), '"Adventuring" Arts Entrepreneurship Curricula in Higher Education: An Examination of Present Efforts, Obstacles, and Best Practices', *The Journal of Arts Management, Law, and Society*, 37 (2): 87–112.

Bennett, D. (2007), 'Utopia for Music Performance Graduates. Is it Achievable, and How Should it be Defined?', *British Journal of Music Education*, 24 (2): 179–89.

Braun, V. and V. Clarke (2006), 'Using Thematic Analysis in Psychology', *Qualitative Research in Psychology*, 3 (2): 77–101.

Bridgstock, R. (2005), 'Australian Artists, Starving and Well-nourished: What Can We Learn from the Prototypical Protean Career?', *Australian Journal of Career Development*, 14 (3): 40–7.

Comunian, R., A. Faggian and S. Jewell (2014), 'Exploring Music Careers: Music Graduates and Early Career Trajectories in the UK', in N. Crossley, S. McAndrew and P. Widdop (eds), *Social Networks and Music Worlds*, 165–88, London: Routledge.

Essig, L. (2017), 'Same or Different? The "Cultural Entrepreneurship" and "Arts Entrepreneurship" Constructs in European and US Higher Education', *Cultural Trends*, 26 (2): 125–37.

Everts, R. and J. Haynes (2021), 'Taking Care of Business: The Routines and Rationales of Early-career Musicians in the Dutch and British Music Industries', *International Journal of Cultural Studies*, 24 (5): 731–48.

Fine, G. A. (2017), 'A Matter of Degree: Negotiating Art and Commerce in MFA Education', *American Behavioral Scientist*, 61 (12): 1463–86.

Frith, S. (2007), 'Live Music Matters', *Scottish Music Review*, 1 (1): 1–17.

Hall, R. (2019), 'An Analysis of Undergraduate Motivations, Perceptions of Value and Concerns in Pursuing Higher Popular Music Performance Education', *International Journal of Music Education*, 37 (2): 327–41.

HBO-Raad (2011), *Focus op toptalent: Sectorplan hbo kunstonderwijs 2012–2016*, Den Haag: HBO Raad.

Hennekam, S. and D. Bennett (2016), 'Self-Management of Work in the Creative Industries in the Netherlands', *International Journal of Arts Management*, 19 (1): 31–41.

Hesmondhalgh, D. and S. Baker (2013), *Creative Labour: Media Work in Three Cultural Industries*, London, New York: Routledge.

Jones, S. (2015), '"You would Expect the Successful Person to be the Man": Gendered Symbolic Violence in UK HE Entrepreneurship Education', *International Journal of Gender and Entrepreneurship*, 7 (3): 303–20.

Kenning, D. (2019), 'Art World Strategies: Neoliberalism and the Politics of Professional Practice in Fine Art Education', *Journal of Visual Art Practice*, 18 (2): 115–31.

McRobbie, A. (2016), *Be Creative: Making a Living in the New Culture Industries*, Cambridge: Polity Press.

Menger, P.-M. (1999), 'Artistic Labor Markets and Careers', *Annual Review of Sociology*, 25: 541–74.

Newsinger, J. and P. Serafini (2021), 'Performative Resilience: How the Arts and Culture Support Austerity in Post-crisis Capitalism', *European Journal of Cultural Studies*, 24 (2): 589–605.

Ordanini, A. and J. C. Nunes (2016), 'From Fewer Blockbusters by More Superstars to More Blockbusters by Fewer Superstars: How Technological Innovation has Impacted Convergence on the Music Chart', *International Journal of Research in Marketing*, 33 (2): 297–313.

Von der Fuhr, S. (2015), *Pop, wat levert het op? Onderzoek naar de inkomsten van popmusici in Nederland*, Tilburg: Cubiss.

Chapter 5

On the Potential of Niche Markets

The Case of Bluegrass Music

Nate Olson

Introduction

In September of 2021, I participated in a meeting of bluegrass music educators at the International Bluegrass Music Association's International Conference held in Raleigh, North Carolina, United States. The consequences of the global pandemic of 2020–1 permeated the conversation. We discussed broad issues facing higher education programmes, in general, and, more pointedly, the perceived, sometimes dire, situation for musics and music programmes considered somewhat on the 'fringe', like many of ours. In response, several participants suggested broadening our offerings – that there simply wasn't enough interest in this music to attract students, and that we should consider teaching courses in audio production, tourism or other fields or add other genres to what we were already teaching (e.g. mariachi, Celtic or pop music) in order to stay viable. Others asserted that we have a responsibility to prepare students to live 'a life in music', and that we should therefore teach courses in graphic design, for example, so that students could 'pivot' effectively when performance or teaching opportunities dried up as they had for many musicians this year. At the forefront of this discussion were the seemingly dwindling markets for musicians in many music-related fields and the precarity of music and music-adjacent programmes and careers (Timberg, 2015).

I imagine that many music educators are having similar discussions: making a living in music has always been challenging and is becoming more so (cf. Everts, Hitters and Berkers, 2022). One could argue that students will need to 'think outside the box', to imagine and conceive of ways of responding to and creating market opportunities that have perhaps never been employed before, in order to find success in an uncertain economic landscape. On the back of that urgency, programmes should also change quickly to orient, or reorient, to rapidly changing markets. While providing more types of classes and ensembles, and more kinds of opportunities (broadening offerings), can be a solution, I want to suggest another approach that capitalizes on the uniqueness of a niche market, the notion that narrowing offerings can feed and fund student passion, and that doing so is not only a sound educational approach but a wise market approach as well. My contention is that many students seek an immersive experience in the musical genre(s) that they are passionate about, and that creating and sustaining programmes, and affording opportunities for students to invest deeply in *their* music, makes sense educationally, institutionally and economically.

A discussion of the orientation of a music education programme to 'the market' (or in this case, the many music 'markets') lends itself to a neoliberal lens, with which one might examine how markets, and free market considerations, shape cultures and economies. Which market considerations have influenced, and continue to influence, curricular choices in a programme that serves bluegrass markets? How does such a programme differ from other, more typical music programmes oriented to more mainstream music industries? What obstacles presented themselves in the development of the programme, and how were they negotiated? What factors contributed to the success of the programme? What are the problems of orienting to a niche market?

To present this case, I will briefly consider neoliberalism and its relationship to the academy and music education in general, and this programme in particular. I will then present a narrative of the development of the Bluegrass, Old-Time, and Roots Music Studies Programme at East Tennessee State University (ETSU), a music education programme closely tied to bluegrass music. The programme is unique among non-classical music programmes in higher education in the United States because it is essentially a stand-alone programme, not an ancillary piece of a larger School of Music (with a dominant Western art music culture) and has consequently been able to focus coursework and student experiences squarely on this specific genre and its associated industries. In this accounting, I am interested in teasing out the ways that the programme, even at its first inception, was keenly aware of and tied to the markets for this music, and that the growing and continued success of the programme is in no small part a result of that focus.

The narrative that I will present is based on several sources of data. I first became aware of this programme during my dissertation research, which I undertook between 2011 and 2014. As part of a broader study (Olson, 2014), I spent a week on campus interviewing students, faculty and administrators both in the music department and in the then-titled 'Bluegrass, Old-Time, and Country Music Studies Programme'. I observed classes, rehearsals and lessons and examined curricula, syllabi and other documents. Upon completing my doctorate in 2014, I was fortunate to secure a position on the ETSU faculty and have been intimately involved in the development of coursework and curricula in the programme since then. I have also spoken with many of the key players who contributed to the evolution of the programme over the past forty years, including directors, department chairs, other administrators, faculty and students. All of that being said, I acknowledge that this is 'a' story of the curricular development of our programme, one that is unavoidably coloured by my own interests, observations and assessments. I do not suggest or pretend that this report is 'the' story about ETSU, or that it can be generalised in any way to reflect broader trends. I further acknowledge at the outset my own biases as an instructor at this very institution, as a lifelong practitioner of bluegrass, old-time and other non-classical musical genres and as an educator who cares deeply about the ways that so-called 'minority musics' are accepted and incorporated in American institutions. I assert that in this case, as Kvale (2007) suggests, my bias is useful:

> Unacknowledged bias may entirely invalidate the results of an [. . .] inquiry. A recognized bias or subjective perspective may, however, come to highlight specific aspects of the phenomenon being investigated and bring new dimensions forward, contributing to a multi-perspectival construction of knowledge. (Kvale, 2007: 86)

Neoliberalism and the Academy

Certainly, neoliberalism, an economic philosophy that can be understood as the 'doctrine' or the 'ideology' of the free market, has coloured and influenced discussions and decisions about education and music education for many years, and perhaps especially in recent years. Harvey (2007) asserts:

> The advocates of the neoliberal way now occupy positions of considerable influence in education. [. . .] Neoliberalism has, in short, become hegemonic as a mode of discourse. It has pervasive effects on ways of thought to the point where it has become incorporated into the common-sense way many of us interpret, live in, and understand the world. (Harvey, 2007: 3)

Researchers have highlighted the entrepreneurial mindset that some programmes espouse and note how career achievement is often linked to success in a music programme (Miller, Dumford and Johnson, 2017). The need to develop 'entrepreneurial attributes' in students is a common theme, as is the need for closer alignment to markets and direct relationships to career preparation (c.f. Kelman, 2020). Some assert that 'skills in entrepreneurship, best business practices, intellectual property, marketing, grant writing, fundraising, creativity, and many others must be a part of a modern performance curriculum', contending that, 'higher education must do a better job in providing relevant career preparation for their performance graduates' (Goodstein, Lapin and McCurdy, 2017: 2). This 'bottom line' becomes ever more important at universities, where new programmes and degree tracks are created to respond to the needs of the market and market forces. These programmes are criticized and closely scrutinized with regard to their ability to prepare students (or not) to 'get far' in the 'real world' (Cantor, 2012).

Others have problematized a neoliberal emphasis in music education. Allsup (2015: 253), for example, acknowledges its influence, 'According to neoliberal principles, universities and schools are markets like any other, and should be treated as such', but goes on to argue,

> After all, most of us pursued music in spite of, not because of, the market. We pursued the study of music because of how it makes us *feel*, because of what it

tells us about who we are, who we think we are, and who we might become. (Allsup, 2015: 255)

Smith (2016) also illustrates the perhaps inauthentic ways that music programmes seek to capitalize on the market by prominently, and often exclusively, highlighting alumni who have found extraordinary commercial success. 'This narrow, false narrative, reinforced throughout years of undergraduate and graduate study in an instrumentalist, vocational paradigm,' he says, 'forces students and graduates into construing their musicality and ambitions in terms of the neoliberal capitalist paradigm and away from choices for a more variegated sense of what success in a life in music could be' (Smith, 2016: 72). Woodruff (2015: 56–7) offers perhaps the most pointed critique, claiming that 'our schools and universities are extensions of the capitalist-corporate system whose function is to prevent the public from realizing that those and other institutions have long been intended and designed to serve the powerful and privileged'.

While a comprehensive discussion of these issues is beyond the scope of this report, for the purposes of this chapter, it is enough to note that markets are an inevitable, if not primary, factor in the consideration of how a course of study in music is conceived. To not consider the economic environment that students will enter would be irresponsible, and indeed there is something to be said for preparing students to be both artistically fulfilled and, at the very least, aware of, and ideally highly conversant with, the markets in which their work will be a part. In the particular example that I share here, the market is always in the background and is often in the foreground of considerations about curricula and the student experience. In some ways, the bluegrass market in the United States is very similar to many popular or mainstream music markets, where practitioners seek new audiences through various means, capitalize on technological advances to capture and deliver musical products and are prone to disruptive practices facilitated by the likes of YouTube, TikTok, livestreaming and social media. But bluegrass also diverges from more mainstream markets in unique and influential ways, and in that divergence is opportunity. For example, a large portion of the bluegrass audience is older, which means that CD sales are still an important revenue stream for many bluegrass musicians, and bluegrass music camps that cater to older, adult students have a robust following. These market peculiarities have undeniably influenced curricula, recruitment and policy in higher education programmes as well as university programme demographics, student outcomes and career trajectories.

Bluegrass and Higher Education

It is against this landscape of the shaping influence of neoliberalism in higher education that I consider the example of bluegrass music. Bluegrass is a subgenre of country music that features close vocal harmonies, intricate instrumental soloing and plaintive, 'lonesome' lyrics that often reflect the American south. Originating in the hills of Kentucky and the aesthetic of Appalachia in the 1940s, the music represents a synthesis of old-time fiddle tunes, Irish and Scottish tunes and songs, blues music, gospel harmony singing and jazz improvisation (Rosenberg, 2005). Percussive mandolin playing, driving bass lines, flashy fiddle solos, scalar bass runs on the guitar and the signature three-finger banjo roll further distinguish the bluegrass sound. As the music has evolved, it has also become increasingly virtuosic and performative. Cantwell (2002) notes:

> This is not the Sunday-afternoon music of miners, farmers, mill or factory workers, heartfelt, gutsy, and powerful as that music was and is, but of crack practitioners with the hands of neurosurgeons and the heads of engineers. [...] They are musicians who have developed from childhood in an environment rich with the sounds of Bluegrass and alive with the entrepreneurial energy of its global community of followers. (Cantwell, 2002: xii–xiv)

Bluegrass also occupies a unique demographic niche in the broader music industry. Practitioners are overwhelmingly white and typically male, a reflection of its roots. 'Country music is a racialized music,' Hammond (2011: 1) asserts, 'though it may be subtle or overt, race has always been a part of its commercial packaging.' As a subset of country music, the same can be said of bluegrass. On the Bluegrass Hall of Fame Museum web page (bluegrasshall.org/inductees), for example, every single inductee is white. The success of Black bluegrass artists in recent years, with releases like 'Black Banjo' by Tray Wellington or the Grammy-winning work of the now-disbanded Carolina Chocolate Drops, underscores that while the demographic is broadening, Black artists in the genre have been atypical. Further, Hardwig (2001: 35) argues that 'typically male recreations were an integral part of the bluegrass culture that surrounded Bill Monroe's band in the 1940s and 50s, and that these recreations influenced the way that musicians conceptualized their music and the presentation of their public images'. These influences are still deeply embedded in bluegrass culture. It would not have been unusual in years past to attend a bluegrass festival where all of the featured bands were made up of white men, though festivals today feature more diverse groups, and all-women bands like Sister Sadie and Della Mae have gained recognition and prominence in the industry and touring circuit.[1]

Recent research shows that the more than 18.5 million bluegrass fans in the United States are also overwhelmingly white and middle class – and commonly southern (Silverstein, 2012). Marketing reports indicate that 42 per cent of listeners are from the area comprising Tennessee, West Virginia, Kentucky, North Carolina and Virginia. About 67.7 per cent are homeowners and 63.3 per cent are more likely to be between the ages of twenty-five and fifty-four, though festival audiences tend to skew older (Silverstein, 2012). As mentioned, the sale of compact discs is still an important source of revenue for most bluegrass bands, as a sizeable portion of their audience is more comfortable with this format. During the eighty years since Bill Monroe founded the Blue Grass Boys in 1938, a thriving culture and industry has built up around this genre that includes hundreds of bluegrass festivals both in the United States and abroad, ubiquitous and regular local jams, summer camps and workshops, contests and conventions, chat groups, Facebook pages, online instruction and commercial recognition. The Grammys have awarded a 'Best Bluegrass Album' since 1989.

The music has also found a place in many institutions of higher education in the United States and a few locations abroad. At the time of writing, the International Bluegrass Musicians Association (ibma.org) identifies forty-nine institutions in the United States that include bluegrass music in some form. This could be a bluegrass club or band run by an enthusiastic faculty member, a course that explores history or performance aspects or at some institutions a full-fledged undergraduate degree in bluegrass music, with course sequences in music theory, music history, performance and sound reinforcement all oriented to the concerns of the bluegrass artist. East Tennessee State University (ETSU), where I work and teach, has perhaps the most extensive coursework of any programme in higher education in the United States, and I will describe its evolution and composition in more detail in the following section.

East Tennessee State University

ETSU is a medium-sized, state-supported school located in the Southern United States. It serves 14,000–15,000 students, many of whom live in the region and commute to the university. Approximately 81 per cent of the student population is white, which matches the demographics of the surrounding area (ETSU Demographics, 2021). The Music Department employs fourteen full-time faculty members and a number of adjuncts and offers degrees in Music Performance and Music Education. The department is accredited by the National Association of Schools of Music. Bluegrass music is taught in the Bluegrass, Old-Time, and Roots Music Studies Programme, a part of the Appalachian Studies Department at ETSU. While the programme and the music department were once combined, they now have virtually no interaction with each other. Courses, faculty, rehearsal spaces, finances and resources are completely separate. The programme employs five full-time tenured or tenure-track professors, one full-time instructor and over twenty adjuncts. More than 100 students are involved with the programme in some way each semester, either by taking private lessons, being involved in ensembles or taking other classes. At the time of writing, the programme hosted twelve bluegrass bands, six old-time bands, two country bands and two Celtic bands. Recently the programme began to offer a major, and approximately fifty students are pursuing a degree in Bluegrass, Old-Time, and Roots Music Studies. While there is an informal audition process for these students, and on rare occasions students have been rejected from the programme based on their perceived ability, most students who desire to study at ETSU are afforded the opportunity to do so. Tuition at ETSU is a little less than $5,000 per semester, and generous out-of-state and in-state scholarships are available.

The programme started when, after many years of commercial and professional success in bluegrass music, Jack Tottle settled in Johnson City, Tennessee, where ETSU is located. In the early 1980s, Jack approached the administrators of the music department to gauge their interest in 'having some guitar/mandolin lessons and possibly some classes in bluegrass and country music' (personal communication).[2] Like most departments of music in the United States at that time, the course offerings focused primarily on the Western classical music tradition. They taught Western music theory, aural skills and the history of classical music; hosted large bands and choirs that performed classical music and jazz; and offered applied instruction on orchestral and jazz instruments. The department responded enthusiastically to Tottle's invitation and happily provided him with space to teach courses in the schedule and adjunct pay. Initially, Jack directed a bluegrass/country music ensemble and taught private lessons on guitar and mandolin, and he soon began drawing students to ETSU keen on studying these musics.

ETSU's location has a long and storied history in American roots music. Several genres trace their origins to this area, and bluegrass, country and what has come to be referred to as 'old-time' music continue to feature prominently in the community and family life of the region. The teaching in the programme reflected these origins. As Dan Boner, the current programme director, described it, Jack's goal was to 'maintain the integrity of how [bluegrass] music is taught, how it's passed down, how it's always been passed down, for students to understand where the music came from, and to be a part of where it goes in the future' (personal communication). To that end, a major facet of Jack's teaching revolved around aural learning. He prized the interaction between a seasoned master and an eager apprentice, exchanging and marinating in tunes together, 'knee-to-knee'. In band classes, they created carefully constructed imitations and alternative versions of standard bluegrass tunes made famous by Bill Monroe, Flatt and Scruggs and the Stanley Brothers, among others. Jack schooled them in the intricacies of the style and helped them capture the subtle nuances of the three-finger banjo roll, the mandolin 'chop' and the groove-heavy backup guitar and bass figures complementing the tight, three-part, 'lonesome' vocal harmonies they were learning.

While Western theoretical concepts form the foundation of bluegrass and country music, they tend to be used differently than in the common practice. Many musicians, for example, use the principles of the Nashville Number System (see Williams, 2019) to talk about structure, form and harmony, and other unique vocabulary norms have evolved over the history of the genre. And obviously the rich history of bluegrass music deserved a comprehensive treatment. Jack Tottle wanted to mentor students into these musical, historical and cultural traditions and, to that end, proposed separate theory, history and other classes for his students so that they could learn concepts and applications as they related to bluegrass and country music. This would require an additional space commitment, an additional time commitment in the curricular schedule and perhaps more teachers to accommodate those classes. It would also require a divergence from the music theory classes already being offered in the music department.

As these classes were adopted, ETSU became known as a place for the rigorous study of these musics and enrollment grew. With time, the ideological and material differences between the programme and the music department became more palpable, even confrontational. To his credit, Jack Tottle was not willing to compromise what he felt were critical elements of bluegrass culture (and, not incidentally, the skills and knowledge valued in the bluegrass industry). After nearly two decades in the music department, the conflict came to a head, and Jack began looking to other entities within the university that might be willing to adopt the bluegrass programme. He approached what was then the Center for Appalachian Studies and Services and inquired if they would be interested in hosting the bluegrass classes and ensembles that he wanted to teach. They were very enthusiastic about this prospect and felt that bluegrass could find a home in the Center. They made the move, and the Bluegrass, Old-Time, and Country Music Studies Programme has been a part of Appalachian Studies since 2001. The Center eventually became a full-fledged department, hosting a unique Appalachian Studies graduate programme as well.

What has happened since 2001 is especially instructive. Freed from the ideological constraints and expectations of the music department and its adherence to the Western classical music tradition, those in the programme constructed a curriculum that closely matched bluegrass culture and its music industries. They developed a three-course bluegrass history sequence and a four-course theory sequence in addition to private instruction and performance-heavy band instruction, with some groups performing twenty times or more per semester. Other coursework included songwriting, vocal and fiddle harmony classes and seminar classes focused on the peculiarities of creativity, career development and living life as an artist within the bluegrass markets. Within a few years, bluegrass was an official minor at the university and then an academic major. Interest in the programme flourished as students found that they could immerse themselves in a rigorous study of bluegrass and country music and make a career out of doing so, and soon the programme incorporated additional emphases, like old-time and Celtic music. Today, more than twenty years after Jack Tottle helped move bluegrass out of the music department, the programme employs six full-time faculty members and numerous adjuncts, hosts nearly thirty performing ensembles and serves just over fifty majors and many more minors. Compared to other institutions that offer bluegrass music in the United States, it is by far the largest and most successful, both in terms of student interest and growth and in the ability to create an immersive experience in the culture of bluegrass. It is telling that, of the schools that I am aware of that offer bluegrass courses, it is the only one that is not attached to a school or department of music.

Recently, the programme underwent a significant overhaul of the major, and questions about how the programme was and could be orienting to bluegrass markets and what students really wanted were on the table in a formal way. Over the years, students had expressed their desire for more opportunities to develop and deepen the skills that they perceived to be valuable to the industry. They especially requested classes that focused on marketing, public relations, legal and finance issues and promotion. We created courses like 'Bluegrass Event Planning and Promotion', which focuses on bluegrass festivals, a critical commercial location in the industry; 'Digital Marketing in Bluegrass Music'; 'Identity and Creative Strategy in Bluegrass Music'; and even history and theory classes even more tightly aligned to bluegrass repertoire and practice. We recognized that, for example, touring bluegrass bands looking to fill a spot in their line-up (positions our students desired) were not as interested in musicians who could play many styles or who had a comprehensive knowledge of complex jazz theory or Western music history. Rather, they looked to hire musicians who were passionate about bluegrass and who had a deep understanding of its history, aesthetics and culture. Other facets of the industry such as labels, public relations, marketing and festival promoters also valued employees who could bring these perspectives to their efforts. The revised major, now titled 'Bluegrass, Old-Time, and Roots Music Studies', features four concentrations including one in Bluegrass Music Industry and one in Audio Production, which is also oriented tightly to acoustic and bluegrass music recording techniques.

Discussion

In his landmark ethnography about a music conservatory, Kingsbury (1988: 19–20) writes, 'my sense is that a conservatory is probably more appropriately compared with a seminary than with a professional school, in that the concentrated focus of conservatory training seems more an inculcation of devotion than a preparation for a career.' He continues, 'The sense of commitment among conservatory students seems more personal, moral, and emotional than professional or economic.' In other words, many, if not most, students who undertake a serious study of music in higher education are driven primarily by their passion for music, and their devotion to it, not necessarily by the career prospects it might afford. As part of making a life in music, industries take on different roles for each individual, and I am reluctant to dictate the acceptable reasons why one might choose to invest in a rigorous study of the music that they love. I resonate with Allsup's (2015: 259) observation that, 'as musicians, we know intimately that the arts have values that are richer, more complex and more confusing, than those attributed to commerce or mere self-identity'. Consequently, rather than assuming the responsibility to prepare students for every eventuality in their musical life and career, there is inherent and multifaceted value in providing rich and immersive opportunities to understand the history, culture, aesthetics and experience of a genre deeply: to take the music and its study seriously and on its own terms. In a sense, our approach belies a neoliberal orientation; we are responding to a desire in students (and the market opportunity around that desire) to invest in an immersion in their passion.

Our programme is not for everyone. We seek to recruit a very particular kind of student, often a student who grew up listening almost exclusively to this music or playing it with family or who found this music in some other way and developed a consuming interest in it. While it is not required for students to have an extensive background in bluegrass to be admitted to the programme, the reality is that most students are attracted to the curriculum because of their previous experience in the music. Students have come to ETSU from all over the world to study in the programme, including Iran, Japan, Scotland, the Netherlands, Germany, Canada and many other locales, and they typically have an extended experience with, or at least a keen interest in, bluegrass music over other genres. A limited number of students with this interest exists, and consequently, if many programmes pursued them, it would likely not be sustainable. As noted, bluegrass music has a strong connection to the area, and community support is a significant factor in the programme's success. A mariachi programme, for example, would likely not survive here but would find more success in an area where that genre has a regional relevance.

Creating a programme like this also requires a significant administrative commitment, which we are fortunate to enjoy at ETSU. For example, most of the instructors in our programme are not credentialed in the same way that many academics are; they tend to be successful bluegrass musicians, 'cultural insiders' who have played for decades and know the markets and cultures of the music intimately. Many do not have university degrees, and we have established other ways that their rich experience can be recognized institutionally. I cannot emphasize enough the critical importance that these faculty have in the programme's growth and success. Authenticity and legitimacy are highly valued by the students who seek out our programme: they want to work with their heroes and sit alongside the culture bearers of the genre. This requires a financial investment to attract those practitioners, and the investment extends beyond the faculty into developing and supporting unique, culturally relevant coursework and programming. I would argue that, in a neoliberal context that orients to market factors, this is a wise investment in our case and could be for other institutions that seek to incorporate non-classical musics. I suspect that one reason many other programmes are not as outwardly successful is in no small part due to the limited investment that is made in faculty, facilities and other resources. A meagre investment cannot create deep immersion.

Are there drawbacks to orienting a music programme to a narrow niche of the music industry in this way? Admittedly, I and other members of the faculty have some reservations. While a strict focus can cultivate expertise, it is necessarily – purposefully – limiting. I worry especially that the primary dedication to one tradition makes it difficult to appreciate other diverse musical cultures or embrace them. We also worry about the viability and sustainability of a career in the bluegrass or old-time music labour markets and whether they will always provide enough opportunities to justify the expense and time commitment of an academic major. (Of course, could one not make these same arguments about the overwhelming focus on classical music at most institutions of higher education?)

What has become clear to us after ten plus years of graduating Bluegrass, Old-Time, and Roots Music Studies majors is that every musician follows a unique career trajectory, incorporating disparate and various elements, which may include performance, teaching, research and writing, marketing, public relations and potentially many other areas of activity. While some students do find success in just one or a few of these areas, in bluegrass music, as in nearly every other kind of marketed music in the United States, including classical music, 'portfolio careers' have become more and more common (cf. Bartleet et al., 2019). And of course, some graduates end up making a living in some other field and pursuing bluegrass opportunities as more of an avocation. In other words, a student's passion for bluegrass music can find expression in many different ways after graduation, and while a neoliberal consideration *may* shape those pursuits for some students, in many cases, other factors weigh more prominently.

That being said, when students invest in the curriculum wholeheartedly and with intention, they undoubtedly cultivate musical expertise: they learn to play and sing well, with good timing, precision and appropriate style. Perhaps just as importantly, they develop a niche expertise in the historical and contemporary landscape of the genre. This knowledge is rare and, in the context of their desired market, valuable. Tellingly, approximately one-third of our students land professional work as performers in bluegrass or old-time bands before they graduate from our programme. The market is small, and our graduates have a reputation. By following and then deepening their love of the music, they can both tap into the intrinsic and rich values that Allsup (2015) intimates and cultivate and capitalize on their unique capacity in a niche market.

Notes

1. A thorough discussion of race and gender in bluegrass music is beyond the scope of this chapter. Readers are directed to the work of Hardwig (2001), Hammond (2011) and Hood (2020), as well as the address given by Rhiannon Giddens at the 2017 International Bluegrass Music Association Conference, for a more nuanced treatment of these topics.
2. All quotes included in this section are drawn from the interviews and personal communication that I conducted as part of my dissertation research (Olson, 2014). Research participants agreed to be quoted in this chapter.

References

Allsup, R. E. (2015), 'The Eclipse of a Higher Education or Problems Preparing Artists in a Mercantile World', *Music Education Research*, 17 (3): 251–61.

Bartleet, B.-L., C. Ballico, D. Bennett, R. Bridgstock, P. Draper, V. Tomlinson and S. Harrison (2019), 'Building Sustainable Portfolio Careers in Music: Insights and Implications for Higher Education', *Music Education Research*, 21 (3): 282–94.

Cantor, M. (2012), 'The 13 Most Worthless Majors', *Newser*, 23 April. Available online: https://www.newser.com/story/144600/the-13-most-worthless-majors.html (accessed 23 April 2012).

Cantwell, R. (2002), *Bluegrass Breakdown: The Making of the Old Southern Sound*, Urbana: University of Illinois Press.

ETSU Demographics (2021). Available online: https://www.etsu.edu/equity/documents/etsu_demographics_and_heed_survey_results_2021_dr_hoff.pdf (accessed 21 February 2022).

Everts, R., E. Hitters and P. Berkers (2022), 'The Working Life of Musicians: Mapping the Work Activities and Values of Early-career Pop Musicians in the Dutch Music Industry', *Creative Industries Journal*, 15 (1): 97–117.

Giddens, R. (2017), *Community and Connection*, Address given at the 2017 International Bluegrass Music Association Conference. Available online: https://www.nonesuch.com/journal/rhiannon-giddens-keynote-address-ibma-conference-community-connection-2017-10-03 (accessed 22 December 2022).

Goodstein, R. E., E. J. Lapin and R. C. McCurdy (2017), 'The Future of Arts Performance in Higher Education', *College Music Symposium*, 57.

Hammond, A. D. (2011), 'Color Me Country: Commercial Country Music and Whiteness', PhD diss., University of Kentucky.

Hardwig, B. (2001), 'Cocks, Balls, Bats, and Banjos: Masculinity and Competition in the Bluegrass Music of Bill Monroe', *Southern Quarterly*, 39 (4): 35–48.

Harvey, D. (2007), *A Brief History of Neoliberalism*, New York: Oxford University Press.

Hood, A. L. (2020), 'How History Books Erased the Marginalized Voices That Built Bluegrass', *Vice*, 19 May. Available online: https://www.vice.com/en/article/dyzzmq/how-history-books-erased-the-marginalized-voices-that-built-bluegrass (accessed 28 February 2022).

Kelman, K. (2020), *Entrepreneurial Music Education: Professional Learning in Schools and the Industry*, Cham: Springer Nature.

Kingsbury, H. (1988), *Music, Talent, and Performance: A Conservatory Cultural System*, Philadelphia: Temple University Press.

Kvale, S. (2007), *Doing Interviews*, Los Angeles: Sage Publications.

Miller, A. L., A. D. Dumford and W. R. Johnson (2017), 'Music Alumni Play a Different Tune: Reflections on Acquired Skills and Career Outcomes', *International Journal of Education & the Arts*, 18 (29): 1–21.

Olson, N. J. (2014), 'The Institutionalization of Fiddling in Higher Education: Three Cases', PhD diss., Teachers College, Columbia University.

Rosenberg, N. V. (2005), *Bluegrass: A History*, Champaign: University of Illinois Press.

Silverstein, B. (2012), 'How to Reach Bluegrass Fans Where they Want to be Reached: A Special Report on Bluegrass and the Internet'. Available online: http://bluegrasstoday.com/wp-content/uploads/pdf/Bluegrass_Today_Special_Report.2012.v1.0.pdf (accessed 22 December 2022).

Smith, G. D. (2016), 'Neoliberalism and Symbolic Violence in Higher Music Education', in L. C. DeLorenzo (ed.), *Giving Voice to Democracy in Music Education: Diversity and Social Justice*, 65–84, New York: Routledge.

Timberg, S. (2015), *Culture Crash: The Killing of the Creative Class*, New Haven: Yale University Press.

Williams, C. (2019), *The Nashville Number System*, Chas Williams Publishing.

Woodford, P. (2015), 'Confronting Innocence: Democracy, Music Education, and the Neoliberal "Manipulated Man"', in L. C. DeLorenzo (ed.), *Giving Voice to Democracy in Music Education: Diversity and Social Justice*, 51–64, New York: Routledge.

Chapter 6

From Merit to Engagement

Moving Music Education to the Next Phase

Mina Yang

Introduction

Music curricula in US higher education are under greater scrutiny today because of pressures from within and without academia. On the one hand, the expansion of the managerial sector in higher education, as a result of the neoliberalization of the university, has amplified demands that the humanities prove their utility or find themselves on the chopping block. On the other hand, scholars who came of age during the rise of feminism and post-colonialism are no longer content with teaching the same Eurocentric curriculum they inherited from earlier generations, and some of them are airing their grievances as part of larger mainstream conversations about social justice. We find ourselves at a crossroads: make a few changes with a new faculty member or two, offer more popular music courses to satisfy both the university bean counters and critics of the Eurocentric bias of the curriculum or ditch the whole model altogether and reinvent music education from scratch. To think through each scenario and to offer recommendations for how to move forward, I will situate recent attempts to reform higher education's music curricula within two different theoretical frameworks: education scholar Wayne Au's (2016) notion of Meritocracy 2.0 and feminist pedagogue Peggy McIntosh's (1997) 'Interactive Phases of Curricular Re-vision'. In surveying course catalogues across music departments in the United States and interrogating the overarching purpose of music education, I ultimately conclude that a wholesale paradigm shift is necessary if music education is to survive the challenges posed by the current cultural climate.

Meritocracy 1.0

Au's label (2016) for today's educational terrain, Meritocracy 2.0 (more on this later), implies an earlier version, a Meritocracy 1.0. Perhaps even more than in general primary and secondary education, music at the university level has and continues to emphasize merit as a prerequisite and objective. Constructed around a belief in the exceptional merit of the music itself, classical music culture reifies Western bourgeois values of individual achievement, and the music programmes that developed around this culture, by extension, have touted the musical equivalent of 'merit' for much of its existence. American universities, created by elites for the scions of the elites, placed the tradition of Western art music firmly at the centre of music education. Whether a student has any affinity for this music or not, a music major would typically study the history of classical music replete with great masters and their masterworks, move through a music theory sequence that would explain why these works – and, by implication, not others – were masterful and hone performance skills to prepare them for cut-throat orchestra auditions, where they would get ranked according to their perceived merit. A select few might even nab the ultimate meritocratic prize of winning a big competition and launching a solo career. Students practice solo excerpts and concertos and receive lessons from illustrious teachers on how to achieve the most flawless finish and just the right level of expressiveness. Blind orchestra auditions only reinforce the prevailing conviction that the classical music world is a meritocratic one, where anyone with the requisite talent and diligence could find success and even a secure livelihood. The core assumption that individual talent and mettle bring about success hides from view the enormous privilege necessary just to meet the minimal requirements of becoming a music major, involving years of musical tutelage, hours of practice and ready access to classical music institutions. Once the standards of evaluating this musical culture were set in place, other musical genres and practices that didn't conform to its standards of merit were seen as less-than, as marginal.

The value proposition of music in higher education replicates the white supremacist agenda of American society at large: those who come from privilege (i.e. white, male, upper class) claim a natural birthright to the rewards of this meritocratic system. In fact, music curricula in many US universities and conservatories are imbued with what Loren Kajikawa (2019) calls a 'possessive investment in whiteness', with required courses in music history and theory and performance ensembles and electives propping up a musical culture that claims to be Music itself, which helps to maintain the privileged position of white elite culture as Culture. Such a 'possessive investment in whiteness' in music education, as well as the considerable desire to challenge and upturn this legacy of whiteness, was demonstrated in the wake of the George Floyd killing, when Americans everywhere were reckoning with the persistence of racial inequity in their fields. In response to Philip Ewell's 2019 plenary talk (publ. 2020) for the Society for Music Theory conference, calling out Heinrich Schenker's racism, which Ewell argued informed the construction of a 'white racial frame' around the field of music theory in the United States, the *Journal of Schenkerian Studies* published a symposium issue (Graf, 2019) that many saw as promoting an anti-Black, white supremacist agenda. Given the timing of the ensuing melee, coinciding with the huge upswing of international sympathy for the Black Lives Matter movement following Floyd's killing by the police, 'Schenkergate' blew up and entered mainstream culture battles. Perhaps it wasn't entirely remarkable that the *New Yorker*'s music critic, Alex Ross (2020), who occasionally dips his toes in academic waters, covered the story; what was truly shocking was that the ultra-conservative, populist *Fox News* gave coverage to a controversy about what a music professor at Hunter College (New York) had to say about a little-known (outside of advanced music studies) Austrian music theorist, repackaging the incident as another example of the Left's 'cancel culture' (Betz, 2020).

The racism that came into public view during Schenkergate was just the latest in a series of controversies that shook the classical music world as the aesthetic cloak that had shielded it from external scrutiny was forcefully yanked off. In the wake of the #MeToo movement, survivors of sexual abuse divulged secrets about a world rife with bad actors, not unlike Hollywood, who hid barely out of sight behind the 'sublime' and 'other-worldly' music of Beethoven and Schubert. Conservatories, which foster notions of the sanctity of the music of the great masters, often resemble halls of worship, with teachers descended from a lineage traceable to the heroes of this hallowed musical tradition and having outsized influence on the careers of their young students. A culture built around such a star system of heroes was primed for abuse. Amidst rape and harassment allegations levelled against celebrity conductors James Levine, Placido Domingo, Charles Dutoit and others, violinist Lara St. John came forward with her story of suffering sexual abuse at the hands of her teacher, Jascha Brodsky, when she was a fourteen-year-old student at the Curtis Institute of Music (Philadelphia, Pennsylvania), only to be followed by many more such stories from others harmed by teachers with 'god status' at conservatories, music departments and music festivals (Fetters, Chan and Wu, 2020).

These recent scandals incontrovertibly demonstrated that music education does not operate at a remove from the rest of society. With the changing demographics of students, as well as the professoriate, in US higher education, the all-classical format of many music departments has become less tenable and more vulnerable to criticism from all sides. Some changes have been made, detailed in the following section, although it is questionable whether these changes have resulted in an abandonment of the kind of 'possessive investment in whiteness' that Kajikawa (2019) perspicaciously critiques.

Meritocracy 2.0

In using the term 'Meritocracy 2.0', Au is mostly interested in how standardized testing is being deployed in primary and secondary education as a means of providing 'objective' and 'anti-racist' data to help consumers choose schools for their children and to enable profit-making interventions in public schools. On our current educational landscape, Au writes: 'This interplay of neoliberalism, the reconstitution of "anti-racism" in ways that deny the structural and material realities of racism, and high-stakes testing coalesce in what I name here as "Meritocracy 2.0"' (Au, 2016: 40). Au is troubled by the ways in which the language around individual 'merit' hides persistent inequities of race and class and justifies the continuation of unequal schooling, now backed by so-called hard data. Although there is not an equivalent of standardized testing in music education, I see recent changes in music curricula that purport to remedy unequal access of the past without dismantling its dominant structure to be analogous to Au's description of schools under the testing regime. In response to criticism about their elitist and resource-heavy curricula, as well as the increasingly challenging professional outlook for their graduates, music schools and departments have begun to make changes that I am identifying henceforth as Meritocracy 2.0 musical style. Two different responses to the problems identified in Meritocracy 1.0 are common in the updated 2.0 version: (1) the addition of elective courses on popular and non-Western musics to the existing curriculum and (2) the emergence of music entrepreneurship programmes. Music schools and departments proffer these 'solutions' to problems of uneven access and opportunities that, akin to standardized tests in Au's Meritocracy 2.0, in fact paper over the issues without adequately acknowledging the structurally unequal foundations upon which Meritocracy 1.0 was built.

On the surface, adding classes from traditions outside of the Western elite culture appears to solve the problem of inclusion. Conceding that more diversity is desirable, music departments across the country have folded in classes on hip-hop, electronic dance music and non-Western music, adding colour to the formerly lily-white curriculum. Although fewer in number than the core classes in Western art music, these classes fill large lecture halls, in effect serving to subsidize the resource-heavy individualized lessons and smaller classes of the more 'serious' musicians. Yet even while fulfilling diversity hiring quotas, many, if not most, of the new faculty teaching these popular and non-Western music classes are part-time and contingent, with little power to change the dominant narratives already in place. Whether these classes come under the heading of 'Popular Practices in Music' or 'Music Cultures of the World' or 'Ethnomusicology', they clump together myriad types of music and are offered as the other to the main fare of Western classical music. While seeming to offer greater diversity and inclusion, the addition of music from outside of the Western art music canon in fact ends up reinforcing the dominant schema, with classical music occupying the centre and other musics pushed to the margins of our musical terrain, no matter that this relationship is actually the inverse of real-life consumption habits outside of academe.

Another 'solution' to the inadequacy of Meritocracy 1.0 music curricula comes in the form of music entrepreneurship classes. To satisfy parents and neoliberal managers who are increasingly demanding that universities provide students with professional readiness, more and more music departments are offering classes on how to start and maintain businesses, write business plans, secure loans, pitch investors, keep and read financial spreadsheets and so on. As Andrea Moore (2016) argues, however, music entrepreneurship is merely freelancing in fancy neoliberal clothes. Rather than provide musicians with paths to secure livelihoods, music entrepreneurship, according to Moore, is promoting professional precarity. Music entrepreneurship classes teach students business skills that will theoretically help them to patch together a career. However, such a career provides little in the way of stability and much in the way of unpaid labour, mostly non-musical, with no guarantee of success, and entails struggling to get by within a capitalistic system that increasingly demands creative content be freely available with diminishing returns for the creators. The language around music entrepreneurship is the language of Meritocracy 2.0. It is up to individuals to make something of their career, and those with merit will rightfully rise to the top. Emphasizing terms like 'individual agency' and 'creative freedom', Meritocracy 2.0 masks the structural inequities built into the cultural capitalistic machinery, which allows very few, mostly those with independent wealth and social connections who are predominantly white and male, to win at this game. Higher education administrators, complicit in the cost-slashing, pro-capitalist agenda of the neoliberal university, point to these classes on entrepreneurship as evidence that they care about the professional success of their students. Graduates who have had to take on large debts to earn their music degrees are left wondering why they need to keep their financial books in order when there is zero money coming in.

Interactive Phases of Curricular Revision

To think about how to move beyond Meritocracy 2.0, I propose adapting and expanding McIntosh's (1997) 'Interactive Phases of Curricular Re-vision' as interpreted by musicologists Cynthia Cyrus and Olivia Carter Mather (1998). In imagining a curriculum for Medieval and Renaissance art music that is sensitive to the lessons of feminist scholarship, Cyrus and Mather reference McIntosh's five phases as a guideline:

1. Womanless History
2. Women in History
3. Women as a Problem, Anomaly, or Absence
4. Women as History
5. History Reconstructed, Redefined and Transformed
   (Cyrus and Mather, 1998: 105)

For the purpose of this chapter, 'woman' will be expanded to include People of Colour, people from the working class and others who have been excluded from the larger historical narratives of Eurocentric elite culture. The first phase, the main fare of universities and conservatories for the last 100 plus years, is what I have been calling Meritocracy 1.0 in US higher education music curricula. Many music programmes are entering into phases two and three, inserting token women and Black, Indigenous and People of Colour (BIPOC) composers and performers into the pre-existing historical narrative in the mode of Meritocracy 2.0, and some are even noting their absence out loud.

A few have made more drastic moves into phases four and five, expanding the representation of previously marginalized people so that they occupy a much more visible (and audible) space in the curriculum. At the New England Conservatory of Music (Boston), for example, the Department of Contemporary Improvisation includes musicians from Turkish, Persian, Chinese, Appalachian, Jewish and many other traditions and is not a mere afterthought to the more standard Western classical fare that was its *raison d'etre*. Harvard University (Cambridge, Massachusetts) went even further into phase five in 2017 with its curricular overhaul, eliminating the core music history and theory sequence for a more flexible and inclusive model that requires only two courses for majors: 'Thinking About Music' and 'Critical Listening'. Acknowledging that its previous curriculum for music majors, with its twin pillars of (Western art) music history and (Western art) music theory sequences, left little room for other musical explorations, music theory professor Alexander Rehding explained:

> We'd been tinkering with the structures for quite a while, and we'd made little changes, and at one point we realized that rather than tinkering with the edges it makes more sense to think through what we're doing as a whole. The other goal is to increase diversity. We know that there are many students at Harvard who don't have a traditional musical background but who are very musical, and it's those people that felt the music curriculum wasn't for them. And that was something that we wanted to address. (Robin, 2017: n.p.)

Perhaps not surprisingly, because this was Harvard and the proposed changes were so dramatic, the Harvard music department received considerable media attention and not a little pushback from the public, even earning grumpy editorials from famous alums like the composer John Adams. A few other schools are also experimenting with the edges of where they were in the not-so-distant past. The music major at Cornell University (Ithaca, New York) 'provides avenues for students to capitalize on the strengths, experiences, and training that they bring to the program as well as opportunities to engage deeply with unfamiliar sounds, traditions, and ways of thinking and behaving musically' (Cornell University, Department of Music, n.d.) and offers Western art music as an option within a wide array that also includes Latin musics, African musics in the diaspora, experimental and digital musics, among others. At Yale University (New Haven, Connecticut), freshmen have the option of taking seminars that didn't exist twenty years ago when I was a graduate student there: 'Noise', 'Cognition of Musical Rhythm', '1000 Years of Love Songs' and 'Music and Human Evolution'. The University of California, Santa Cruz, now offers three tracks for music majors, 'Contemporary Practices', 'Global Musics' and 'Western Art Music', in an acknowledgement that what we call classical music is but one of the major musical traditions of the world (though this one tradition admittedly receives as much attention as all the rest of the globe put together).

In my survey of dozens of music curricula at universities and colleges – from the most exclusive Ivies to the most accessible community colleges – I found that a majority of music programs in the United States are still stalled at phase one or two.

The Higher Education Arts Data Summaries (HEADS) in Music, a compilation of data from annual reports submitted by member institutions of the National Association of Schools of Music, provide a broader picture: In the charts for 'Total Music Student Enrollment', the HEADS reports list the most common music majors, such as violin, piano, voice, music theory and musicology, which rely on the Eurocentric approach to music education outlined earlier. The only majors that diverge from this approach are guitar, jazz studies and other (unspecified). A comparison of the 2000 Summary to the 2020 Summary shows the majors remaining unchanged and the numbers moving only slightly – in 2000, 173 of 366 (47 per cent) reporting institutions offered guitar, 84 (23 per cent) jazz studies and 91 (25 per cent) other; in 2020, 164 (39 per cent) of 425 institutions offered guitar, 121 (28 per cent) jazz studies and 93 (22 per cent) other (HEADS, 2001, 2021) – suggesting that little has changed in the past twenty years. It is more urgent than ever to ask what music education should be doing, and the answer currently is that it is buttressing a musical culture with less and less relevance to contemporary life, that supports a power structure with questionable moral claims and that fails most musicians in preparing for a meaningful and sustainable professional career. Harvard University's new programme, as well as a handful of the other programmes described earlier, strives to do better with its goal of cultivating a thinking musician. My proposal is that we add to our music educational aspirations one more qualifier for the end product – that we educate to produce an *engaged*, thinking musician. As a group that has been especially harmed by the neoliberal economy, musicians must learn how to fight the system and turn the tide. This brings us to the sixth phase, yet to be conceived and implemented.

The Sixth Phase

Heeding Alejandro Madrid's (2017) call to refuse complacency in the face of the incremental changes of the recent past, I advocate for the addition of a sixth phase to McIntosh's (1997) original five, called 'The Present Critiqued, The Future Reimagined'. Madrid characterizes much of the recent curricular revisions as so much tokenism, the satisfaction of quotas without challenging the fundamental values represented by the traditional model. Although the intention behind the inclusion of more music by marginalized people may be well-meaning, the result is not so different: the reinforcement of a historical narrative that foregrounds exceptional individuals and their masterpieces. If anything, with the values of (a certain kind of) quality and (a specific) teleological perspective left intact, the addition of the Others seems to only justify why the canon is what it is and why the token inclusions are less-than and should remain marginalized. Madrid calls for a transhistorical, critical approach that examines why we do what we do and interrogates the assumptions and judgements that inhere in the canon and its aesthetic criteria. Finally, he advocates for a music curriculum that 'allows us to establish new connections, based on common issues, among a variety of moments in the space-time continuum as opposed to fixating on the type of teleology that the current archetype privileges' (Madrid, 2017: 126). Madrid sees music scholarship and curricula as a form of 'critical intervention' that can help us to understand the world and better relate to one another. McIntosh's (1997) fifth phase, 'History Reconstructed, Redefined and Transformed', likewise calls for such a critical approach, but Madrid goes beyond her final phase, questioning the validity of the historical foundation of much of the musical curricula still being taught at most universities and conservatories.

Above and beyond Madrid's insightful critique and call to action, I would add one more consideration. Beyond learning why and what *is*, young musicians should learn what *could be*. Except for a small number of those who are extremely 'lucky' or independently wealthy, musicians can no longer sustain a stable and sufficient musical livelihood in this era of free content and an ever more cut-throat gig economy. Musicians need to learn how neoliberalism and other larger socio-economic trends impact where, when, how and why music is deployed. By understanding how music supports or challenges power, who gets rewarded and why and then gaining the tools to become more politically engaged, new generations of musicians may actually have a fighting chance of changing the system for better, for rolling back the deleterious effects of neoliberal policies, for recognizing and tapping into their potential as agents of sociopolitical change.

I propose two courses that would serve as the bedrock of a new musical curriculum that seeks to educate thinking, engaged musical practitioners. The first is a course on the neoliberal economy and the history of labour organization. For many young adults, the socio-economic system they grew into seems like a part of the natural environment and therefore immutable. By learning about how music became a commodity in the modern economy, its transition from commodity to 'free content' in the neoliberal economy and the implosion of the performing arts sector during the pandemic, budding musicians can begin to recognize the fluid nature of socio-economic systems. By learning about how labour movements have won concessions from capital that made work tolerable and even enjoyable for many workers in the past, musicians might envision the possibility of organizing into unions and other collectives to be able to more effectively demand from Big Tech companies like Google and Amazon and concert promoters like Live Nation fair remuneration for their time and labour. Once music students learn about how they might organize to effect positive change in their own lives, they might consider using their political will and musical abilities to bring about transformation for others. A second required course would focus on how music can play a role in social justice movements. Students will read theories of community formation and resistance and read case studies about the power of music in political movements of the past, such as the anti-apartheid movement and the Civil Rights Movement. They might learn to critique the implication of Western art music in the classist, white supremacist projects of the past (e.g. Levine, 1997) or discover how music is integral to the formation of digital communities built on common cultural affinities (e.g. Jenkins, Ito and boyd, 2016). They might become inspired by women like Nina Simone or Miriam Makeba, who used their music to face down racism, or be amazed at how a Bollywood soundtrack can so dramatically shape-shift within the South Asian diaspora. Music can change lives and communities, but most music students today are too focused on the next audition or jury to be conscious of just how much impact they may have in the world beyond the concert hall.

With classes on music as labour and music and social change as the cornerstone of a new music curriculum, students will go into their other classes and onto their professional lives with a firmer sense of why they make music and how they can continue to make music and live fulfilling, relevant lives well into the future.

Conclusion

The music profession is in a state of crisis. This is bad not only for those of us who are music professionals but for all of humankind. Music is one of the few things that sets humans apart from other living things, and music can carry us beyond mundane routines to add magic to our lives. Although we now have more music recorded and archived than a single music aficionado could listen to in an entire lifetime, there is infinitely more music to be imagined, reimagined, recontextualized and played in live performances that could change the course of humankind.

This precious cultural practice is under threat from multiple fronts. Union-protected jobs in orchestras are becoming an endangered species, and even some of the most prestigious and secure of them, such as tenured positions with the Metropolitan Opera, left musicians high and dry during the Covid-19 pandemic lockdown. With Big Tech monopolistically controlling creative content for the near future, musicians can expect to reap little reward for their musical output even if they're more readily able to put it in front of global audiences. Live performances, with their merchandise sales and ancillary commerce, were the one lifeline that many musicians clung to in the post-Napster era, but that, too, proved vulnerable to the Covid-19 shutdown. Still, students show up at universities and conservatories wanting to study music because music engenders that kind of excitement and commitment. What a waste to not channel this passion by shepherding these young people into fulfilling and financially rewarding careers, connected to the communities in which they reside. This is why we must completely overhaul our music curricula, to educate the thinking, engaged musicians of today and tomorrow. This is no longer (if it ever was) about conservatives and liberals or about whether we should reserve a hallowed space or cancel the inherited canon of dead white men but rather whether we value music at all and want to continue to cultivate an ecosystem that includes living musicians for the future of humanity. With that goal in mind, let's dismantle our current music curricula, based on false ideals of meritocracy, and construct a new educational paradigm that educates the entire musical person – heart, mind and soul as well as the music-making bits – and provides for young musicians the tools that can sustain them and prop them up. A tall order, but if we don't rise up to meet the challenge, there may be no music curricula at all in the not-so-distant future.

References

Au, W. (2016), 'Meritocracy 2.0', *Educational Policy*, 30 (1): 39–62.

Betz, B. (2020), 'Music Faculty at Texas College Stokes Ire for Suggesting Music Theory Isn't White Supremacist', *Fox News*, 4 August. Available online: https://fxn.ws/3kk4HDp (accessed 29 August 2021).

Cornell University, Department of Music (n.d.), 'Undergraduate Studies'. Available online: https://music.cornell.edu/undergraduate-studies-0 (accessed 29 August 2021).

Cyrus, C. J. and O. C. Mather (1998), 'Rereading Absence: Women in Medieval and Renaissance Music', *College Music Symposium*, 38: 101–17.

Ewell, P. (2020), 'Music Theory's White Racial Frame', *Music Theory Online*, 26 (2). Available online: https://mtosmt.org/issues/mto.20.26.2/mto.20.26.2.ewell.pdf (accessed 29 August 2021).

Fetters, A., J. C. Chan and N. Wu (2020), 'Classical Music Has a "God Status" Problem', *Atlantic Monthly*, 31 January. Available online: https://www.theatlantic.com/education/archive/2020/01/conservatories-sexual-harassment-abuse/604351/?utm_source=email&utm_medium=social&utm_campaign=share (accessed 29 August 2021).

Graf, B., ed. (2019), *Journal of Schenkerian Studies*, 12.

Higher Education Arts Data Services (2001), *Music: Data Summaries, 2000–2001*. Reston. Available online: https://nasm.arts-accredit.org/wp-content/uploads/sites/2/2022/09/M-2000-2001-HEADS-Data-Summaries-for-Website.pdf (accessed 29 August 2021).

Higher Education Arts Data Services (2021), *Music: Data Summaries, 2020–2021*. Reston. Available online: https://nasm.arts-accredit.org/wp-content/uploads/sites/2/2022/04/M-2020-2021-HEADS-Data-Summaries.pdf (accessed 29 August 2021).

Jenkins, H., M. Ito and d. boyd (2016), *Participatory Culture in a Networked Era. A Conversation on Youth, Learning, Commerce and Politics*, Cambridge: Polity Press.

Kajikawa, L. (2019), 'The Possessive Investment in Classical Music: Confronting Legacies of White Supremacy in U.S. Schools and Departments of Music', in K. Crenshaw, L. C. Harris, D. Martinez HoSang and G. Lipsitz (eds), *Seeing Race Again: Countering Colorblindness Across the Disciplines*, 155–74, Berkeley: University of California Press.

Levine, L. W. (1997), *The Opening of the American Mind: Canons, Culture and History*, Boston: Beacon Press.

Madrid, A. (2017), 'Diversity, Tokenism, Non-canonical Musics, and the Crisis of the Humanities in U.S. Academia', *Journal of Music History Pedagogy*, 7 (2): 124–30.

McIntosh, P. (1997), 'Interactive Phases of Curricular Re-vision: A Feminist Perspective', in J. Q. Adams and J. R. Welsch (eds), *Multicultural Prism: Voices from the Field*, 3, 18–34. Available online: https://files.eric.ed.gov/fulltext/ED414585.pdf#page=19 (accessed 29 August 2021).

Moore, A. (2016), 'Neoliberalism and the Musical Entrepreneur', *Journal of the Society for American Music*, 10 (1): 33–53.

Robin, W. (2017), 'What Controversial Changes at Harvard Mean for Music in the University', *National Sawdust Log*. Available online: https://www.nationalsawdust.org/thelog/2017-04-25-what-controversial-changes-at-harvard-means-for-music-in-the-university (accessed 29 August 2021).

Ross, A. (2020), 'Black Scholars Confront White Supremacy in Classical Music', *New Yorker*, 21 September. Available online: https://www.newyorker.com/magazine/2020/09/21/black-scholars-confront-white-supremacy-in-classical-music (accessed 29 August 2021).

Part II

Power Relations, Alternative Pedagogies and Activism

Chapter 7

Classical Music After #MeToo

Is Music Higher Education a 'Conducive Context' for Sexual Misconduct?

Anna Bull

Introduction

Despite high-profile sexual harassment scandals (e.g. Stewart and Cooper, 2020), it has been argued that in classical music, #MeToo has led to less of a reckoning than in many other industries (Madonna, 2019). Higher music education institutions, which historically and to some extent today have been dominated by classical music, have also seen only a limited amount of scrutiny. Nevertheless, there is plenty of evidence that sexual harassment and misconduct – often teachers targeting students as well as bullying and emotional abuse (Bull, 2019) – does occur in higher music education (e.g. Kopelman, Boylan and Kashti, 2020; Pidd, 2013). Despite this evidence in the public domain, there remains little academic research on abuse in music education (although see Baker and Cheng, 2021; Gisler and Emmenegger, 1998; Hoffmann, 2015; Pace, 2013a; Simpson, 2010). Similarly, in the classical music industry, researchers have only recently begun to document sexual harassment (Hennekam and Bennett, 2017; Incorporated Society of Musicians, 2018; Keil and Kheriji-Watts, 2022; Scharff, 2020). This chapter provides a theoretical framing for studying sexual misconduct in higher music education by analysing the context that enables its occurrence in higher classical music education institutions, focusing on the UK to exemplify this discussion.

It has been suggested that neoliberal reforms of higher education have created a climate in which fears of reputational damage lead to 'institutional airbrushing' (Phipps, 2018: 230), whereby higher education institutions cover up instances of abuse by silencing victims and protecting high-profile members of the institution. Phipps draws on a broad understanding of neoliberalism as a form of 'rationality in which everything is understood through the metaphor of capital' (2018: 3). This is in line with widely used definitions of neoliberalism in this context as 'the encouragement of market mechanisms in public HE' (McCaig, 2018: 17). However, I follow McCaig (2018) in arguing that this broad definition does not accurately describe recent policy developments in higher education in many countries, such as the UK. Instead, 'neoliberalism in this context [. . .] implies the use of market incentives by governments within a regulated system in an effort to change behaviours, be they institutional, academic or student behaviours' (McCaig, 2018: 18). Furthermore, while neoliberal reforms in higher education, in particular marketization, have indeed had profound impacts, sexual harassment – and inadequate institutional responses to it – has longer histories that go back earlier than neoliberal reforms (as documented by Pace (2013a)). Therefore, I argue that the role of neoliberal market reforms in creating a conducive context for sexual misconduct in higher music education in the UK context is contradictory and uneven. This means that rather than looking to neoliberalism as a key factor explaining the context in which sexual misconduct remains unaddressed, it is necessary to examine how cultures of gendered hierarchy, authority and power in classical music, as elsewhere, create a climate that enables abuse. These cultures are embedded into the social relations, technologies and materialities that create classical music's aesthetic and enter into its institutions and, to some degree, its repertoire (Bull, 2019). This means that while paying attention to the impacts of neoliberal reforms, we have to primarily look to the longer histories of the genre and its institutions to make sense of sexual harassment and abuses of power in classical music.

To this end, in this chapter, I draw together my research across two areas – classical music's cultures and inequalities and sexual misconduct by staff/faculty[1] in higher education – in order to examine the context for sexual harassment and misconduct carried out by teachers or authority figures in higher classical music education. I focus on the UK context as neoliberal developments within this context have been influential internationally in reform agendas in higher education (Marginson, 2018: 26). I use the term 'sexual misconduct' not only to encompass sexual harassment as defined in equalities legislation such as the UK Equality Act 2010 but also to include wider sexualized behaviours that constitute professional misconduct and cause harm but may not be 'unwanted' as is required by standard definitions of sexual harassment (see Page, Bull and Chapman, 2019). It should be noted that these terms include sexual and gender-based violence such as rape or sexual assault as well as 'grooming' behaviours (Bull and Page, 2021a) and gender harassment (National Academies of Sciences, Engineering and Medicine, 2018). While some of these arguments may also apply to higher music education more widely, I focus specifically on classical music here in order to pay attention to its specific culture(s) and modes of authority. I draw on Kelly's (2016) idea of the 'conducive context' for abuse to move away from ideas of classical music's 'exceptionalism' and instead identify specific aspects of classical music cultures that might enable misconduct. By 'exceptionalism' I refer to an often-tacit discourse that classical music is fundamentally different from – and superior to – other musical genres. Christina Scharff and I have described this as its 'unspoken and uncontested value' as evidenced by its privileged status in cultural funding, discourses of its 'complexity' and 'emotional depth' and its historical and contemporary associations with the white middle and upper classes (Bull and Scharff, 2017: 14). In order to make this argument, the chapter firstly discusses existing research on sexual misconduct in higher education and in classical music education, then outlines the presence of 'institutionalized authority and gendered power' in classical music and examines the extent to which there exists an 'external challenge' to these power-knowledge systems, before briefly discussing ways forward to address this issue.

Staff/faculty Sexual Misconduct in Higher Education

Sexual harassment by staff/faculty towards students in higher education has been overlooked until recently (with exceptions; see Carter and Jeffs, 1995). However, large-scale surveys of students in Australia and the United States in recent years have revealed its prevalence, finding that between 5 and 10 per cent of students are subjected to sexual harassment by staff during their studies, and women students, postgraduate students and LGBTQ+ students are much more likely to be targeted (Australian Human Rights Commission, 2017; Cantor et al., 2019). Nevertheless, there are differences between disciplines and institutions in how prevalent this is; in the United States, medicine and engineering have been found to have substantially higher rates of sexual harassment by faculty/staff than other disciplines (National Academies of Sciences, Engineering and Medicine, 2018: 281), although this study was not able to reveal reasons why this was the case. Similarly, the Australian Human Rights Commission study reported finding different rates of sexual harassment by staff across different institutions (Bagshaw, 2017). These studies highlight the role of institutional cultures in creating an environment where harassment is normalized and invisibilized (Jackson and Sundaram, 2020) or challenged.

Not all students are equally at risk of sexual misconduct from staff/faculty. One-to-one teaching between postgraduate research students and their supervisors appears to be a particular risk factor for abuse to occur (Bull and Rye, 2018; Whitley and Page, 2015). In addition, inequalities relating to gender, institutional roles, racialized identities, class and disability have been identified as enabling staff/faculty to perpetrate sexual misconduct (Bull and Page, 2021a; Whitley and Page, 2015). However, structures for reporting sexual harassment or assault in higher education appear to rarely be fit for the purpose, leading students who attempt to report through a lengthy, emotionally draining and ultimately ineffective process, which fails to achieve safety for themselves or others (Bull and Page, 2021b; National Academies of Science, Engineering and Medicine, 2018).

In higher music education, these wider patterns intersect with the genre cultures of different music worlds, such as classical music. For example, in my research with young people playing in classical music ensembles in the south of England (Bull, 2019), four out of the thirty-seven young people I interviewed told me about teachers – whether at conservatoires or in pre-tertiary music education – who had engaged in bullying or emotionally abusive behaviours. Young people in my study did not label this as bullying but instead took responsibility themselves for their teachers' behaviour, explaining that it was justified or needed because they were not good enough, not working hard enough or not mature enough. Around the same time that I was carrying out these interviews in 2013, sexual abuse scandals in classical music education institutions in the UK were breaking. Chetham's School of Music, a specialist secondary school that enrols pupils aged eleven to eighteen for intensive classical music education, was exposed as having employed teachers between the 1970s and 2010 who had sexually abused pupils (Pidd, 2013, 2021). My research had shown how bullying and abuse could be normalized, accepted and invisibilized within classical music's culture through being taken for granted as typical behaviour within the one-to-one master-apprentice teaching relationship and/or camouflaged within the gendered patterns of authority and control between conductor and musicians. The emerging scandals within music schools suggested that this normalization could also extend to sexual abuse. As a result, after finishing my PhD, I worked with campaigner and musicologist Ian Pace to organize a series of events for the music education sector to discuss how to tackle abuse (Bull, 2015, 2016a, 2017).

Focusing primarily on specialist music schools – secondary schools for eleven- to eighteen-year-old musicians – Pace, an alumnus of one of these schools himself, has documented cases of abuse in classical music education in the UK (Pace, 2013a). He argues that elite classical music training is characterized by 'a systematic pattern of domination, cruelty, dehumanization, bullying and emotional manipulation from unscrupulous musicians in positions of unchecked power, of which sexual abuse is one of several manifestations' (Pace, 2015: n.p.). He outlines various factors within specialist classical music education that create an environment where abuses – sexual, physical, psychological – can occur. The first factor is a culture of 'great musicians', which institutions' reputations draw on to accrue prestige (Pace, 2013b). Secondly, the particular emotional landscape of classical music draws on values and attitudes 'rooted in the 19th century' (Pace, 2013b). Thirdly, the sexualization of musical performance and performers' dress creates an environment where sexuality is foregrounded and ever-present (Pace, 2013b). He also points to other factors, including the lack of training for music teachers and the intensity of one-to-one teaching relationships in classical music education (Pace, 2013b). Despite these critiques, Pace defends the aesthetic values and conventions of classical music more widely, arguing against attempts to challenge notions of musical 'standards' (Pace, 2017).

While many of these points are convincing, this chapter critically reflects on them. Firstly, Pace's argument that the sexualization of musical performance contributes to abuse risks being aligned with a victim-blaming approach, mistaking sexual misconduct as being about sex rather than power and implying that 'respectable' feminine dress is a possible solution. Secondly, as I have argued elsewhere (Bull, 2019), the aesthetic of classical music contributes to producing the social relations – including the power relations – that characterize this space. Therefore, Pace's argument that the aesthetic qualities of the music must not be part of a wider social change is to align with a position where the music is seen as more important than the people who make it (Cheng, 2020). As outlined later, this risks taking a position of what I am calling exceptionalism rather than looking for the common factors across all institutions and cultures that enable abuses of power to occur. Finally, and most importantly, Pace's analysis focuses on aspects of classical music's culture that are distinctive to the genre, thus implying that there is something unique about classical music that creates an environment where sexual misconduct can occur. Instead, in this chapter, I argue that we need to examine the common factors that exist in contexts where sexual misconduct occurs, including classical music education, rather than suggesting that classical music is special or different.

Liz Kelly's concept of the 'conducive context' was formulated to understand what similarities there are between different social spaces where violence against women and girls occurs (2016). Kelly suggests two main factors that such sites might have in common. First, they are characterized by 'institutionalized power and authority', where this authority is 'gendered'. This can be understood as a distribution of power within an institution (or set of institutions) whereby positions of authority are disproportionately held by men and/or cultural norms of masculinity confer authority (similarly to Connell's 'gender regimes' (2006)). Second, there is 'limited external challenge', that is, these gendered forms of power and authority are not challenged by other forms of authority existing outside the institution (Kelly, 2016: n.p.). An example that illustrates these points is the family, which has historically been characterized by strong male authority while also being a space that is private and outside the jurisdiction of the state or other forms of social control. In the rest of this chapter, I analyse the culture of classical music in higher education in relation to these aspects of the conducive context: first, 'institutionalized power and authority', which is gendered; and second, that such forms of authority cannot be challenged by competing forms of power outside the institution.

Institutionalized Authority and Gendered Power in Classical Music

Institutionalized gendered power relations have been relatively well documented within the classical music industry and classical music education (Bull, 2016b; Green, 1997; O'Toole, 1994; Scharff, 2015, 2017). Leadership and authority positions are disproportionately held by white men, despite higher numbers of predominantly white middle- and upper-class girls learning classical music as children (Bull, 2021; Green, 1997; Scharff, 2017). In the UK, for example, recent studies have found that as few as 1.5 per cent (Scharff, 2017) to 5 per cent (Royal Philharmonic Society, 2019) of professional conductors working in the UK are women, and other prestigious roles such as orchestral section leaders or conservatoire teachers are more likely to be held by men than women (Scharff, 2017).

The operatic canon – widely used in classical music education – normalizes male violence against women and girls through frequent, often racialized depictions that glorify or minimize it (Bull, 2019; Vincent, 2023). Within cultures of classical music practice more widely, institutionalized power and authority is also well evidenced through reverence to the authority of the composer and the score (Goehr, 1992; Kingsbury, 1988; Nettl, 1995), which in turn gives authority to the teacher, both in the one-to-one lesson and in public masterclasses. This also occurs through the social organization of canonic repertoire that institutionalizes the role of the conductor (Lambeau, 2015) and the ongoing weighting of programming towards dead white male composers (Bain, 2019; Donne, 2021). Analysing the microsocial dynamics of how this authority is constructed and normalized can help to understand how it is perpetuated and reproduced (Bull, 2019: 114–19; O'Toole, 1994).

Furthermore, it is not only conductors but also teachers (of all genders) who perpetuate conditions where they wield power and authority. As Barton (2020) describes in his study of private instrumental teachers in the UK, teachers maintained that they were giving pupils choice and control over their learning but in fact prescribed very narrowly the possible choices that pupils could make. Others have also noted that power relations exist in the master-apprentice model of instrumental tuition (Gaunt, 2011; Haddon, 2011; Rakena, Airini and Brown, 2016). More widely, Perkins's (2013) study of a conservatoire documented a 'star system' in which hierarchies were created and perpetuated within the student body whereby students were valued or devalued based on both musical and extra-musical qualities. These forms of authority are institutionalized; if students wish to access higher classical music education, they cannot avoid participating in spaces that are characterized by these forms of gendered, racialized power.

However, this discussion reveals an apparent contradiction in that, for freelance classical musicians, despite the formal structures of authority and power within institutional spaces, the *informality* of modes of getting work can compound gendered, classed and racialized patterns of inclusion and exclusion (Hennekam and Bennett, 2017; Scharff, 2020; Wang, 2015; Yoshihara, 2008) while also failing to address normalized patterns of sexual harassment (Scharff, 2020). As Hennekam and Bennett (2017) outline in their study of sexual harassment among creative industries workers in the Netherlands, competition for work, industry culture, gendered power relations and informal networks create a context where there is a tolerance for sexual harassment. However, these informal networks are, in the case of classical music, underpinned and supported by formal institutions in which institutionalized authority and gendered power are reproduced. These institutions play a major role in conferring and legitimizing the charismatic authority of arts leaders (Nisbett and Walmsley, 2016). It appears, therefore, that this gendered power can operate through both institutionalized authority and informal networks. However, both have in common the limited external challenge to their culture.

Limited External Challenge to Institutionalized Authority

In addition to institutionalized authority and gendered power relations, a second characteristic of the 'conducive context', as Kelly (2016) describes, is 'limited external challenge' to institutionalized authority and entitlement. This could be understood in (at least) two senses. First, this could relate to the governance structures in a particular field and their accountability to external bodies. Second, it could be understood in relation to the existence of competing modes of authority that can challenge the power-knowledge systems that exist within a particular context.

Addressing the first point around governance structures, a strong value across European higher education is institutional autonomy – the freedom to self-govern across financial, staffing, organizational and staffing decisions. This has until recently been most fully realized in the UK (Erçetin and Yılmaz Fındık, 2016). However, this institutional autonomy is now being challenged. First, market reforms have introduced a level of state regulation that was hitherto absent (e.g. the Higher Education Reform Act of 2017 introduced a regulator for higher education in England). In this way, in the UK, the marketization of higher education has occurred through an *increase* in state regulation and control, with less autonomy for higher education institutions (McCaig, 2018) and greater external challenge. This includes proposed statutory requirements for higher education institutions to address sexual misconduct (Office for Students, 2021).

A second challenge to institutional autonomy comes from discourses and practices relating to student 'employability'. Within UK conservatoires, competing discourses between the musical values of classical music and the discourse of employability have been documented, as Ford (2010) describes, through competing ideals of the 'professional' musician. In her study, some students and teachers in conservatoires espoused a discourse of 'art for art's sake' whereby 'the intrinsic worth of the canon was held up as a justification for being a professional, and the maintenance of these [values] was seen as the goal' (Ford, 2010: 208). A 'competing image of the professional' was articulated by those who upheld the discourse of employability: 'one which measured the professional's worth in terms of earning money' (Ford, 2010: 208). The pressures on institutions towards 'employability' are incentivized through the use of national metrics to measure graduate employment, thus further diluting institutional autonomy and demonstrating external influence through the institutions of the market.

As these examples show, in the UK, the marketization of higher education has occurred through an increase in state regulation and control. Such regulation also includes proposed legal requirements on higher education institutions to address sexual misconduct (Office for Students, 2021). These requirements can be seen as a 'mode of authority' that aims to shape institutional actions within a wider marketized context in order to address the sexual misconduct and harassment that occurs in higher education. However, while there have been steps towards addressing sexual misconduct in UK conservatoires (e.g. Kopelman, Boylan and Kashti, 2020), these steps have not challenged the established forms of authority in classical music that might disrupt the conducive context.

Indeed, the second way of understanding 'external challenge' further illuminates this point: the question of whether there exist competing modes of authority that can destabilize the power-knowledge systems that shape students' and staff subjectivities within conservatoires. These power-knowledge systems rely on the intensive, lengthy period of socialization that is normal for classical musicians on entering higher music education (Bull, 2019; Hall, 2018; Wagner, 2015). This socialization tends to create closed social and musical worlds and strong identities as classical musicians (Bull, 2019). These closed social worlds that classical music students inhabit means that they are not exposed to challenges to the modes of authority that exist within music higher education institutions. Therefore, while higher music education institutions may be increasingly subjected to external challenge through marketization and employability discourses, it appears that the social and 'genre worlds' of music students are not. The way forward therefore lies not in replacing patriarchal conservatoire authority with neoliberal practices but, instead, as the next section explores, in rethinking the pedagogic and gendered relationships within the conservatoire.

Ways Forward

Ways forward on addressing this issue need to tackle both prevention and response. Firstly, as students who are subjected to sexual misconduct or abuse only rarely report it to their institution, institutions should take proactive steps to encourage and support reporting and to adequately deal with reports (Bull, Calvert-Lee and Page, 2020). In addition, higher music education institutions should lead on prevention and response work within the wider music industries, especially as many part-time faculty/staff in conservatoires work across industries and educational levels.

However, the focus on the conducive context shows that 'raising awareness' is not enough; the structures of gendered and racialized power also need to change. This requires working towards greater equality of representation and voice among the staff and student body across different marginalized groups. For example, to address sexual misconduct, working towards greater gender equality is an important aspect of prevention, and this includes recognition of gender identities beyond binary gender as well as proactive steps for inclusion of trans people and other minoritized or marginalized groups, including students and faculty of colour.

Finally, however, it is necessary to tackle the ways in which the conducive context is created in the first place, that is, to challenge institutionalized gendered and racialized power and authority. Simply extending access for women, non-binary people and People of Colour to the existing structures of authority is not sufficient, as neither established conservative modes of authority nor emergent neoliberal logics sufficiently challenge the power structures that exist in conservatoires (such as the master-apprentice model). Instead, this step requires pedagogic reforms to teaching and learning practices in music education. Challenging the master-apprentice model of one-to-one teaching, supporting peer and group learning and developing student voice in music education are all factors that can play a role in creating a context that works against harassment or abuse occurring (see e.g. Gaunt and Westerlund, 2013; Mayne, Bull and Raven, 2022). It is necessary to minimize the hierarchies that are taken for granted within the normal conventions of the genre and to reimagine and transform classical music's culture and institutions.

Conclusion: Moving Beyond Classical Music's Exceptionalism

This chapter has analysed cultures and institutions of higher classical music education to ask whether it creates a 'conducive context' that enables sexual misconduct to occur. There are various factors that suggest that classical music does indeed constitute such a context due to its high levels of institutionalized power and authority, including gendered power relations. While there are increasing external challenges to institutional governance structures due to the marketization of higher education, it is not clear that this challenge extends to students' subjectivities, as it appears that classical musicians still inhabit closed genre worlds.

The theorization of the 'conducive context' can make visible the similarities across sites that normalize sexual misconduct and violence against women. Therefore, while this chapter has outlined specific aspects of classical music's cultures that enable sexual misconduct, this is not intended as an argument that there is something distinctive about classical music higher education that makes sexual misconduct more likely to occur in this space. Indeed, this idea of classical music's exceptionalism – the discourse that classical music is fundamentally different from other social and cultural spaces – can contribute towards the conducive context by suggesting there is something special and valuable about classical music that makes it better and different from other musical or social scenes. This helps create an environment where there is limited (although increasing) external challenge to institutionalized power.

Instead, the theorization of the conducive context allows us to move beyond exceptionalism and to acknowledge that sexual harassment and misconduct and other forms of power-based abuse happen everywhere in society, but that there are factors that can make them more or less likely to happen. The discussion in this chapter also opens up questions around how the informal networks required to access work in the creative industries might enable sexual misconduct, as well as formal structures of gendered power. However, while these factors may occur in distinctive ways in classical music higher education, they are also present in other sites where sexual abuse and misconduct have been documented, such as elite sports education or the entertainment industry.

Finally, the extent to which neoliberal market reforms in higher music education in the UK context have played a role in creating a conducive context for sexual misconduct is contradictory and uneven. There is now more external challenge to the institutionalized authority of classical music, but this external challenge is pushing institutions towards greater accountability according to a narrow set of metrics, which does not fundamentally challenge structures of power and exclusion. Furthermore, the factors discussed earlier that create a conducive context in classical music were in place long prior to the introduction of market reforms into this space. Ironically, in the UK, the marketization of higher education has led to an *increase* in state regulation and control, with less autonomy for higher education institutions (McCaig, 2018). Nevertheless, these reforms also compound and intensify 'star' systems of staff and students as documented by

Perkins (2013) in the UK before the most recent round of legislation increasing marketization. Classical music higher education was not, then, innocent before neoliberalism took hold, and it does not appear that neoliberal reforms have, as yet, fundamentally shifted the previous cultures of classical music higher education documented in the 1980s (Kingsbury, 1988; Nettl, 1995). In acting to address sexual misconduct in higher music education, it is therefore important to remain vigilant as to the influence of market reforms while also working to challenge cultures of institutionalized power and authority that have older and deeper roots.

Note

1 In the United States, the term 'faculty' refers to academic employees and 'staff' to non-academic employees, while in the UK, the term 'staff' covers both. Here, I use both terms in order to indicate that my discussion encompasses academics across all jurisdictions.

References

Australian Human Rights Commission (2017), *Change the Course: National Report on Sexual Assault and Sexual Harassment at Australian Universities*, Sydney: Australian Human Rights Commission.

Bagshaw, E. (2017), '"We Should All Be Shocked" Leader of University with Worst Results Comforts Students', *The Sydney Morning Herald*, 2 August. https://www.smh.com.au/politics/federal/more-than-20-per-cent-of-students-at-australias-top-universities-sexually-harassed-by-staff-20170801-gxmwyz.html (accessed 22 October 2022).

Bain, V. (2019), 'Counting the Music Industry'. Available online: https://vbain.co.uk/research.

Baker, G. and W. Cheng (2021), 'The "Open Secret" of Sexual Abuse in Venezuela's Famous Youth Orchestra Program Is Finally Exposed', *Washington Post*, 27 May. https://www.washingtonpost.com/opinions/2021/05/27/venezuela-me-too-yo-te-creo-sexual-abuse-el-sistema-youth-orchestra (accessed 22 October 2022).

Barton, D. (2020), 'The Autonomy of Private Instrumental Teachers: Its Effect on Valid Knowledge Construction, Curriculum Design, and Quality of Teaching and Learning', PhD diss., Royal College of Music.

Bull, A. (2015), 'Abuse in Music Education: Event Overview'. Available online: https://annabullresearch.wordpress.com/2017/01/02/abuse-in-music-education-event-overview-september-2015 (accessed 22 October 2022).

Bull, A. (2016a), 'Safeguarding and Youth Voice in Music Education'. Available online: https://annabullresearch.wordpress.com/2016/11/28/safeguarding-and-youth-voice-in-music-education (accessed 22 October 2022).

Bull, A. (2016b), 'Gendering the Middle Classes: The Construction of Conductors' Authority in Youth Classical Music Groups', *The Sociological Review*, 64 (4): 855–71.

Bull, A. (2017), 'Abuse in Music Education: Institutional Perspectives'. Available online: https://annabullresearch.wordpress.com/2017/01/02/abuse-in-music-education-institutional-perspectives-event-overview (accessed 22 October 2022).

Bull, A. (2019), *Class, Control and Classical Music*, New York: Oxford University Press.
Bull, A. (2021), 'La "Respectabilité" et La Musique Classique. Étudier Les Intersections de Classe, de Genre et de Race Pour Comprendre Les Inégalités Dans Les Formations Musicales', *Agone*, 65: 43–64.
Bull, A., G. Calvert-Lee and T. Page (2020), 'Discrimination in the Complaints Process: Introducing the Sector Guidance to Address Staff Sexual Misconduct in UK Higher Education', *Perspectives: Policy and Practice in Higher Education*, 25 (2): 72–7.
Bull, A. and T. Page (2021a), 'Students' Accounts of Grooming and Boundary-Blurring Behaviours by Academic Staff in UK Higher Education', *Gender and Education*, 33 (8): 1057–72.
Bull, A. and T. Page (2021b), 'The Governance of Complaints in UK Higher Education: Critically Examining "Remedies" for Staff Sexual Misconduct', *Social & Legal Studies*, 31 (1): 27–49.
Bull, A. and R. Rye (2018), 'Silencing Students: Institutional Responses to Staff Sexual Misconduct in Higher Education', The 1752 Group/University of Portsmouth. Available online: https://1752group.files.wordpress.com/2018/09/silencing-students_the-1752-group.pdf (accessed 22 October 2022).
Bull, A. and C. Scharff (2017), '"McDonald's Music" Versus "Serious Music": How Production and Consumption Practices Help to Reproduce Class Inequality in the Classical Music Profession', *Cultural Sociology*, 11 (3): 283–301.
Cantor, D., B. Fisher, S. Chibnall, S. Harps, R. Townsend, G. Thomas, H. Lee, V. Kranz, R. Herbison and K. Madden (2019), *Report on the AAU Campus Climate Survey on Sexual Assault and Misconduct*, Association of American Universities. Available online: https://www.aau.edu/key-issues/campus-climate-and-safety/aau-campus-climate-survey-2019 (accessed 22 October 2022).
Carter, P. and T. Jeffs (1995), *A Very Private Affair: Sexual Exploitation in Higher Education*, Ticknall: Education Now Books.
Cheng, W. (2020), *Loving Music Till It Hurts*, New York: Oxford University Press.
Connell, R. (2006), 'Glass Ceilings or Gendered Institutions? Mapping the Gender Regimes of Public Sector Worksites', *Public Administration Review*, 66 (6): 837–49.
Donne (2021), 'Equality and Diversity in Concert Halls'. Available online: https://donne-uk.org/wp-content/uploads/2021/03/Equality-Diversity-in-Concert-Halls_2020_2021.pdf (accessed 22 October 2022).
Erçetin, Ş. Ş. and L. Yılmaz Fındık (2018), 'Autonomy in Higher Education', in Ş. Ş. Erçetin (ed.), *Chaos, Complexity and Leadership 2016, Springer Proceedings in Complexity*, 463–75, Cham: Springer International Publishing.
Ford, B. (2010), 'What are Conservatoires for? Discourses of Purpose in the Contemporary Conservatoire', PhD diss., Institute of Education, University of London.
Gaunt, H. (2011), 'Understanding the One-to-One Relationship in Instrumental/Vocal Tuition in Higher Education: Comparing Student and Teacher Perceptions', *British Journal of Music Education*, 28 (2): 159–79.
Gaunt, H. and H. Westerlund, eds (2013), *Collaborative Learning in Higher Music Education*, Burlington: Routledge.
Gisler, P. and B. Emmenegger (1998), 'Die Grenze ist ja, wie wir wissen, furchtbar schwer zu ziehen… Geschlechtsspezifische Schließungsprozesse und Sexualität am Beispiel zweier Organisationen der höheren Ausbildung', *Zeitschrift Für Personalforschung / German Journal of Research in Human Resource Management*, 12 (2): 143–66.

Goehr, L. (1992), *The Imaginary Museum of Musical Works: An Essay in the Philosophy of Music*, Oxford: Clarendon Press.

Green, L. (1997), *Music, Gender, Education*, Cambridge: Cambridge University Press.

Haddon, E. (2011), 'Multiple Teachers: Multiple Gains?', *British Journal of Music Education*, 28 (Special Issue 01): 69–85.

Hall, C. (2018), *Masculinity, Class and Music Education: Boys Performing Middle-class Masculinities through Music*, London: Palgrave Macmillan.

Hennekam, S. and D. Bennett (2017), 'Sexual Harassment in the Creative Industries: Tolerance, Culture and the Need for Change', *Gender, Work and Organization*, 24 (3): 417–34.

Hoffmann, F. (2015), *Panische Gefühle: Sexuelle Übergriffe im Instrumentalunterricht*, London: Schott Music.

Incorporated Society of Musicians (2018), *Dignity at Work: A Survey of Discrimination in the Music Sector*, Incorporated Society of Musicians. Available online: https://www.ism.org/images/images/ISM_Dignity-at-work-April-2018.pdf (accessed 22 October 2022).

Jackson, C. and V. Sundaram (2020), *Lad Culture in Higher Education: Sexism, Sexual Harassment and Violence*, New York: Routledge.

Keil, M. and K. Kheriji-Watts (2022), *#MeToo in the Arts: From Call-outs to Structural Change (Gender and Power Relations)*, Shift Culture. Available online: https://cultureactioneurope.org/download/?filename=https://cultureactioneurope.org/files/2022/04/SHIFT-Gender-and-Power-Relations-Report-2022.pdf (accessed 22 October 2022).

Kelly, L. (2016), 'The Conducive Context of Violence against Women and Girls', *Discover Society*, 1 March. https://archive.discoversociety.org/2016/03/01/theorising-violence-against-women-and-girls (accessed 22 October 2022).

Kingsbury, H. (1988), *Music, Talent, and Performance: A Conservatory Cultural System*, Philadelphia: Temple University Press.

Kopelman, P., M. Boylan and R. Kashti (2020), *Review of Safeguarding Arrangements*, Royal Academy of Music, University of London. Available online: https://s3.eu-west-1.amazonaws.com/whitespace-ram-production/Review-of-Safeguarding-Arrangements.pdf (accessed 22 October 2022).

Lambeau, C. (2015), 'As a Chief Needs Men, so Men Need a Chief', trans. M. Jones, *Transposition. Musique et Sciences Sociales*, 5 (September): 1–24.

Madonna, A. Z. (2019), 'Classical Music Saw a #MeToo Backlash in 2019 – The Boston Globe', *The Boston Globe*, 19 December. https://www.bostonglobe.com/2019/12/19/arts/classical-music-saw-metoo-backlash-2019 (accessed 22 October 2022).

Marginson, S. (2018), 'Global Trends in Higher Education Financing: The United Kingdom', *International Journal of Educational Development*, 58: 26–36.

Mayne, I., A. Bull and J. Raven (2022), *Embedding Youth Voice in Classical Music Pedagogy*. London: Sound Connections. Available online: https://issuu.com/soundconnections/docs/the_music_lab_-_toolkit (accessed 22 October 2022).

McCaig, C. (2018), *The Marketisation of English Higher Education*, Bingley, West Yorkshire: Emerald Publishing Limited.

National Academies of Sciences, Engineering and Medicine (2018), *Sexual Harassment of Women: Climate, Culture, and Consequences in Academic Sciences, Engineering, and Medicine*, Washington: The National Academies of Sciences, Engineering, and Medicine.

Nettl, B. (1995), *Heartland Excursions: Ethnomusicological Reflections on Schools of Music*, Urbana: University of Illinois Press.

Nisbett, M. and B. Walmsley (2016), 'The Romanticization of Charismatic Leadership in the Arts', *The Journal of Arts Management, Law, and Society*, 46 (1): 1–11.

Office for Students (2021), 'Statement of Expectations', 19 April. https://www.officeforstudents.org.uk/media/d4ef58c0-db7c-4fc2-9fae-fcb94b38a7f3/ofs-statement-of-expectations-harassment-and-sexual-misconduct.pdf (accessed 22 October 2022).

O'Toole, P. (1994), 'I Sing In A Choir But I Have No Voice!', *The Quarterly Journal of Music Teaching and Learning*, IV (5): 1–26.

Pace, I. (2013a), 'Reported Cases of Abuse in Musical Education, 1990–2012, and Issues for a Public Inquiry', *Desiring Progress*. Available online: https://ianpace.wordpress.com/2013/12/30/reported-cases-of-abuse-in-musical-education-1990-2012-and-issues-for-a-public-inquiry (accessed 22 October 2022).

Pace, I. (2013b), 'The Culture of Music Education Lends Itself to Abuse', *Times Educational Supplement*, 11 May. https://www.tes.com/magazine/archive/culture-music-education-lends-itself-abuse (accessed 22 October 2022).

Pace, I. (2015), 'Music Teacher Sentenced to 11 Years in Prison as Abuse Film Whiplash Prepares for Oscars', *The Conversation*. http://theconversation.com/music-teacher-sentenced-to-11-years-in-prison-as-abuse-film-whiplash-prepares-for-oscars-37786 (accessed 22 October 2022).

Pace, I. (2017), 'The Insidious Class Divide in Music Teaching', *The Conversation*, 17 May. http://theconversation.com/the-insidious-class-divide-in-music-teaching-77574 (accessed 22 October 2022).

Page, T., A. Bull and E. Chapman (2019), 'Making Power Visible: "Slow Activism" to Address Staff Sexual Misconduct in Higher Education', *Violence against Women*, 25 (11): 1309–30.

Perkins, R. (2013), 'Learning Cultures and the Conservatoire: An Ethnographically-informed Case Study', *Music Education Research*, 15 (2): 196–213.

Phipps, A. (2018), 'Reckoning Up: Sexual Harassment and Violence in the Neoliberal University', *Gender and Education*, 21 (2): 1–17.

Pidd, H. (2013), '39 Manchester Music School Teachers Face Inquiry', *The Guardian*, 7 May, sec. UK news. https://www.theguardian.com/uk/2013/may/07/manchester-music-schools-teachers-investigation (accessed 22 October 2022).

Pidd, H. (2021), 'Chetham's School of Music "Facilitated" Sexual Abuse of Pupil, Says Judge', *The Guardian*, 27 May, sec. UK news. https://www.theguardian.com/uk-news/2021/may/27/chethams-school-of-music-facilitated-sexual-abuse-of-pupil-says-judge (accessed 22 October 2022).

Rakena, T., O. Airini and D. Brown (2016), 'Success for All: Eroding the Culture of Power in the One-to-One Teaching and Learning Context', *International Journal of Music Education*, 34 (3): 285–98.

Royal Philharmonic Society (2019), 'Women Conductors'. Available online: https://royalphilharmonicsociety.org.uk/performers/women-conductors (accessed 22 October 2022).

Scharff, C. (2015), *Equality and Diversity in the Classical Music Profession*, King's College London. Available online: https://www.impulse-music.co.uk/wp-content/uploads/2017/05/Equality-and-Diversity-in-Classical-Music-Report.pdf (accessed 22 October 2022).

Scharff, C. (2017), *Gender, Subjectivity, and Cultural Work: The Classical Music Profession*, London: Routledge.

Scharff, C. (2020), 'From "Not Me" to "Me Too": Exploring the Trickle-down Effects of Neoliberal Feminism', *Rassegna Italiana Di Sociologia*, LX (4): 667–91.

Simpson, R. E. (2010), 'An Examination of the Relationship of Teacher Certification Area to Sexual Misconduct: Florida as a Case Study', *Journal of Music Teacher Education*, 20 (1): 56–65.

Stewart, J. B. and M. Cooper (2020), 'The Met Opera Fired James Levine, Citing Sexual Misconduct. He Was Paid $3.5 Million', *The New York Times*, 21 September. https://www.nytimes.com/2020/09/20/arts/music/met-opera-james-levine.html (accessed 22 October 2022).

Vincent, C. (2023), 'Staging a Loose Canon: Scripture, Tradition, and Embedded Exclusion in Opera Production', in A. Bull, C. Scharff and L. Nooshin (eds), *Voices for Change in the Classical Music Profession: New Ideas for Tackling Inequalities and Exclusions*, 102–11, New York: Oxford University Press.

Wagner, I. (2015), *Producing Excellence: The Making of Virtuosos*, New Brunswick: Rutgers University Press.

Wang, G. (2015), *Soundtracks of Asian America: Navigating Race through Musical Performance*, Durham: Duke University Press.

Whitley, L. and T. Page (2015), 'Sexism at the Centre: Locating the Problem of Sexual Harassment', *New Formations*, 86: 34–53.

Yoshihara, M. (2008), *Musicians from a Different Shore: Asians and Asian Americans in Classical Music*, Philadelphia: Temple University Press.

Chapter 8

History, Narrative and Equality, Diversity and Inclusion in the Music Conservatoire

Uchenna Ngwe

Introduction

Following almost twenty years as a freelance musician and educator (among other roles), I decided to return to higher education in 2018 as a doctoral student at Trinity Laban Conservatoire of Music and Dance in London, UK. In contrast to my time as an undergraduate at the same institution, this was an opportunity for me to explore my own heritage and development as a British Nigerian oboist within the context of a higher music education institution. My research focused on uncovering and performing the work of African diasporic musicians who had been active in the Western classical tradition prior to 1970.

Initially facing bemusement from many of my musical colleagues, global events in 2020 such as the reaction to the murder of George Floyd and increased awareness of the global Black Lives Matter movement forced a reckoning among music professionals and educators at all levels. Activist movements raised awareness of the challenges faced by Black communities around the world as, with other higher education institutions, British music conservatoires were called on to show their support for the diverse student bodies they had been cultivating for years. In this context, my research topic (previously seen as an extremely niche topic by many of my peers) suddenly grew in importance as music institutional Equality, Diversity and Inclusion (EDI) frameworks were updated and Eurocentric curricula began to be interrogated on a larger scale.

Through their development as independent sites of cultural learning, specialist music higher education institutions in the UK have become standardized as training grounds attempting to balance the needs of students, industry and the wider society. Traditionally, curricula in these spaces have focused on developing musical technique and instilling narrow canonical knowledge that does not necessarily align with the life of a contemporary working musician (Palmer and Baker, 2021). Within this, concepts of inclusivity and equity are new considerations for industry-focused pedagogies, and methods of incorporating EDI into advanced music curriculum and career development are still emergent. In cases where Black musicians are being discussed rather than actively included, EDI committees have relied on generalized cultural assumptions with an 'emphasis on racism and discrimination' (Johnes, 2020), rather than understanding the need for incorporating a range of narratives across the curriculum.

My aim with this chapter is to reflect on how an understanding of African diasporic connections with British higher music education can provide effective narratives for engaging with Black students in these spaces today. I begin by briefly outlining the development of British music conservatoires and examination boards in Britain and their use in colonial contexts (part one). Emerging from this development are the stories of various composers of African descent who have largely been forgotten despite their musical innovations. Themes of forgetting, suppressing and silencing are present throughout this chapter, as is the importance of an inclusive understanding of musical histories to counteract this (part two). In the next sections, I explore how placing equity at the heart of curriculum development and EDI supports building sensitive learning communities (part three), giving students agency through inclusive teaching frameworks and alternative narratives (part four). The final section considers a selection of initiatives focused on the diversification of Western classical music research, including my own *plainsightSOUND* project that promotes the history of Black British classical music (part five).

Looking to the Past

Despite its importance in understanding the development of advanced training and pedagogy within British classical music, the origins of conservatoires and their connections to colonialism are frequently overlooked. The British music conservatoire emerged from within the Victorian desire for status as a global authority on Western classical music. Intended to counteract its reliance on continental European performers and composers, the nineteenth-century British musical establishment – including figures such as Arthur Sullivan (1842–1900) and George Grove (1820–1900) – saw this as an opportunity for the nation to prove itself. Despite the founding of the Royal Academy of Music in 1822 as a centre for musical training in London, however, the British had not yet begun to take formal music education seriously. In these early years, its inability to distinguish between the educational needs of professional and amateur musicians, or between performers and teachers, led to British musicians deciding that institutional training was not a necessary route into the profession. Many preferred private tuition, informal training or travelling to mainland Europe instead. In fact, prior to 1870, only approximately 10 per cent of Britain's professional musicians studied at the Royal Academy of Music (Ehrlich, 1985: 96–9; Wright, 2005: 237–8), positioning it as a school for amateurs and teachers rather than professional performers.

However, this era was central to what has since been called the 'English Musical Renaissance' (Hughes and Stradling, 2001) – a period of renewed serious musical engagement by the middle and upper classes in the late nineteenth and the mid-twentieth centuries. Advanced musical training spread rapidly throughout Britain, with opportunities particularly concentrated in London – a place where the ideals of cultural and social modernization through imperialism and colonialism were in full effect. In this environment, new institutions emerged that portrayed themselves as arbiters of national musical quality. The Royal Military School of Music at Kneller Hall (established 1857) created an innovative model of standardized efficiency that made it the most successful music college of the nineteenth century (Wright, 2013: 31). The development of routine, infrastructure and certified courses of study was vital to the success of this endeavour. Trinity College of Music (1872), Guildhall School of Music (1880) and the Royal College of Music (1882) were among the institutions intending to show that this new focus in advanced music education was something to be taken seriously in the capital. By the 1890s, London had become the site of a music institutional growth based on certification. As Johnson-Williams (2015: 36) writes, 'The mass production of music examinations in the British free trade market . . . impacted upon (and one might say unraveled) the way that music was consumed and desired.' Progression towards certification of graded music exams such as those developed by the Associated Board of the Royal Schools of Music (ABRSM), which was initially set up as an examinations partnership between the Royal Academy of Music and the Royal College of Music in 1889 (Wright, 2005: 258–60), and Trinity College London, built upon a public mood for the centralization of academic frameworks that was verified by continued financial investment from candidates. Low pass rates and high fees ensured an exclusivity based on the assumption that the qualification must be desirable if the standard is difficult to achieve. Such perceptions provided a regular income from students who frequently failed but would continue to re-enter the examinations until passing, paying additional fees each time (Wright, 2013: 57–9; Johnson-Williams, 2015: 36–7).

The popularity of these certifications was also crucial to a model of imperialistic control and surveillance developed in Britain and exported to British colonies by music examination board officials. The Royal College of Music emerged as a new model of advanced British music education amidst the nationalistic fervour that had arisen just over thirty years earlier during the Great Exhibition of 1851. The Royal Family supported several other London exhibitions (Richards, 2017), with these events presenting imperialism as an inspirational motif. What had begun as a supposedly positive and hopeful British patriotism shifted to competitive sentiments of chauvinistic national dominance and rivalry over the years. This was reflected in colonial contexts where European 'classical' cultural signifiers were strongly promoted, while local, traditional cultures were suppressed under the guise of civilizing progress. In the nineteenth century, a European West African elite developed, closely linked to Christian missionaries and a Church that had placed itself in opposition to traditional African cultural practices (Nketia, 1979: 13–5). Collusion between colonialists and missionaries strongly encouraged formal schooling that focused on learning English (reading, writing and speaking), arithmetic and, later, music (Flolu, 1994: 59–65). This approved an education that 'emphasised Western hymns, school music, and art music' (Nketia, 1979: 15) and enshrined Eurocentricity as a major aspiration from childhood. Local music teachers were encouraged to follow ABRSM, Cambridge or London GCE examination syllabuses, further fostering a bond forged in a coerced embrace of European customs.[1]

Several talented West African and Caribbean musicians who were identified through this training attended British higher education music institutions from their inception. For them, success abroad meant further proof of their abilities and the majority eagerly returned home following their studies, ready to continue sharing and developing their skills as accredited musicians. Conservatoires had clearly defined models of talent and success and created new pathways towards achieving and demonstrate these ideals around the world. By the 1890s, these institutions had developed standards that produced a reliable number of highly skilled professional British and colonial musicians as well as knowledgeable amateurs who would be the future paying audiences that sustained the industry. A respectable route through formal music education had been constructed, and conservatoires were firmly at its centre.

Diverse Histories and Anti-racism

At all levels of education, scholars and educators have fought for the restoration of missing Black narratives to their rightful places in core curricula. Yet in the histories of the London conservatoires, early Black British and African students are rarely acknowledged. Nigerian musician and composer Fela Sowande (1905–1987), the Ghanaian ethnomusicologist and composer J. H. Kwabena Nketia (1921–2019) and Nigerian composer, musicologist and pianist Akin Euba (1935–2020) all studied at Trinity College of Music in the first half of the twentieth century. Among ethnomusicologists, they are known for their pivotal academic work, but through 'strategic silencing' (Gilroy, 2002: 50–1) little attention has been paid to their more artistic innovations, which include the development of distinct musical subgenres such as African Pianism.[2] Strategic silencing determines what we acknowledge about Blackness in British history and society, hiding narratives that do not centre whiteness and insisting that some people did not exist in certain historical spaces. Other stories include African American composer Edmund T. Jenkins (1894–1926), whose popularity as a Royal Academy of Music student resulted in him becoming the first editor of *The Academite* – their student magazine. Amanda Aldridge (1866–1956), daughter of the pioneering African American Shakespearean actor Ira Aldridge and his Swedish wife, studied at the Royal College of Music before embarking on a career as a singer, pianist, teacher and composer under the name Montague Ring. Among Afro-British classical musicians of the early twentieth century, only Samuel Coleridge-Taylor (1875–1912) – a composer and conductor of part white British and part Sierra Leonean heritage who also studied at the Royal College of Music – remains relatively well known. These are just a few of the pioneering musicians who bridged traditional

African or African diasporic and European art music cultures, but there remains 'a deeply ingrained tradition of considering British culture while ignoring the presence of black and brown people' (Harris, 2009: 486). Although their names are recorded in archives, having cultural or ethnic origins outside of Europe means that their presence in certain spaces continues to be overlooked. Other than concerted efforts to recognize forms of Blackness, such as during Black History Month, the musical achievements of Black Britons are rarely celebrated or even acknowledged in higher music education institutions. This reflects Paul Gilroy's (2002: 48–51) discussion of how the narrow conversations around race in Britain focus on immigration stories and perceptions as 'new peoples' rather than exploring long-standing historical and cultural identities.

In an increasingly globalist society, organizations are starting to understand the importance of changing such narratives, but if meaningful change is to be achieved, social justice must be at the core of the work. This must be recognized alongside a focus on 'resisting its appropriation as an institutional tool to be operationalized within an increasingly marketized, bureaucratized environment' (Gabriel, 2020: 5). Following the murder of George Floyd in 2020 and the subsequent rise in awareness of the Black Lives Matter movement, some higher education music institutions initially appeared to be acting swiftly. Rapidly defining their own versions of social justice, they finally began to acknowledge the global protests that had begun years prior. In many cases, however, the outcomes were insubstantial. Diversity initiatives were hastily announced, with speakers and consultants often invited to address faculties that lacked awareness and lived experience of the challenges being addressed. They also frequently lacked engagement with Black students and staff – the people most directly affected by these issues.

EDI boards, once seen as niche groups, have become more visible in higher music education institutions, leading to increased workloads for marginalized staff. Consisting of staff members in higher music education institutions that are already limited in terms of diversity, they centre the experiences of the majority while requiring increased input from the most marginalized. Such committees, when tasked with developing anti-racist or decolonizing curriculum policies, tend to rely on a tiny pool of the same people: staff members of colour or external consultants, who are given overarching responsibilities to identify and solve these embedded issues on behalf of the institutions. In order to sufficiently challenge the institutional structures that reinforce exclusion, it is necessary to create room for the voices of excluded groups to be heard while ensuring individuals are adequately supported and not overloaded with additional, unpaid labour.

Institutional appropriation of anti-racist concepts in neoliberal frameworks is not new. As wider society confronts certain challenges, it becomes profitable for corporations to present minimized methods of engaging with challenging topics, and despite utopian ideals, higher music education institutions are committed to the same marketization. Higher music education institutions balance their goals of preparing students for the professional music labour markets with their immediate needs. But how can they support students from a range of diverse backgrounds and with differing intersectional needs? Although not all graduates will work in the music industries, higher music education institutions aim to produce graduates who can enter the labour market. For this reason, it benefits conservatoires to adopt any initiatives and systems that they see as modelling future working conditions, if they are also institutionally beneficial.

Diversifying the Western classical music curriculum in higher education presents an interesting challenge for institutions due to the neoliberal restructuring and marketization of higher music education institutions as a means of cultural reproduction within postcolonial societies. A more open, diverse society is emerging, but more recent demographic analyses point to Western classical music's institutional and industry-based resistance to these changes (Black Lives in Music, 2021; Scharff, 2015; Spence, 2021). Without interrogation, such environments encourage the dismissal of non-Western musical cultures and non-canonical connections. To counter this positioning, the complicated cultural histories of Britain and Europe, along with the still-resonating effects and influences of colonialism, must be acknowledged, and integrated into our pedagogical frameworks.

As early as 1999, a major inquiry into the racist murder of Stephen Lawrence, a Black teenager from South London, recommended that a deeper understanding of cultural diversity and anti-racist training should be embedded in school curricula (Macpherson, 1999: 67–9). To date, British history still excludes Black British and colonial histories, resulting in a limited understanding of everyday racism and its related challenges. It is a positioning that confines most of its references to the transatlantic slave trade and the arrival of Caribbean immigrants on the *Empire Windrush* in 1948. It is unsurprising that people who do not experience racism and rely on a solely theoretical knowledge of race are unable to fully grasp the impact of racism on racialized individuals and communities. Without a basic understanding of this, institutional EDI frameworks focusing on race frequently remain a 'vast net with gaping holes that catches very little at all' (Ahsan, 2022). Rushed policies constructed by hastily gathered, unrepresentative and inexperienced committees provide limited positive impact, in some cases unintentionally reinforcing the damage inflicted on marginalized groups.

Creating spaces for sharing information and understanding various cultures and experiences at all levels of education can help move towards improving these imbalances. The *Black Curriculum* report (Arday, 2021) explored the systematic exclusion of Black British history from the UK national curriculum in schools. Reiterating points raised in the Stephen Lawrence Inquiry, it notes that '[e]ducation remains a central microcosm of society, and when thought of in this way, the onus to reflect the hybridity of historical identities and diversities is paramount' (Arday, 2021: 9). Again, recommendations include supporting the 'contribution of Black History into the canon, as a body of legitimate knowledge' and broadening perceptions of Black History to 'support our society towards unlearning negative tropes and relearning more accurate discourses situated around race and racism' (Arday, 2021: 3). These approaches support an understanding that the responsibility for teaching Black histories does not lie solely on Black individuals. Instead, a more inclusive sense of history and culture should be instilled across society.

Conservatoire Training and EDI

Music conservatoires offer specialist training that initially developed within Western art music and now encompasses a range of musical genres. Conservatoires UK (CUK), the representative body for conservatoires, lists eleven institutions nationwide dedicated to music and other performing arts. Given the history of higher music education institutions, and CUK positioning itself as 'the voice of Conservatoires in the UK' (Conservatoires UK, 2023), this raises an additional question: *How can antiracist and inclusive curricula be developed within such exclusionary spaces?* Although each member institution is independent, this body exists to ensure that common goals are achieved. A major benefit of such consortiums is that institutions can easily share examples of good practice, and in the case of EDI, solutions need to be tailored to their specific environment. The challenges faced by marginalized students and staff need to be addressed directly and specifically to ensure that any support offered is not just 'Endless Distraction and Inaction' (Ahsan, 2022). EDI needs to be more than a fashionable buzzword used to attract students while remaining mindful of the need for relevant practical strategies to remove barriers.

Even prior to reaching higher education, music lessons have become more difficult for state school children to access. Secondary school students typically enter higher education music courses following A Level music, but if the current rate of decline continues, there will be no students on these courses by 2033, if not sooner (Whittaker and Fautley, 2021). This downturn results from changes in the Conservative Party's governmental policies that encourage schools to focus on science, technology, engineering and mathematics (STEM) subjects as more 'employable', therefore pushing arts and creativity into the domain of private schooling. Learning a Western musical instrument requires significant financial investment from an early age, rapidly increasing the proportion of music undergraduates arriving from private or specialist music schools. These are among the few places where the arts are still thriving, which creates a perception of the conservatoire as being only for those from privileged socio-economic backgrounds or with access to support via charitable foundations or local music education organizations from an early age. In terms of ethnic diversity, data sets provided by UCAS Conservatoires (UCAS, 2022) show that out of 1,040 applicants accepted to the UK conservatoires in 2012, 1.4 per cent – a total of fifteen music students – identified as being Black. By 2021, this had risen to 2.35 per cent (40 out of 1,700), still far below figures shown in the Annual Population Survey (Cox and Kilshaw, 2021: 12–4). Even if only considering economic factors, we can see that without bespoke support and guidance, students entering such environments from outside of privileged 'bubbles' (where they are less well represented) are less inclined to stay (Bull and Scharff, 2017). Regardless of the increase in diversity initiatives, if staff and student bodies do not reflect their own positionality and society in general through a variety of lenses, they will remain functionally disconnected from the diversity they are trying to introduce.

For decades, academics have worked to not only theorize but also to create new models of practice that directly consider and include the experiences of all students in higher education. In *Teaching to Transgress*, bell hooks (1994) described the importance of creating open learning communities that acknowledge and support the contributions of all present. Building on this and referencing the work of Hurtado and Carter (1997), Deborah Gabriel (2020: 10) highlights that for students of colour, 'a sense of belonging is not solely dependent on interaction within the academic environment but also on the external interactions with key support networks'. The *Black Curriculum* report (Arday, 2021) outlines the importance of this sense of belonging in school teaching, which is even more pronounced in higher music education settings where postgraduate progression and success depend largely on the ability to network with peers and engage with paying audiences in order to survive. We cannot ignore the importance of this cultural capital in the music and cultural industries, which are so hierarchically structured and based on social inequalities (Brook, O'Brien and Taylor, 2020). The intersections of class, race, gender and disability make conversations around EDI challenging for higher education performing arts institutions whose core curricula still revolve around canons and notions of hegemonic and cultural supremacy.

Focusing on EDI as a concept rather than its practical application in higher music education institutions can be limiting if wider historical and social contexts are not fully considered. As Sara Ahmed (2012: 128–9) argues, diversity initiatives often fail to bring about social change due to a lack of 'institutional will'. Consequently, without concerted efforts across organizations and the wider music and cultural industries, EDI schemes can never be entirely successful. This therefore requires a deep understanding of where the issues lie within higher music education institutions.

Teaching Frameworks

In the performing arts, practice-based or practice-as-research methodologies allow researchers to use their creative skills as investigatory tools. For musicians, this can include areas such as composition, performance, pedagogy or curation. Recognizing the diverse research currently emerging from higher music education institutions is essential in the move away from market-driven cultural reproduction and towards broader investigations of historical and contemporary music cultures. This intertwining of artist practice and research has encouraged musicians from a range of backgrounds to engage with research outside of traditional musicological or ethnomusicological frameworks. In these contexts, the work of performer-scholars (straddling dual careers as artists and academics), who can challenge and disrupt the hierarchical hegemonies embedded in the foundations of music conservatoires, is essential (Gaunt, 2010: 54). Also active in higher music education institutions, and often intersecting the work of performer-scholars, are scholar-activists. These are academics who have become empowered by their lived experiences, research and chosen art forms to explore alternative modes of engagement directly with audiences, participants and organizations. Musicians in these roles might incorporate community engagement as well as collaborative cross-genre and research-based projects into their practice, highlighting and curating underperformed repertoire. Many scholar-activists modify and construct their own relevant frameworks to respond to social justice challenges due to the limitations of existing models. Academic recognition of this work has been overdue, but practitioners moving towards scholarship can now centre their own, often complex, experiences of culture and heritage in building inclusive methods of knowledge gathering and creation.

The Black Curriculum (Arday, 2021) highlights the importance of empowering students by developing a sense of belonging among them as learners. This is also a central theme of hooks's exploration of 'engaged pedagogy' (1994) and an inspiration for inclusive teaching frameworks such as 3D Pedagogy. Devised by Deborah Gabriel (2020: 6) to 'liberate the curriculum and democratize the cultural environment in which teaching and learning takes place', 3D Pedagogy centres cultural democracy, with the promotion of social justice and critical race pedagogies at its core. It focuses on ensuring positive learning experiences for minoritized students rather than hoping for them as a supplemental outcome of a modified (diversified) Eurocentric curriculum. By placing justice and equity as fundamental building blocks in education, rather than emphasizing individualism, awareness is raised across social groups and outside of tokenistic programmes. Such transformative models amplify the voices of marginalized students, repositioning their experiences at the core of everyday learning. As a result, institutions become comfortable hosting complex conversations about identity, power and inequalities, leading to more nuanced exchanges.

There are many opportunities for teachers and students to integrate 3D pedagogical practice into music teaching in higher education. We might conceptualize belonging by supporting student-initiated performance events, organizing study days to explore marginalized music creators or developing seminars that incorporate broader socio-political-historical understanding alongside music theory. Caution should be exercised to ensure these interactions are implemented safely and to prevent causing additional harm through our own ignorance, no matter how well intentioned. In supporting marginalized students, it is important to understand where we can draw on lived experience and where other external methods of support would be appropriate. For example, as a Black female classically trained music professional, I am part of a tiny minority teaching academic courses in UK higher education music institutions. Many of my students have never been taught by a Black person previously. Like any teacher, I frequently draw from my own experiences while asking students to contextualize their own positions as burgeoning musicians, and it is important that I remain mindful of any internal biases that I might hold. Class discussions not only reflect traditional Western music history topics but also encourage students to examine these threads through additional lenses such as race, gender, disability, sexuality and class. Incorporating broader critical thinking into core areas of the curriculum supports students and teachers in challenging the status quo and seeking alternative stories of representation. Embracing engaged pedagogical frameworks as a key institutional aim of higher music education institutions would support collaborative learning communities that constructively interrogate existing curricula and welcome oppressed cultures into conventional spaces.

Counter-storytelling and Online Art Music Activism

Challenging accepted cultural hegemonies in higher education music institutions requires acknowledging the realities of marginalized people, demonstrating 'that they are not alone in their position' (Solórzano and Yosso, 2002: 36). Black and other marginalized students, who frequently navigate narratives projected onto them by others, may find this shift complicated in practice. Counter-storytelling, a methodological framework developed from critical race studies (Hess, 2019; Hingorani, 2018; Solórzano and Yosso, 2002), can be a useful exploratory tool. It repositions and centres unheard voices, highlighting alternative world views and validating the complexities of societal differences and expectations. Music students engaged in musicology or researching repertoire might search for the peers of colour when exploring canonical composers or cross-cultural production from a non-Western perspective. Music texts such as *Music on the Move* (Fosler-Lussier, 2020) support this work by presenting music history as a series of global 'human connections' rather than as a commodity that only some can understand. Creating interrelated communities facilitates the search for alternate histories and the imagining of radical creative possibilities.

Music scholar-performer-activists inhabit multiple roles incorporating research, musical performance, teaching and public advocacy – the outputs of which are increasingly being documented through online projects. *DONNE, Women in Music*[3] and *Inclusive Early Music*[4] provide materials for researching, performing and teaching Western art music outside of the canon. The *Musical Representations of Disability Database*[5] focuses on representations of disability in musical works. *Mae Mai*,[6] a blog by Jon Silpayamanant, explores music and post-colonialism. From a West African perspective, Edewede Oriwoh's *African Composers Database*[7] highlights and creates networks for contemporary African composers.

My personal development as a scholar-performer-activist began in 2017 with the creation of *plainsightSOUND*. As I mentioned in the introduction, my research was borne out of the frustration I encountered as a freelance oboist. This research project became a way for me to connect with my West African heritage and share my research into African diasporic musicians who had been active in British classical music. With the exception of Joseph Bologne and Samuel Coleridge-Taylor (both of mixed heritage), these were not musicians I had performed or heard of previously, but the importance of protecting and promoting these stories was clear. I decided to focus on historical musicians, chose 1970 as a cut-off date and gathered information through archival research, interviews and social media connections. The website was developed first as a stand-alone project, before becoming an integral part of my PhD study.[8] Counter-storytelling is integral to the purpose of *plainsightSOUND*, as can be seen most obviously in two main areas: (1) a visual timeline with brief biographies of the musicians included in the project so far, and

(2) the *plainsightSOUND* database, which lists over 400 pieces by Black musicians in Britain. The aim of this element is to provide support to those who wish to diversify their classical music programming but are unsure of how to begin this process.

The reactions to *plainsightSOUND* have been extremely positive. My students and colleagues are regularly surprised by the range of musicians featured on the website. Although many scores by Black composers, particularly from early-twentieth-century British publishers, are no longer in print, established musicians and music students actively seek out diverse, advanced repertoire. Demand for information has increased in recent years, and as projects like *plainsightSOUND* raise awareness of individuals, publishers are beginning to reissue selected pieces, and exam boards are commissioning new, diverse composers (Wilson, 2022a,b,c). Amidst the narrow confines of higher music education, these online platforms are useful teaching, research and performance tools. They allow us to disseminate new or rediscovered information easily, while helping to foster curiosity and belonging for musicians at all levels.

Conclusion

Since the early days of music conservatoires in the UK, studying a musical instrument or voice to an advanced level has been considered in terms of potential employment. Today, there is largely a broader institutional understanding of what this employment might be and who is included within it. As higher music education institutions are forced to address their foundational origins and the barriers to fair learning pathways, methods of supporting marginalized students must be interrogated. By implementing engaged and transformative pedagogical strategies, we can explore the placement of teaching and performance in relation to social change, justice and equity in knowledge production. Conceptualizing counter-storytelling through projects like *plainsightSOUND* can be used to support students in their own investigations of alternatives to the canon. As educators, we can empower marginalized students in higher music education institutions to openly explore their identities and histories while equipping them with the tools for individual and collaborative creativity as future musicians.

hooks (1994) wrote that teaching 'is meant to serve as a catalyst that calls everyone to become more and more engaged, to become active participants in learning' (hooks, 1994: 11). An essential part of this process is understanding that all participants need to feel part of their learning communities and institution. In higher music education, the creation of positive and collaborative learning communities is a vital factor as we progress towards ensuring inclusive spaces for all.

Notes

1   The first African ABRSM music examinations were held in South Africa in 1894 (Wright, 2013: 93). This was fortified decades later by their West African adoption in the Gold Coast (Ghana) in 1933 (Nketia, 1979: 15).

2 Akin Euba (2005: 86) defined African Pianism as 'a style of keyboard composition and performance that is influenced by African traditional practices (as found, for example, in the music of drums, xylophones and "thumb pianos")'. Many of its earliest proponents had begun to explore its possibilities as conservatoire students.
3 https://donne-uk.org
4 https://inclusiveearlymusic.org
5 https://www.lsu.edu/faculty/bhowe/disability-representation.html
6 https://silpayamanant.wordpress.com
7 https://www.africancomposers.com
8 Interestingly, as this took place shortly before the surge in interest of Black issues, I was unable to find any funding support for *plainsightSOUND*. The project remains independent and is supported by occasional small donations via the website.

References

Ahmed, S. (2012), *On Being Included: Racism and Diversity in Institutional Life*, London: Duke University Press.

Ahsan, S. (2022), '"EDI": Endless Distraction and Inaction', *The Psychologist*, 16 February. Available online: https://thepsychologist.bps.org.uk/edi-endless-distraction-and-inaction (accessed 2 March 2022).

Arday, J. (2021), *The Black Curriculum: Black British History in the National Curriculum*, The Black Curriculum. Available online: https://static1.squarespace.com/static/5f5507a237cea057c5f57741/t/5fc10c7abc819f1cf4fd0eeb/1606487169011/TBC+2021++Report.pdf (accessed 5 February 2023).

Black Lives in Music (2021), *Being Black in the UK Music Industry, Just the Data: Music Creators – Part 1*, Black Lives in Music. Available online: BLIM.org.uk (accessed 20 March 2023).

Brook, O., D. O'Brien and M. Taylor (2020), *Culture Is Bad for You: Inequality in the Cultural and Creative Industries*, Manchester: Manchester University Press.

Bull, A. and C. Scharff (2017), '"McDonald's Music" Versus "Serious Music": How Production and Consumption Practices Help to Reproduce Class Inequality in the Classical Music Profession', *Cultural Sociology*, 11 (3): 283–301. Available online: https://doi.org/10.1177/1749975517711045.

Conservatoires UK (2023), 'Home, Conservatoires UK'. Available online: https://conservatoiresuk.ac.uk (accessed 20 March 2023).

Cox, T. and H. Kilshaw (2021), 'Creating a More Inclusive Classical Music: A Study of the English Orchestral Workforce and the Current Routes to Joining It'. Available online: https://www.artscouncil.org.uk/sites/default/files/download-file/Executive_Summary.pdf (accessed 5 February 2023).

Ehrlich, C. (1985), *The Music Profession in Britain Since the Eighteenth Century: A Social History*, Oxford: Clarendon Press; New York: Oxford University Press. Available online: http://archive.org/details/musicprofessioni0000ehrl (accessed 5 February 2023).

Euba, A. (2005), 'Remembering Joshua Uzoigwe: Exponent of African Pianism (1946–2005)', *Journal of Musical Arts in Africa*, 2 (1): 84–8. Available online: https://doi.org/10.2989/18121000509486703.

Flolu, E. J. (1994), 'Re-tuning Music Education in Ghana: A Study of Cultural Influences and Musical Developments, and of the Dilemma Confronting Ghanaian School Music Teachers', PhD diss., University of York.

Fosler-Lussier, D. (2020), *Music on the Move*, Ann Arbour: University of Michigan Press.

Gabriel, D. (2020), 'Teaching to Transgress through 3D Pedagogy: Decolonizing, Democratizing and Diversifying the Higher Education Curriculum', in D. Gabriel (ed.), *Transforming the Ivory Tower: Models for Gender Equality and Social Justice*, 5–17, London: Trentham Books.

Gaunt, H. (2010), 'One-to-one Tuition in a Conservatoire: The Perceptions of Instrumental and Vocal Students', *Psychology of Music*, 38 (2): 178–208. Available online: https://doi.org/10.1177/0305735609339467.

Gilroy, P. (2002), *There Ain't No Black in the Union Jack: The Cultural Politics of Race and Nation*, 2nd edn, London: Routledge.

Harris, R. (2009), 'Black British, Brown British and British Cultural Studies', *Cultural Studies*, 23 (4): 483–512. Available online: https://doi.org/10.1080/09502380902950971.

Hess, J. (2019), 'Moving beyond Resilience Education: Musical Counterstorytelling', *Music Education Research*, 21 (5): 488–502. Available online: https://doi.org/10.1080/14613808.2019.1647153.

Hingorani, D. (2018), 'Performing Difference: Diversity, Representation and the Nation', in A. Breed and T. Prentki (eds), *Performing and Civic Engagement*, 41–68, London: Palgrave Macmillan.

hooks, b. (1994), *Teaching to Transgress: Education as the Practice of Freedom*, New York: Routledge.

Hughes, M. and R. Stradling (2001), *The English Musical Renaissance, 1840–1940: Constructing a National Music*, Manchester: Manchester University Press.

Hurtado, S. and D. F. Carter (1997), 'Effects of College Transition and Perceptions of the Campus Racial Climate on Latino College Students' Sense of Belonging', *Sociology of Education*, 70 (4): 324–45. Available online: https://doi.org/10.2307/2673270.

Johnes, M. (2020), 'Race, Archival Silences, and a Black Footballer between the Wars', *Twentieth Century British History*, 31 (4): 530–54. Available online: https://doi.org/10.1093/tcbh/hwaa023.

Johnson-Williams, E. G. (2015), 'Re-examining the Academy: Music Institutions and Empire in Nineteenth Century London', PhD diss., Yale University, New Haven.

Macpherson, W. (1999), *The Stephen Lawrence Inquiry*, London: Home Office, February. Available online: https://assets.publishing.service.gov.uk/government/uploads/system/uploads/attachment_data/file/277111/4262.pdf (accessed 5 February 2023).

Nketia, J. H. K. (1979), *The Music of Africa*, New York: W. W. Norton & Company Inc.

Palmer, T. and D. Baker (2021), 'Classical Soloists' Life Histories and the Music Conservatoire', *International Journal of Music Education*, 39 (2): 167–86. Available online: https://doi.org/10.1177/0255761421991154.

Richards, J. (2017), 'Teaching the Lessons of Empire: Exhibitions and Festivals', in J. Richards, *Imperialism and Music: Britain 1876–1953*, 117–210, Manchester: Manchester University Press.

Scharff, C. (2015), *Equality and Diversity in the Classical Music Profession*, King's College London. Available online: https://www.impulse-music.co.uk/wp-content/uploads/2017/05/Equality-and-Diversity-in-Classical-Music-Report.pdf (accessed 5 February 2023).

Solórzano, D. G. and T. J. Yosso (2002), 'Critical Race Methodology: Counter-storytelling as an Analytical Framework for Education Research', *Qualitative Inquiry*, 8 (1): 23–44. Available online: https://doi.org/10.1177/107780040200800103.

Spence, S. (2021), *Equity Diversity Inclusion: A Research Report Exploring Workforce Diversity and Representation in London Music Education Hubs Through the Lens of Racism*, Music Mark. Available online: https://www.musicmark.org.uk/wp-content/uploads/Music-Mark-EDI_Report-1.pdf (accessed 5 February 2023).

UCAS (2022), *UCAS Conservatoires End of Cycle 2021 Data Resources*, UCAS. Available online: https://www.ucas.com/data-and-analysis/ucas-conservatoires-releases/ucas-conservatoires-end-cycle-2021-data-resources (accessed 5 February 2023).

Whittaker, A. and M. Fautley (2021), 'A Level Music: Going, Going, Gone?' *Music Teacher*. Available online: https://www.musicteachermagazine.co.uk/features/article/a-level-music-going-going-gone.

Wilson, R. (2022a), 'Examining Change: What is ABRSM doing to Decolonise?', *Music Teacher*, 1 April. Available online: https://www.musicteachermagazine.co.uk/features/article/examining-change-what-is-abrsm-doing-to-decolonise (accessed 7 June 2022).

Wilson, R. (2022b), 'Examining Change: What is LCME doing to Decolonise?', *Music Teacher*, 1 May. Available online: https://www.musicteachermagazine.co.uk/features/article/examining-change-what-is-lcme-doing-to-decolonise (accessed 7 June 2022).

Wilson, R. (2022c), 'Examining Change: What is Trinity College London doing to Decolonise?', *Music Teacher*. Available online: https://www.musicteachermagazine.co.uk/features/article/examining-change-what-is-trinity-college-london-doing-to-decolonise (accessed 20 May 2022).

Wright, D. (2005), 'The South Kensington Music Schools and the Development of the British Conservatoire in the Late Nineteenth Century', *Journal of the Royal Musical Association*, 130 (2): 236–82. Available online: https://doi.org/10.1093/jrma/fki012.

Wright, D. C. H. (2013), *The Associated Board of the Royal Schools of Music: A Social and Cultural History*, Woodbridge: The Boydell Press.

Chapter 9

Other Acts of Intervention through Hip-Hop Studies
Teaching and Reflecting

Fernando Orejuela

Introduction

I photographed the two images in this chapter on two separate occasions. Once at the beginning of April 2021 and again in late June. They are photographs of two free walls on a bridge that connects the main campus of Indiana University Bloomington to the street where most of our fraternity and sorority houses reside. 'Graffiti bridge' is a place where students can paint non-offensive messages that typically praise a graffitist's fraternity or sorority or offer some expressions of goodwill or good times. The bridge had been painted over with tan paint early in spring semester 2021, which is normal, but this time the sanctioned graffiti shared a uniform style and corresponding sentiments on each wall of the bridge that reflected the current attitudes and normalization of the Black Lives Matter (BLM) movement. The walls read, 'THIS BRIDGE BELONGS TO ANTI-RACISTS' (see Figure 9.1) and 'NONE ARE FREE 'TIL ALL ARE FREE. BLACK LIVES MATTER' (see Figure 9.2).

I tried locating the persons responsible for writing the messages but failed. Since it is the students' wall, I suspect students painted the messages, even though we were mostly interacting remotely from home due to the Covid-19 pandemic.

Graffiti bridge is a highly visible space, given the number of people who traverse it to get to the main campus. The sentiment painted on the walls is performative; however, the statements address a value that was not embraced in the recent past. The summer of 2021 in multiple ways represents a 'crossing over' – a beginning to return to normal with the promise of combatting the two pandemics that paralysed Americans in 2020: the highly infectious respiratory disease and an ongoing disease of deadly racism in the United States that resonated with other colonized people around the world. In this chapter, I, a Latinx instructor at a predominantly white institution, focus on an interventionist approach to reify the presence of Black music theory and African American and African diasporic folk verbal art traditions in hip-hop music through the students' listening practices outside the classroom. Having students engage in leisure listening by way of *gaming* (covertly doing classwork as games) and *testifying* (overtly displaying a comprehension of

Figure 9.1 The eastern-facing wall of 'Graffiti Bridge'. © Fernando Orejuela.

culture-specific concepts studied in class) can address the issue of unintentional Black cultural erasure in popular music consumption, therefore helping students make connections between the course and the world around them to boost intrinsic, tactical listening in everyday life.

Take It to the Bridge

The metaphor of a bridge as an in-between space is not lost on me. The bridge's writers could have chosen to scribe current, standardized affirmations similar to the mass-produced signs posted in front of homes throughout the predominantly white, liberal neighbourhoods surrounding the university, with messages such as 'Hate does not live here' or 'Black Lives Matter'. Reading a statement like 'Hate does not live here' reminds me of Sara Ahmed's critique of institution's public statements that perform an imaginary ideal of diversity, inclusion or justice. Such diversity work ultimately becomes document machinery and a superficial corrective (Ahmed, 2012: 115–9). If statements of diversity, inclusion or justice do not do what they say, then if a resident or visitor describes an experience of 'hate' (read here as racism) that person must be the problem because 'hate' does not happen here. The graffitists' statements, while still performative, mark more than goodwill or allyship. The term anti-racist is trending again as a result of Ibram X. Kendi's (2019) *How to Be an*

Antiracist and the graffitists' application recognize that the work is all of ours to do. Instead of just defining racism as occasional acts of hatred, the statements recognize that racism is a practice of everyday life that affects all. I struggle with symbolic gestures of goodwill, but, done efficaciously, they can be important.

However, the bridge is not a shrine. In fact, between April 2021 and the time I took the second picture in June, the word 'ALL' on the western-facing wall was defaced and was quickly painted over with tan paint; however, the lettering was not repainted (see Figure 9.2), perhaps to remind us that it was defaced. By June 2021, the far end of the east wall was getting tagged with the traditional graffitied tokens celebrating good times and the neighbouring houses' Greek letters. This begins the gentler process of making the normative happen again. Creeping back from a year-long isolation of pandemic proportions there was a sense of Covid-19 relief by way of vaccination and fewer restrictions to co-mingle with friends and family have helped that shift to normalcy, and, for some, the conviction and light sentence of former Minneapolis police officer Derek Chauvin for the murder of George Floyd signalled a false sense that justice had been served. Accountability might be more accurate than justice.

George Floyd's murder resonated differently for Americans who had been witnessing video-recorded violence in recent history since – at least – the brutal beating of Rodney King in 1991 and even more recently with the great number of recorded incidents that have been shared on social media, especially since the

Figure 9.2 The western-facing wall of 'Graffiti Bridge'. The defacing element on the word 'ALL' had been painted quickly. © Fernando Orejuela.

2014 murder of Michael Brown – the moment that the BLM movement garnered national attention but not national support. Unlike the mid-2010s, an estimated 15 to 26 million people in the United States participated in demonstrations over George Floyd's murder and other victims between May and July 2020 (Buchanan, Bui and Patel, 2020). The 2020 summer protests took folks out of the safety of their homes during a highpoint of the Covid-19 pandemic to march through cities *and* suburbs and travel to the very neighbourhoods where the violence took place. Similarly, three days after Floyd's recorded murder went viral, nearly 8.8 million Twitter users tweeted #BlackLivesMatter, which according to Pew researchers made it the highest number of uses for this hashtag in a single day since the Center started tracking its use (Anderson et al., 2020). All this to say, yes, a conviction almost never happens, but the list of Black people dying at police hands grows even after the Chauvin verdict, which should remind us that this too shall pass. A reflective moment, for me, in the middle once again, forces me to ask myself to (re) consider the way I think about anti-racism in my teaching, especially regarding the impact of BLM and critical race theory today versus five years ago.

The 2010s were highlighted by frustrations I harboured as an academic trying to do anti-racism in my classroom. Additionally, I acknowledge my frustrations were nothing compared to the frustration of my Black students, who were streaming the killings of young Black men and women on social media, confronting the systemic, structural violence done by way of laws and protections that support such detestable acts as acceptable. On a more local level, they were being silenced and invisibilized by their own university, where they needed to be heard and seen. It was the actions of the protestations that prepared us for the necessary, painful, yet productive expressions of anger to be discussed by way of writing assignments in my hip-hop classes at a predominantly white institution. Many Indiana University students want to promote the idea that hip-hop belongs to everyone, while avoiding a discussion of how self-identified allyship is a luxury and self-identifying as an ally could further silence by tuning out the reality narratives performed by the very hard-core and political rap artists they favour, whether it is 'classic rap' by N.W.A, Public Enemy and Tupac or contemporary rap by, for example, Noname, Mach-Hommy and Lil Baby. Claiming that hip-hop is universal or belongs to everyone erases Black experiences as well as Black culture and creativity.

The protests that emerged in 2015 were impossible to ignore and helped promote again the uncomfortable conversation about racism in America. BLM as a movement slowly took shape. Alicia Garza, a labour organizer for the National Domestic Workers Alliance, made a moving pronouncement on a social media account moments after the 2013 acquittal of George Zimmerman for the murder of Trayvon Martin. Along with activist and community organizer Patrisse Khan-Cullors, whose hashtag named the inspirational message, and Ayo (Opal) Tometi, a former director of Black Alliance for Just Immigration who spearheaded the social media campaign, the three women helped plan and mobilize a mass protest for Michael Brown's injustice. Black college students not only started organizing and participating in national protests against lethal police violence but also started unpacking the diversity and inclusivity measures by their universities that were not doing what they claimed.

At my university and other American universities, students stood in solidarity with one another to protest along with BLM activists but also by situating racist practices and the tolerance of unjust treatment of Black students among other kinds of violence against Black people. On my campus, a town hall was organized with approximately 100 students, the dean of students and the provost to discuss race and racism on our campus (Orejuela, 2018). At the same time, the definition of Black Lives Matter was hijacked by conservative media outlets and personalities who identified the organization as a terrorist group and restructured the narrative regarding race-related crimes in order to deny racism in the United States. I am reminded of *Fox and Friends* morning news anchor Elizabeth Hasselbeck, who reclaimed the mass racial killings of worshipers at the historic Emmanuel AME Church in Charleston, South Carolina, on 17 June 2015. Instead, she called it an attack on Christian faith – ignoring the shooter's celebration of Confederate imagery as well as his racist manifesto posted on his social media accounts and again dismissing a history of racial violence in South Carolina and the United States in general.

Bridging the Gap

The rap music course that I inherited from my mentor, Portia K. Maultsby, an African American ethnomusicologist who specializes in Black music studies, was my way of continuing her legacy of not doing music appreciation that focuses too heavily on the industry, celebrity, songs, dates and audiophilia but rather a music education course that tackles issues on this particular Black music form by approaching it socioculturally, politically and historically. I still teach that course as an issue-based, discussion-centred teaching course limited to thirty students. However, in 2003, I developed a survey of hip-hop course, because much of the basics – the early history and foundations, development of styles, chronology, cultural and subcultural components, among others – were becoming less familiar. Additionally, it forced students to locate hip-hop's history and culture within the context of American history, the legacy of enslavement and structural racism we had legislated and/or practiced. From Dr Maultsby, I learned that teaching Black music *as* music is an intervention and that a music education that prioritizes genre-and-celebrity knowledge acquisition discourages critical thought outside of style features and encourages complacency, which perpetuates the narrative that Black art forms are the consumers' art forms.

Listening as performance is often located in the sonic elements as much as it is in the narrative yet can still get heard incorrectly in order for fans to claim affiliation with the hip-hop musical community at large. For example, many of our white students in the 1990s and the 2000s heard, and claimed for themselves, N.W.A's 'F--- tha Police' as a song of rebellion and not a song protesting the police's invasive and violent confrontations with Black youth in south-central Los Angeles.

In pursuing a social rather than a more familiar psychological theory of learning, Jean Lave (1996) asks about the 'what' that learners are learning (Facts? Knowledge? Skill?), reminding me to move beyond the stuff of an educated person and investigate a more crucial way to characterize what can go on in my teaching. Following Lave, I compartmentalize my teaching as 'schooling', the workplace of the teaching, but also a call-and-response style of educating basic facts; for example:

- 'Who developed the Merry-Go-Round technique?'
  – 'Kool Herc'.
- 'How?'
  – 'Observing and Responding to the dancers wait for the break beat of tune'

Additionally, there has to be an appreciation of 'learning' that individuals do in their heads and through their bodies that allows them to tap into repositories of experiences, best practices, performance competencies and so on, in class and on qualitative exams. This puts the 'schooling' taught in the institution to use by applying it to activities happening in the world now and asking students to confront their own positionalities. In terms of modelling, I remind my students at the beginning of the semester and before each writing assignment that they are learning about hip-hop from a professor who identifies as Latino, cisgender male, mid-fifties and that my position and experiences in this world affect my assessment process.

My research and teaching draw on direct engagement with performance studies, critical race theory, intersectional approaches, sound analysis and sound studies, as well as queer and feminist studies, all in an effort to pursue a lifelong project of best methods for teaching culture and artful expressions and experiences. I am careful not to teach tolerance, for nobody wants to be tolerated, but I am also careful not to over-emphasize a celebration of diversity, because describing culture is not enough. My goal is to get students to begin to recognize the importance of positionality, both inside the classroom and out, with a move towards becoming active (as opposed to passive) citizens in their post-baccalaureate lives. Does my teaching do that? Not entirely, of course; it is a goal – maybe a dream. If my teaching is a kind of pedagogy of activism, it is one that is born from acts of interventions.

In the fall of 2015, I created a writing assignment, in the same semester as the student-led activism on our campus, the Michael Brown case and the growing BLM movement, to hear tactically how Black musicians in hip-hop respond to the recurrence of violence to Black bodies and challenge my students in my Diversity in the US courses to discuss, at a minimum, a couple of basic tenets of critical race theory: that racism happens in our everyday practices and the social construction thesis, which holds 'that race and races are products of social thought and relations and not based on biological or genetic reality' (Delgado and Stefancic, 2012: 7–8). Kendi's often-quoted line, 'The only way to undo racism is to consistently identify it and describe it – and then dismantle it' (2019: 9), sets up the site where I do my work in the classroom. My teaching attempts to intervene in the spirit of Sumi

Cho, Kimberlé Williams Crenshaw and Leslie Mc Call's interventionist 'response to the institutional and political discourses that largely ignored these issues' (2013: 790). What follows is a 'pedagogy of unlearning' to undo the misleading messages that everyone, according to our American Declaration of Independence, is 'created equal', but treated equally is altogether more complicated in our history.

The term 'post-race', which entered the US popular vernacular around 2008, was born over the course of a typical inharmonious electoral campaign that resulted in this nation electing its first African American president, has arguably lost its popularity in the late 2010s; however, the term quietly lingers in the imagination. For example, the hyper-visibilizing of underrepresented students at a predominantly white campus by way of brochures and websites somehow legitimizes colour erasure – and perhaps class erasure, too – because meritocracy works, and we can move past that now even though the percentage of African American students remains very low for a state school. Since fall 2020, students have pushed back less when I lecture on the BLM movement and music. To date, the counterargument is that an expression (and movement) that proclaims Black Lives Matter does not read Black Lives Matter *more than yours* to students today. Stating Black Lives Matter is a succinct statement observing the way Black people in the United States experience institutionalized discrimination, systemic oppression and state-imposed violence; furthermore, not all Americans live with such conditions or question if they are being deprived of such basic human rights. Such a concept might be clearer today, but the work is not done. Therefore, the course of action is to disrupt that desire to 'return to normal'. Such an expression reveals more about an unwillingness to think of systemic problems as systemic and that we as citizens must continuously confront them. Breaking the habitual deference to the hegemony of dominant US culture is processual, so exercising conscientious acts as a goal puts into practice ways of anti-racism in other everyday activities, such as listening to music.

Creating writing assignments to do this in a large class is troublesome. What I offer my students is a series of three writing assignments: two traditional essays and a worksheet on cultural-tradition retention, which is the focus of this chapter. In every case, the student is asked to consider the past with their living, present period. The assignments situate students in such a manner as to pay attention to the ways that they have been practicing tactical, intersectional listening habits in the classroom – tactical, drawing on Deborah Kaphan's definition, meaning a kind of listening to effect pedagogical and political change (2017: 5), and intersectional, as a concept, was born from critical race theorist and legal scholar Kimberlé Williams Crenshaw's analytic method for exposing the multiple layers of systemic and structural oppression experienced particularly by Black women as well as other marginalized people, but more to the point, Alison Martin's use of 'intersectional listening' as a commitment to the 'both/and' rather than the 'either/or' when studying the relationship between categories of identity and systems of oppression by way of sound (2020: 12).

In the classroom, we practice tactical, intersectional listening: for example, hearing Black Nationalism coded musically on Sylvia's 'It's Good to be Queen' by incorporating the first four bars of the Black National Anthem 'Lift Ev'ry Voice and Sing' before she raps about her success as a Black business owner, producing a new Black pop genre, supporting Black employees and so on, or hearing the Black Panther Party's ideology clearly in Ice Cube's 'Who Got the Camera?', or listening to or watching police injustice practiced at the end of Grandmaster Flash and the Furious Five's 'The Message' song and video. The two essays are assigned at the beginning and at the end of the semester in structurally familiar territory for most first-year undergraduate students but with an emphasis to keep in check our positionality, our claim and reasonable research materials to support such claims.

The first assignment asks students to demonstrate the ability to explain and assess the changing perspective on the meaning of arts and humanities traditions, in this case, the term 'hip-hop'. It is an opinion paper that follows with a critique of the definitions we explore in the first few weeks by scholars and by members of the first-generation, South Bronx pioneers and subsequently a self-critique to address some of their own assumptions before taking the class. Something brought them to this course – some specific engagement with something called 'hip-hop'. Perhaps it is because they listen to hard-core trap exclusively or they make hip-hop-inspired beats for aspiring rappers, or perhaps because they were not allowed to listen to rap music as a child and want to learn more about it. In addition to starting with their pre-course definition (or assumptions), they must draw on the definitions of 'hip-hop' in our textbook, the discussion and development of the youth music scene and the coining of the term from the lectures and the quotes from some of the earliest pioneers. They then must write an essay discussing and critiquing how these definitions inform their updated ideas about defining hip-hop in these first few weeks of the semester. As a first essay, I provide as much structure as possible and require a section in the introduction to acknowledge their positionality and reflect on how their own perceptions of the world are typically based on how we identify ourselves and the experiences we have. It is important to recognize the factors which impact how we experience and understand different ideas, concepts, events and so on and how our own biases differ from those of other people. How might a scholar's position impact their defining a cultural phenomenon like 'hip-hop'? How might a person who was there as it emerged impact it? How might students today deal with their experience consuming, producing and defining a 'hip-hop' that has been practiced for almost fifty years? My hope is for students to wade through the murkiness of origin stories and artefacts as well as who get to make declarations that come to be treated as fact.

The second assignment's goal is to examine hip-hop spaces and write an essay based on how songs represent the complex and varied ways that rap artists have addressed and continue to address social inequality and systemic racism in the United States, especially in the years after conscious rap and g-style narratives became clearer from pioneering artists (ca. 1984–96) like Public Enemy, Ice-T, 2pac, Geto Boys, Queen Latifah, Lauryn Hill and De La Soul, then link to current rap artists living alongside the development of BLM as a movement. Thus, students are connecting the recent past to this contemporary movement's fight for human rights, life and dignity by way of current songs such as Kendrick Lamar's 'Alright', Joey Baa$$'s 'Land of the Free', Lil Baby's 'The Bigger Picture' or HER's 'I Can't

Breathe', ultimately, encountering Black music for consumption as it intersects with Black music as lived experience. Another goal is for students to demonstrate the ability to develop arguments, ideas and opinions, grounded in rational analysis, about forms of hip-hop musical expressions. Tactical, intersectional listening as a technique aims to transform consumptive listening habits into culturally engaged listening and invites students to contextualize this current movement for basic human rights with rap artists' negotiation and expressions of Black resistance.

The in-between assignment differs in that it is a worksheet more so than a formal essay that allows for Lave's (1996) ideas to be incorporated – tapping into the familiar, the socially situated, that what they do. In essence, a listening scavenger hunt seeking African American and African diasporic tradition art and musical folk forms reconfigured in modern meaningful ways in the music that they or their contemporaries listen to right now. The in-between assignment is no less conscious-raising or political than the formal essays that contain it, but it is performed by doing something for fun, listening to rap music and feeling like a gaming activity more so than a formal writing assignment.

Bridges

Some context is necessary. Teaching these past few years, but especially the academic year 2016–7, coincided with a contentious political moment and a political party debating vociferously whom to select for their presidential candidate. From that event, one of the unruliest presidential campaigns by Donald Trump and his team, produced the Republican nominee. Many conservative citizens and the *formerly* subaltern white supremacists found a reliable agent in Trump. The violent and unapologetically white supremacist language that emerged from those debates trickled onto multiple rumour-like platforms ranging from the debates themselves to an arsenal of social media applications. In the classroom, white supremacy was typically not overtly evident, but alt-right groups had been making their presence known with a more palatable forms of white nationalism. This included Identity Evropa (currently the American Identity Movement), whose members plastered flyers on the office doors of Black and Latinx faculty and graduate students in February 2017. The copy I encountered stated 'OUR FUTURE BELONGS TO US: IDENTITY EVROPA'. On the back read a menacing message that the group will not be dispossessed and the instructors will be surveilled (Davis, 2017). Such moments could have emboldened more students to recentre attention away from the current discussion on BLM and towards meritocracy and overstatements of discrimination and injustice as false narratives, but that mostly did not happen.

In general, student pushback has decreased every year since 2016, but without interviewing the students, I must draw on other happenings around the country, especially since a more generous understanding of what the BLM movement stood for was becoming more mainstream in the United States. Additionally, students in the 2020–1 academic year were affected differently by the murders of George

Floyd and Breonna Taylor, among others. Black Lives Matter was demonized far less and, again, many millions more participated in protests in the United States and around the world compared to the thousands who protested in 2015 and 2016. The National Football League, an organization that actively quieted the injustices of police brutality led by Colin Kaepernick, turned 360 degrees and began painting Black Lives Matter on end zones. Students on my own campus, while slim in numbers due to the pandemic, were responsible for painting the bridge I mentioned earlier, and over the 4 July weekend in 2021, Indiana University students painted a Black Lives Matter street mural in front of our Black Culture Center.

Multiple cities across the country painted Black Lives Matter murals on their streets, including one leading to the White House during the last year of the Trump presidency; as of December 2021, that street mural is being maintained and has been named Black Lives Matter Plaza (Northwest). The campus climate seemed more consistent during the 2020–1 school year than in years before, but, again, without in-depth interviews, it is hard to know if this is a genuine change or a kind of trending tolerance for Black Lives Matter as fashion depicted on T-shirts and yard signs or social media markers such as hashtags or Blackout Tuesday on Instagram. Also, between 2016 and 2020, a series of BLM-centred rap and R&B songs came out in full force via live performances, videos and the Instagram app. The pool to draw on was readily available. I will add that overtly anti-BLM rap songs also came out but largely from one artist: the former professional wrestler-turned-rapper Tom MacDonald from Canada released several songs in 2021, including 'Fake Woke' and 'No Lives Matter', which have yet to make an appearance in my classroom but have charted on *Billboard's Hot 100* (Rutherford, 2021). There are interventionist moments I have incorporated into my lectures, such as anticipating that students get most excited to reify Afrika Bambaataa's motto, 'Peace, Unity, Love and Having Fun', which was incorporated into the lyrics of his song with James Brown in 1984, 'Unity Part 2 (Because It's Coming)', which feels inclusive and marks those early parties as safe spaces for all. To dissuade the students from over-romanticizing that hip-hop is universal, I state and restate that hip-hop is hyper-particularly rooted in African American and African diasporic lore and musicianship and not a well-meaning but colour-blind and tone-deaf universal.

For this reason, the in-between worksheet becomes important and is mindful of BLM objectives that are also incorporated into the two writing assignments. Hearing Black lives, Black life and Black music and listening to culture and not just subculture represents an attempt to reconcile or connect African American and African diaspora folk traditions and Black music theory to their listening habits. This becomes especially significant as my students are coming to hip-hop today by way of international pop stars and white American rappers.

The Bridge is Over

The assignment is called Cultural Connections, but, more recently, I've amended the title to African American and African Diasporic Cultural Connections, given the diversity of performers from around the world doing hip-hop as a style often without acknowledging their debt to R&B and hip-hop greats or why they narrate, pose, diss or pronounce their art coached in African American Vernacular English and other traditions. The assignment is built around the folk narrative traditions in verbal arts we study in class, such as:

- Toasting is a folktale tradition that praises the heroic acts of a character who might be identified as a 'baadman/baadwoman' who disrupts oppressive situations, is just bad to be bad or is a 'trickster' who lives by his or her wits.
- Ritual Insults games, sometimes called *playing the dozens, joning, roasting, ribbing* and so on, are duelling games that push boundaries by exchanging witty insults back and forth until one loses their cool, loses momentum or fails to amuse the audience. It is largely credited for providing the structure for diss or response rap songs in the commercial era.
- Call and Response, engaging the students in antiphonic play in culturally specific ways, either musically (percussive/instrumental pattern alternation) or within the verbal art tradition (oratory with a caller leader and respondents).
- Girl Gaming, which is a broad category informed by ethnomusicologist Kyra Gaunt's work *The Games Black Girls Play* (1998), which they read in class, on handclap, jump-rope rhymes and double-dutch. Thus, accessing women's use of aural-oral-kinetic performances in their songs and videos or the appropriation of girl gaming by men (e.g. Nelly's 'Country Grammar' and the use of the handclap game 'Down, Down Baby').

Students will select a rap song or songs that were released in the last six years and identify any three of the African American and African diaspora traditions listed earlier. I do stress that they select rap songs, even though we are in the middle point of our semester and are discovering that hip-hop is blurry when treated as a musical genre. However, I do so because I have received essays using country, blues and rock song, and while all those song styles also have roots in African American musicking, this is a hip-hop course, and it helps my graders to keep their focus on what we are doing in our lectures and readings. The assignment has a template:

Name of song:
Name of artist or group:
Recording details (provide links):
Write-up (about 250 to 300 words) for Toasting: This is *not* a toast but a rap song that draws on elements that are like the folk narrative tradition's structure

I provide an example in the assignment prompt, but I also demonstrate in class how to do each option. By completing this assignment, students apply what they have learned about African American narrative and verbal art traditions recast in a modern context. I make musical examples of call and response an option – by the way of turntablism or studio producing – but have yet to have a student make the attempt. I argue that students will gain an understanding of the symbolic expressions and narrative conventions that are used in hip-hop lyrics and are rooted in African American and African diasporic cultures. Some results have been very eye-opening in their willingness to think outside the box; for example, one student wrote a clever write-up on Kendrick Lamar's 'Compton' as a toast imaginatively rethinking and anthropomorphizing the city of Compton as the *baadman*. I embraced the metaphor and the attention to detail in making such a claim.

Is this anti-racist pedagogy? I argue that it is, because it intervenes in the habitual, perhaps unintentional, blurring and/or erasure of African American cultural traditions that are the raison d'être of hip-hop musicking and dance culture. The exercise moves beyond a complacent acceptance that rap music and hip-hop culture are mainstream and, therefore, go beyond Black music-making. Here we confront that, as a class, we have 'decolonized' our listening habits. It is an opportunity to put into practice how contemporary hip-hop continues to address the values and tastes of African American and African diaspora vernacular culture in modern ways. In addition, it lends itself to a discursive space for students to question and answer what it means when, for example, Korean pop stars BTS's 'Life Goes On' draws on some of these folk traditions and what it means when they shift into Blaccenting (i.e. imitating African American vernacular English) while rapping in Korean. Additionally, the assignment's gaming activity continues throughout the rest of the semester, and I welcome the interruptions when a student interjects that a song we are listening to is also part of a beef and therefore a diss rap, too, or that one rapper is taking on the attributes of a baadman character or asks if Migos's adlibs are another way of talking about call and response, or . . . .

I understand some music scholars will disagree with my approach and will argue for us to move to disassociate hip-hop from African American and African diaspora culture largely rooted in the messiness of authenticity or origin stories that are too grounded in problematic essentialist debates regarding racial Blackness. Studying the foundations is not for excluding, gatekeeping or suggesting that hip-hop participants – performers or consumers – must be Black. Rather, the focus is on respect and remembrance for hip-hop narratives, and musical sensibilities are associated with a political disposition to counterargue against a legacy of oppression, silencing and invisiblizing that formed movements towards Black freedom in the United States. If I commit to doing a pedagogy of anti-racism, then I must commit to doing the work.

Conclusion

For a different project on trans and non-binary youth, I turned to an old monograph from which I got the title for this chapter: *Acts of Intervention: Performance, Gay Culture, and AIDS* (1998) by David Román. The performance artist Douglas Crimp's timely declaration and critique of the AIDS crisis and art in the 1980s rings true for me today in the 2020s, one year into the Covid-19 pandemic that coexisted with the ongoing BLM movement to change our other pandemic of systemic violence, injustices and deaths experienced by many African Americans. Crimp's stated, 'We don't need to transcend the epidemic; we need to end it' (quoted in Román, 1998: 40). Much of the discourse in 2020–1 revolved around the two pandemics in the United States: the respiratory disease and the brutal killings of African Americans magnified by George Floyd's murder and pronouncement 'I can't breathe', which was heard much louder than when Eric Garner said it in a viral video about six years earlier. Teaching anti-racism in the classroom is teaching community and a community-based pedagogy that confronts and accepts hard histories that we have to own. Its aftermath is one that values progressive social change and takes on the heavy lifting to end racism and white supremacy.

References

Ahmed, S. (2012), *On Being Included: Racism and Diversity in Institutional Life*, Durham: Duke University Press.
Anderson, M., M. Barthel, A. Perrin and E. A. Vogels (2020), '#BlackLivesMatter Surges on Twitter after George Floyd's Death', Pew Research Center, 10 June. Available online: https://www.pewresearch.org/fact-tank/2020/06/10/blacklivesmatter-surges-on-twitter-after-george-floyds-death (accessed 19 April 2021).
Buchanan, L., Q. Bui and J. K. Patel (2020), 'Black Lives Matter May Be the Largest Movement in U.S. History', *New York Times*, 3 July. Available online: https://www.nytimes.com/interactive/2020/07/03/us/george-floyd-protests-crowd-size.html (accessed 19 April 2021).
Cho, S., K. Crenshaw and L. McCall (2013), 'Toward a Field of Intersectionality Studies: Theory, Applications, and Praxis', *Signs Intersectionality: Theorizing Power, Empowering Theory*, 38 (4): 785–810.
Davis, B. (2017), 'The New White Nationalism's Sloppy Use of Art History, Decoded: Identity Evropa has been Terrorizing Campuses across the Country', *ArtNet*, 7 March. Available online: https://news.artnet.com/art-world/identity-evropa-posters-art-symbolism-881747 (accessed 23 October 2017).
Delgado, R. and J. Stefancic (2012), *Critical Race Theory: An Introduction*, New York: New York University Press.
Gaunt, K. (1998), *The Games Black Girls Play: Learning the Ropes from Double-Dutch to Hip-Hop*, New York: New York University Press.
Kapchan, D. (2017). 'Listening Acts: Witnessing the Pain (and Praise) of Others', in D. Kapchan (ed.), *Theorizing Sound Writing*, 277–93, Middletown: Wesleyan University Press.
Kendi, I. X. (2019), *How to Be an Antiracist*, New York: One World.
Lave, J. (1996), 'Teaching as Learning in Practice', *Mind, Culture, and Activity*, 3 (3): 149–64.
Martin, A. (2020), 'Sonic Intersections: Listening to the Musical and Sonic Dimensions of Gentrification in Washington, DC', PhD diss., ProQuest Dissertations Publishing, 27993839.

Orejuela, F. (2018), 'Black Matters: Black Folk Studies and Black Campus Life Matters', in F. Orejuela and S. Shonekan (eds), *Black Lives Matter and Music: Protest, Intervention, Reflection*, 34–54, Bloomington: Indiana University Press.

Román, D. (1998), *Acts of Intervention: Performance, Gay Culture, and AIDS*, Bloomington: Indiana University Press.

Rutherford, K. (2021), 'Sueco, Tom MacDonald & Chris Stapleton Crown Rock Sales Charts', *Billboard*, 26 August. Available online: https://www.billboard.com/articles/business/chart-beat/9620688/sueco-tom-macdonald-chris-stapleton-rock-sales-charts (accessed 31 August 2021).

Chapter 10

Access and Technology in Music Education

Negotiating Neoliberalism During a Pandemic Within a Graduate Popular Music Pedagogies Course

Kyle Zavitz, Rhiannon Simpson and Ruth Wright

Introduction

The closure of schools and the move to online learning in response to the Covid-19 pandemic forced many music educators to rethink previous practices. A small case study was conducted with participants in the graduate summer course 'Understanding Progressive Methods in Music Education'. Redesigned due to the pandemic and held online during the last two weeks of July 2020 at a Canadian university, the course adapted popular music education (PME) pedagogies for online delivery, blending synchronous and asynchronous learning. It was intended that the course would support educators in developing pedagogies they could use in the continuing pandemic; this course therefore aimed to serve as a practical introduction to online PME and its pedagogies. Real-time, group popular music-making activities were reshaped as technology-based, online PME experiences framed by extensive academic reading and discussion.

Careful consideration was given to how the course could be designed to model engaging, equitable and inclusive online instruction. A flipped classroom model – 'a specific type of blended learning that uses technology to move traditionally class-based learning outside the classroom, freeing class time for interactive, group-based, problem-solving activities' – was adopted (Ojala, 2017: 63). This model allowed the application and development of technological skills to take place outside of allotted instruction time, providing flexibility for task completion for students without stable internet access. Tasks included individual and group aural learning of music recorded in the digital audio workstation (DAW) BandLab, a multiscreen audiovisual recording project using the application Acappella, a remix project using pre-recorded loops in the DAW and a songwriting project. In addition, all students designed a fully resourced teacher planning document for several weeks of student instruction exploring music technology and PME. BandLab was chosen as the preferred pedagogic tool for this course due to its accessibility on most popular operating systems (Windows, iOS and Linux) and across multiple devices (smartphones, tablets, Chromebooks and computers). It ensured that instruction was accessible to all students, but that the skills learned were applicable to available technologies in different schools regardless of school socio-economic status (SES). The software was also free, with all the online applications employed in this course – including Flipgrid and Acapella – incurring no cost to the students.

A wide range of reading was assigned for the course, providing background and context for the development of PME (Green, 2001, 2008). The sources examined the role of PME and technology in redressing inequities of race, ethnicity, class, gender and sexual diversity in music education by disrupting existing patterns of exclusion for students who had not previously seen themselves or their musical capital as legitimate within the dominant models of music education. Also addressed were the social distribution of access to the twenty-first-century North American 'technotopia' and the educational plethora of technology-based resources (Wright, 2017), as well as strategies for countering such inequities. Critical reflection on the issues raised in the readings and the applicability of technologies to different contexts took place during synchronous class time. Students also posted critical reflection videos on each practical task using Flipgrid and each led a seminar, preparing a pre-recorded video examining one of the required readings.

In the following sections of this chapter, we present important contextual information on issues of inclusion and exclusion as they relate to music education and popular music, neoliberalism and education, particularly as it applies to music, and some detail concerning the problems the Covid-19 pandemic presented for North American music educators. We use this material as a platform from which to discuss some of the data obtained in our case study of the participants' views on the course. In the conclusion, we consider how PME and the technotopia might help reshape school music curricula, including and affording access to more socially diverse students. In this connection, we discuss the participants' views on the course and their comments relating to neoliberalism, inclusion and access to music education.

Inclusion, Exclusion and Popular Music Education

Matters of inclusion and exclusion have been dominant in the music education literature since the beginnings of sociological thinking in the field (cf. Green, 1988; Shepherd and Vulliamy, 1983; Small, 1977). The traditional 'triumvirate' of band, orchestra and chorus has long remained the central North American curricular model for most music – and therefore music teacher education – programmes (Montemayor, Coppola and Mena, 2018). Scholars have criticized this model for marginalizing certain students and limiting the inclusion of marginalized voices. As Bradley (2015: 190) explains, 'Within traditional paradigms of band, choir, and orchestra, participating students continue to be predominantly White, even in multi-ethnic, multi-racial schools and communities.' This paradigm reifies Western art music and has been accused by scholars of hegemonic cultural elitism for advantaging of more economically privileged backgrounds. In addition, these approaches are accused of promoting a masculine, conductor-centred pedagogy, resulting in the exclusion or self-exclusion of many students with diverse racial, ethnic and gender/sexuality backgrounds from music as a school subject (Wright et al., 2021). For these reasons, a shift in pedagogic models away from band, orchestra and chorus (and its predominant Western art music repertoire) towards PME incorporating technology may provide a means for including students with more diverse backgrounds and identities (Butler and Wright, 2020; Wright et al., 2021).

Green's (2001, 2008) seminal research exploring the ways in which authentic popular music pedagogy could be introduced into school curricula – a key element of the Musical Futures[1] programme in the UK (musicalfutures.org) – gave considerable impetus to the PME movement. Popular music pedagogies have developed as a legitimate alternative to traditional music education in many countries; the informal learning models they frequently embody are hailed for their focus on the legitimation of diverse students' musical experiences. Such pedagogies are particularly compelling for their reach to students who, for reasons of class, race/ethnicity or gender, may not see themselves or their musical capital as legitimate within the school (Wright, 2015).

Informal music learning (Green, 2001) involves students working in groups, selecting music to learn with which they are familiar and engaged – often popular music – and learning this music by ear, commonly through copying recordings. This approach to music education often utilizes peer-to-peer learning in a non-linear form, dictated by the curiosity and interests of the students. Such elements, when introduced to school music pedagogy, have been shown to result in increased motivation and engagement in music by students from disadvantaged groups such as those with a low socio-economic and/or marginalized racial, ethnic and gender status. Students have also demonstrated increased achievement in academic core subjects (Butler and Wright, 2020; Hallam, Creech and McQueen, 2011).

Despite the growing legitimacy of PME methods globally and success within the music classroom in many countries, North American music teacher education largely continues – with a few notable exceptions – to feature band, orchestra and chorus as the gold standard of legitimate music education. In order to engage in critical reflection on the sociological implications of these music pedagogies and their relationship to neoliberal discourses, we will next examine scholarship on neoliberalism in music education and show how neoliberalism manifests itself within curricula and policy.

Neoliberalism and Education

While an exact definition of 'neoliberalism' is difficult to pinpoint due to its complex and ever-changing nature, we adopt Hall, Crawford and Jenkins's (2021: 122) conception of an 'institutionalised framework founded in economic liberalisation that most commonly manifests in privatisation, deregulation, rationalism and free-marketisation'. The result of such influences upon education, Apple (2006) writes, is an education system whose goal is to prepare students as efficiently as possible to engage in the global labour market economy to improve their 'employability'. Scholars further argue that neoliberal policies maintain a myopic view of access to education that continues to disadvantage traditionally marginalized students and effectively reproduces social inequities (Boyles, Carusi and Attick, 2009).

The shift towards neoliberal policies and the repositioning of the purposes of education towards the economic (Hall, Crawford and Jenkins, 2021) have contributed to a widespread increase in competition through the development of ranking systems to assess the 'efficiency', 'quality' and 'authenticity' of education (Horsley, 2014). With a similar focus on rivalry, contest and ranking, large ensemble competitions are the primary means by which the quality and excellence of school music programmes can be evaluated and assured in North America (Montemayor, Coppola and Mena, 2018). Allsup and Benedict (2008) argue that the focus on achieving high scores at such competitions leads to music programmes that are dominated by large ensemble performance instruction. We argue that the conflation of visible, measurable and quantifiable outcomes such as band competition rankings or music examination scores with quality highlights the influence of neoliberal education discourses on music teacher practice in school and studio. Such discourses may not encourage critical reflection regarding the level of engagement, cohort diversity or cultural relevance within music programmes. Through such a focus, Montemayor, Coppola and Mena (2018: 10) suggest, 'teachers effectively neglect to acknowledge the intensely diverse array of musical potentials that might exist in places no further than their students' own homes and communities.'

Questions of authenticity have long dominated debates about expanding the canon of music education repertoire. Fear of inauthentic engagement with other musics has been presented as a barrier to greater curricular musical diversity in respect to genres such as popular music and musics of other countries and ethnicities. It has been suggested that unless classroom music can engage 'authentically' with other musics in terms of instrumentation and deep knowledge of the particular tradition, it may do more harm than good. As Bradley (2015: 190–1) notes, however, racism 'hides within the myth of "authenticity" in music education practices, which too often serves as a barrier that prevents the inclusion of musics other than Western art musics (predominantly by male composers) in the curriculum'. Racial and socio-economic diversity alone suggest that Western art musics may be far from the music experienced in students' homes. In a similar way, we suggest that classism hides behind authenticity discussions in relation to popular musics, such music often accused of being 'lowbrow', simplistic and unchallenging and lacking the features of complexity that distinguish art music as superior. Questions of authenticity can then undermine estimations of quality in alternative models of music education. The combination of dominant, competitive models of music education and barriers such as racism, misogyny, homophobia and classism, disguised as concern about the possibility of authentic engagement with musics outside the Western art music canon, limits diversity in the field of music education in terms of race, ethnicity, class and gender/sexuality. Students whose experiences or values do not align with these dominant models may not see themselves or their musical knowledge as of value (Bernstein, 2000).

The earlier factors, alongside the focus on competitive ranking and perceptions of quality in music education, underwritten by neoliberal rationality, have played a crucial role in impeding alternative genres and pedagogies such as PME from finding legitimacy within the North American music education model. In this way, neoliberal policies have disproportionately impeded the inclusion of students from diverse and marginalized backgrounds, resulting in the strengthening and perpetuating of the exclusionary features of dominant paradigms.

With the arrival of the Covid-19 pandemic, however, data from our case study suggest a new evaluation from teachers of that 'cost-effective' or 'rational' pedagogy. Prior to the pandemic, a progressive pedagogies course (addressing technology-based pedagogic models delivered with popular music) such as that of the case study might not have had the same impact on graduate students' or in-service teachers' willingness to diverge from the traditional model of large ensemble instruction. We consider that the previous legitimation of instruction centred on large ensemble performance practices throughout university music teacher education, paired with ready support for these models from existing school processes and instrumental resources, has formerly led to an easy rationalization of paradigmatic practices through neoliberal discourses of efficiency and practicality. The arrival of the pandemic disrupted the influence of such neoliberal educational policy by making the previously dominant pedagogies impossible. These circumstances, we suggest, provided a window of opportunity for students and teachers to examine alternative approaches more thoroughly, due to need. In turn, this presented an opportunity to disrupt the hegemonic dominance of Western art music-based pedagogies and to afford positive teacher attitudes towards alternative pedagogies and inclusion of the diverse student populations whom these pedagogies serve.

Covid-19 and Music Education

As a result of the Covid-19 pandemic, teachers were required to reconsider how and in what ways music education would take place the following year using digital technologies. In 2017, Wright argued that the educational 'technotopia' in which many students find themselves could offer the potential for greater access to and inclusion in music education within PME informal music learning models. She suggested, however, that consideration of the social distribution of access to such resources was crucial to a successful reshaping of music education to maximize the inclusive potential of PME and music technology. As we shall now see, the case study of the course afforded further opportunity to examine this issue.

Table 10.1 Demographic Data of Interview Participants

Name	Pronoun	Age	Ethnicity	SES of School[a]
Monica	She/Her	25–29	Polish-Canadian/Caucasian	Low
Riley	He/Him	35–39	Caucasian	Medium
Jordan	He/Him	30–34	Caucasian	High
Tiffany	She/Her	25–29	Caucasian	Medium
James	He/Him	30–34	Caucasian	Medium

[a] This refers to the socio-economic status of the school where the participant taught. It is gauged by the average salary and occupations of adults in the community. The status information was given by the teachers and is generally known by teachers in Canadian schools. It affects parental ability to contribute to and fundraise for school resources and activities and also tends to reflect the amount of parental pressure on school administration to achieve results and provide resources. Generally, schools in higher SES neighbourhoods and children in those schools in Canada have access to more and better-quality resources and facilities.

Research Questions

The research questions that guided the case study related to student experiences in the course, their willingness to employ technology and PME methods within their own practices and the extent to which they have used or plan to use these methods in their future teaching. The relationship between the responses and the socio-economic status of the school and teacher was also ascertained. We will first present the participant student demographics ($n = 5$) and responses to the earlier research questions, then interrogate the issues of access to technology, neoliberalism and student inclusion (Table 10.1).

Students were full- and part-time school educators, private music instructors and full-time students, working to earn their master's degrees through the faculty of music ($n = 27$). Many students worked as in-service teachers preparing curriculum for potential online instruction.

Technotopia for All, or Merely for Some?

One of the areas we explored with our respondents was the extent to which they had access to the educational technotopia discussed previously and whether this bore any relationship to the demographic of their school. In responding to questions concerning availability of technology in the music class, both Jordan and Monica made specific note of how resource allocation within different socio-economic contexts can be made visible through access to technology. Jordan notes:

> My school population is generally drawn from a fairly high socioeconomic bracket of the community. I can count on every kid having a device, and for the five or six exceptions that don't, we have enough devices in the school that one can be loaned to them for the purposes of doing this online learning. So, there is not a problem with technology connection. We contrast this to some people I know – my mother's a teacher, and she has a class of Grade 2/3 students, like eighteen kids, and I think ten of them have little or no access to technology and

it's just very, very different. So, it's kind of an artifact of our privilege as a school, but we're going to use it if we got it. (Jordan)

Whereas Jordan describes greater access to technological resources in a 'fairly high' socio-economic context, Monica reveals the ways her school's socio-economic status present challenges for students and how they overcome them:

[Students] ask when they come through the door, 'Are we doing BandLab today?' and they see the laptops and they're like 'Yes! Yes!' They're so happy. I encourage them to bring headphones, but I teach in a low socioeconomic school, so a lot of them would likely not have access to things like headphones. [. . .] But a lot of them, after two weeks of doing BandLab on their own, they took the initiative to find headphones at their home. Like they're actually taking that initiative, which to me is awesome. (Monica)

These responses highlight the hard truth that, as Wright (2017) explains, the distribution of educational resources, including technology, tends to follow patterns of socio-economic privilege. Bernstein (2000) observes that the resource-to-need ratio is often inverted: students who come from less socially privileged homes have more need of resources but often attend schools where these resources are frequently less available, and vice versa. For some students from disadvantaged socio-economic backgrounds to have access to music technology, as was the case with Monica's students, who had to provide their own headphones, they must take the initiative to find the necessary resources. A critical reading of Monica's story might position it as another indication of the effects of neoliberalism on education. In education systems wherein the state has a more clearly defined role in providing equality of access to resources to all schools and therefore all students, such a situation as that of Monica's students would be seen as a failing of the system. From the neoliberal educational perspective, however, the requirement for students to show initiative and provide their own resources would be framed as positive and students would be congratulated for their resourcefulness, exercising the initiative to provide for their own needs. What appears obvious from Monica's experiences, however, is that the lack of resources in school presents a barrier to participation for students who cannot afford to provide their own supplies.

One key aspect of this research was a focus on the willingness of participants to employ technology within their music teaching practice. Of the total interview participants, three indicated that this course increased their readiness to employ technology in their school music practice and two indicated that it did not change their inclination; one was already using it and one preferred to revert to the previous band pedagogy. No respondents indicated that their motivation decreased. When asked how this course affected their disposition to employ technology, James noted:

It increased it obviously, because so much more is possible. Like obviously everyone loves live music, [. . .] but when you really can't do live, it opens the opportunity for DAW tinkering and for, you know, online collaboration with other musicians. (James)

Here, James noted that this course provided an opportunity to explore methods that increased the 'possibilities' within their classroom. In this way, more time was made available to engage students individually and as groups with other approaches to music-making, such as technology like DAWs, and to other types of music.

Monica, on the other hand, saw beyond the mere provision of new experiences for students. She viewed these new PME technology practices as a pathway to engagement for every student:

> It motivated me to use more technology because I found a way to engage kids. [. . .] I truly one hundred percent feel for the first time that I'm able to reach *every single kid* [noting emphasis] and it's been a really great experience so far. (Monica)

This statement suggests that her previous pedagogies had not engaged every one of her students and that the use of technology-based PME practices served to include students who had previously been excluded.

In addition, Monica noted that prior to the course, she felt a certain level of 'guilt' when employing popular music approaches (in lieu of more traditional methods) within her teaching. She went on to explain that she felt the set course readings and their focus on equity and inclusion helped alleviate some of this guilt. In contrast to her undergraduate degree, which she felt instilled an expectation to continue with traditional methods, this course legitimated her use of PME and technology-based approaches. She saw this as facilitating student motivation and engagement, which connects to her earlier statement about being able to reach every single learner.

> I think my vision as a music teacher changed when we did all those readings on popular music. I've always loved pop music, I never saw myself as a traditional music teacher, I barely do classical music [. . .], but I found that I always felt guilty about doing more 'pop' stuff with my kids [. . .]. Cause when I talk to other music teachers [. . .] a lot of them are like, 'Oh yeah, we're looking at Beethoven right now' [. . .]. I'm not really doing that and I almost felt guilty because [in my] undergrad [. . .] you're taught all this classical stuff and I almost felt guilty like, 'am I doing enough theory?' [. . .] But this course made me feel a lot better about teaching popular music because it is worthwhile; you can learn so many skills and motivate and engage with learners so much more easily [than] with classical music. (Monica)

The analysis of the respondents' data was conducted from multiple perspectives. One particularly useful approach was to read participant responses in relation to their reported self-identification as musicians/teachers through their own music education experiences. Like Monica, Jordan confronted his own preconceived notions of the legitimacy of popular music education teaching within the classroom, sharing concerns that he might reproduce the values of his former higher music education to his students. Jordan self-identified as a 'wind-band' instructor and jazz musician who used PME methods within his classroom. He noted that the course did not markedly influence his willingness to employ PME methods within his pedagogy and imagined that he will likely return to his wind-band model of instruction when the Covid-19 restrictions are lifted. However, he noted that he had begun to expand his playing test assessments to include popular music in order to challenge what he perceived as hegemonic assumptions of value. Jordan explained:

> I don't want someone to have to question whether or not their music is okay. And one of the things that that's led to is: [. . .] for at least one of their live tests [. . .] they get to pick whatever they want to play for me [. . .]. Play me anime music that you learned by ear from YouTube without ever knowing the notes. Play me something from your favourite movie that you looked up the sheet music for online. Play me something that you translated from guitar tab to clarinet. I don't care. Play me something that you are interested in that you learned, and that's part of my conscious effort to not have what I had to struggle with happen as much to my kids. (Jordan)

Jordan's shift to position learner-selected materials and informal learning pedagogies as legitimate corresponds to the philosophies and values of PME pedagogies and their focus on student autonomy, social justice and inclusion as experienced in the course readings. It is possible that by allowing space for other ways of learning music and alternative musical genres in his lessons, Jordan might open the door to marginalized students previously alienated from school music.

Monica, Riley, Jordan and Tiffany all noted that they implemented popular music methods to a varying extent within their teaching prior to taking this course. Riley self-identified strongly as both a popular music teacher and as a popular musician. When asked about his willingness to implement PME methods, Riley laughed and responded: 'I only want to use it. I don't want to use anything else.' He explains:

> I've always had little bands at school and they tour, and they learn about PA systems [sound systems] and recordings and that whole stuff, cause that's what I do as well on the side, I play in my own band and do all that kind of stuff so I would just connect both together. (Riley)

Riley continued, noting that while this course exposed him to particular methods he had not experienced – namely the use of BandLab – his interest had been and would likely continue to be in popular music instruction and methods. James noted that this was the first PME course he had taken and that he was unaware of the size and scope of the field. He explained:

> Well, I had never taken any kind of formalized courses on popular music education and I didn't realize the extent to which it had sort of broken in to – not just academia – but primary and secondary education throughout the world ... So, that was [...] very encouraging and exciting for me, because as a person who's come more from popular music [...] it sort of reflected my own journey of being a self-taught musician in many respects, although I've had classical training as well. (James)

James continued by explaining that the course encouraged him to focus on such methods for his final Master's Capstone project.[2] In this inquiry-based learning project (a form of teacher practitioner action research), he chose to explore the effects of using virtual methods, primarily BandLab, to teach students to create music for the video games they design in a Grade 10 coding class.

Neoliberalism

One interesting observation from our reading of the data concerned comments by the respondents that relayed an implicit internalization of neoliberalism. The effects of neoliberalism could be seen strongly throughout the data. Monica and Jordan noted that the previous dominance of Western art music in their formal educational experiences may have predisposed them to employ formalized methods. This intersects with neoliberal educational discourses that support the use of existing knowledges, resources and materials in the name of efficiency and practicality. Such discourses coalesce with previously discussed discourses of assuring quality and excellence through competition. In this way, formalized teaching that focuses on product over process, art music over popular and musics of other cultures and 'excellence' over 'inclusion' often goes unquestioned by teachers and parents and is rewarded externally by school league tables and administration. This 'product' assures quantifiable, rank-able assessment results that tangibly demonstrate to school management and parents the 'quality' of the music programme.

However, the participants reported that both the pandemic and this graduate course served as a catalyst for questioning these previously implicit paradigms. As in-person instruction was often not possible within pandemic protocols, teachers were forced to evaluate the extent to which formalized practices and their related musical genres could – or should – be introduced into a digital space. This, paired with a critical engagement with issues of social justice, inclusion and access in literature and instruction, encouraged students to consider the ways in which popular music and technology-focused teaching and learning music might foster outcomes that are less easily quantified. These included student engagement in class with the musical/creative process, cultural responsiveness and relevance to students' experiences. This course served to announce technologically mediated PME as one way to overcome the barriers associated with online learning and combat issues of social justice, access and inclusion that have previously excluded marginalized students from traditional models of music education. Our findings indicate that, for at least some of the teachers who took the course, this message was received and implemented.

Participants identified that a major determinant of how they perceived the value of the course was in how it prepared them for teaching in a pandemic world. In particular, participants foregrounded the value of 'practicality' and 'relevancy' of the course and its content. Thus, pandemic protocols allowed the designers of the course and the students who attended it to both critique the aspects of neoliberalism that lead to issues of social injustice, exclusion and a lack of access to music education and appeal to the neoliberal discourses that inform institutional decision-making.

Conclusion

This chapter highlights the ways in which inclusion and access are tied inextricably to the pedagogic models and musical content music educators employ: 'what' is taught and how it is taught have implications for 'whom' is served. From an understanding that the traditional conductor-focused, Western art music-centred large ensemble models rationalized through neoliberal discourses have historically excluded students of diverse backgrounds from music, we have explored the ways in which the pandemic may contribute to a 're-rationalization', leading to a legitimation of alternative PME, technology-based pedagogic models. We suggest these approaches may be better suited to recognize and include the students' diverse voices and knowledges within music. We have also explored the ways access to the technotopia available to some twenty-first-century students is tied to the socio-economic status of schools derived from the communities in which they are located. Monica showed that her students in a lower SES school context chose to include themselves within her technology-based PME model by taking the initiative to secure headphones. However, the declining relationship between student need and societal provision of educational resources, such as music technology, accelerated by neoliberal education policy that places the focus on individual resourcefulness and initiative, raises large questions about access for less privileged students to more costly forms of music technology. The technotopia Wright (2017) previously referred to may indeed only be available to some, as she suggested. It would be tragic if resource issues were to negate the inclusive and social justice potential of technology-based PME for already disadvantaged students.

This chapter also highlighted the need for nuance when engaging with critical discussions of neoliberalism, its effects and how it manifests within North American music education. Teachers recognized that the use and adoption of digital technologies to teach PME could provide a means to reject neoliberal ideologies within music education. Interviews with participants in this study affirmed, however, that pre- and in-service teachers who found themselves teaching within the pandemic valued 'practical', 'efficient' and 'relevant' higher music education, which they felt gave them the confidence and technical skills to engage with their students in a new, virtual way. Practicality and efficiency are qualities closely associated with neoliberal ideology; therefore, teachers both espoused the liberatory potential of PME and music technology while justifying their positive opinions in terms of neoliberal discourse. This is an interesting juxtaposition.

That courses such as the one researched are embedded within a largely neoliberal higher education framework does not discount their ability to help us renegotiate the values of the institution and the field of music education more broadly. It may be these methods and technologies that become conditions for the inclusion and access of marginalized students within music education, legitimating a broader diversity of voices, experiences and knowledges. While the pandemic altered what 'normal' music education looks like in many North American schools and higher music education institutions, we may also see it as a hopeful and critical step towards rethinking 'which' music education and for whom.

Notes

1 Now a global phenomenon, Musical Futures began as an action research project whose aim was 'to devise new and imaginative ways of engaging young people, aged 11–19, in music activities' (Hallam, Creech and McQueen, 2011: 13). The informal learning project led by Green mostly concentrated on the use of self-selected popular music by students and was the most successful of the three project strands of Musical Futures.
2 According to the university website, the Capstone project 'provides an opportunity for students to engage in high-level work focusing on an area of specialization within the profession. Capstone projects will be inquiry and practice-centred and will draw upon areas of interest to the student. All capstones aim to bridge theory and practice and are aimed to have an impact on the professional life of students whether they work in classrooms, studios or community spaces' (Western University, Don Wright Faculty of Music, n.d.).

References

Allsup, R. E. and C. Benedict (2008), 'The Problems of Band: An Inquiry into the Future of Instrumental Music Education', *Philosophy of Music Education Review*, 16 (2): 156–73.

Apple, M. W. (2006), *Educating the 'Right' Way: Markets, Standards, God, and Inequality*, London, New York: Routledge.

Bernstein, B. (2000), *Pedagogy, Symbolic Control and Identity: Theory, Research, Critique*, rev. edn, Lanham: Rowman and Littlefield.

Boyles, D., T. Carusi and D. Attick (2009), 'Historical and Critical Interpretations of Social Justice', in W. Ayers, T. Quinn and D. Stovall (eds), *Handbook of Social Justice in Education*, 30–42, London: Routledge.

Bradley, D. (2015), 'Hidden in Plain Sight: Race and Racism in Music Education', in C. Benedict, P. Schmidt, G. Spruce and P. Woodford (eds), *The Oxford Handbook of Social Justice in Music Education*, 190–203, New York: Oxford University Press.

Butler, A. and R. Wright (2020), 'Hegemony, Symbolic Violence, and Popular Music Education: A Matter of Class', in I. Peddie (ed.), *The Bloomsbury Handbook of Popular Music and Social Class*, 97–116, New York: Bloomsbury.

Green, L. (1988), *Music on Deaf Ears: Musical Meaning, Ideology, Education*, Manchester: Manchester University Press.

Green, L. (2001), *How Popular Musicians Learn: A Way Ahead for Music Education*, Aldershot: Ashgate.

Green, L. (2008), *Music, Informal Learning and the School: A New Classroom Pedagogy*, Aldershot: Ashgate.

Hall, C., R. Crawford and L. Jenkins (2021), 'Questioning Convergences between Neoliberal Policies, Politics, and Informal Music Pedagogy in Australia', in R. Wright, G. Johansen, P. A. Kanellopoulos and P. Schmidt (eds), *The Routledge Handbook to Sociology of Music Education*, 121–35, New York: Routledge.

Hallam, S., A. Creech and H. McQueen (2011), *Musical Futures: A Case Study Investigation*, Final Report, Institute of Education, London: University of London.

Horsley, S. (2014), 'A Comparative Analysis of Neoliberal Education Reform and Music Education in England and Ontario, Canada', PhD diss., Western University, Ontario, Canada. Available online: http://ir.lib.uwo.ca/etd/1873 (accessed 7 November 2022).

Montemayor, M., W. J. Coppola and C. Mena (2018), *World Music Pedagogy*, vol. 4, New York, London: Routledge.

Ojala, A. (2017), 'Developing Learning through Producing: Secondary School Students' Experiences of a Technologically Aided Pedagogical Intervention', in G. D. Smith Z. Moir, M. Brennan, S. Rambarran and P. Kirkman (eds), *The Routledge Research Companion to Popular Music Education*, 60–73, London, New York: Routledge.

Shepherd, J. and G. Vulliamy (1983), 'A Comparative Sociology of School Knowledge', *British Journal of Sociology of Education*, 4 (1): 3–18.

Small, C. (1977), *Music, Society, Education*, Hanover: Wesleyan University Press.

Western University, Don Wright Faculty of Music (n.d.), 'Capstone'. Available online: https://music.uwo.ca/departments/music-education/capstone.html (accessed 7 November 2022).

Wright, R. (2015), 'Music Education and Social Reproduction: Breaking Cycles of Injustice', in C. Benedict, P. Schmidt, G. Spruce and P. Woodford (eds), *The Oxford Handbook of Social Justice in Music Education*, 340–56, New York: Oxford University Press.

Wright, R. (2017), 'A Sociological Perspective on Technology and Music Education', in S. A. Ruthmann and R. Mantie (eds), *The Oxford Handbook of Technology and Music Education*, 345–50, New York: Oxford University Press.

Wright, R., G. Johansen, P. A. Kanellopoulos and P. Schmidt, eds (2021), *The Routledge Handbook to Sociology of Music Education*, New York: Routledge.

Chapter 11

The Surge Towards 'Diversity'

Interest Convergence and Performative 'Wokeness' in Music Institutions

Juliet Hess

Introduction

As of late, interest in so-called 'diversity' initiatives in schools of music across the United States and Canada has exploded. Schools that had demonstrated very little interest in equity previously are forming committees on the topic and releasing statements to students that affirm that Black Lives Matter. Mainstream music conference organizers are actively selecting equity as the conference theme.[1] This surge of diversity work occurred largely in the summer of 2020, following the brutal murder of George Floyd in Minneapolis, Minnesota, by police officer Derek Chauvin. In the midst of the Covid-19 pandemic, this murder, after so many others before and after it,[2] seemed to be the threshold for white America. Suddenly concerned with racial justice, white people sent Ibram X. Kendi's (2019) book *How to Be an Antiracist* and Robin DiAngelo's (2018) *White Fragility: Why It's So Hard for White People to Talk about Racism* to the top of the *New York Times* bestseller list in attempts to educate themselves about the subject. Schools of music and their leadership in the United States and Canada followed suit and took preliminary steps to enact 'diversity' work in their institutions. As a long-time member of the diversity committee at the music school where I work, I am relieved to see the surge of interest in matters of race and racism. I am, however, also wary of the motivations behind these moves and the seeming performativity in which music schools seem to be engaged. Nonetheless, given the momentum towards diversity work that began in summer 2020, I am anxious to see music schools capitalize on this moment and work towards meaningful change.

In this chapter, I explore Derrick Bell's (1995) principle of interest convergence – a key tenet of critical race theory (CRT) – to consider the interests at play in this surge towards diversity work in music schools. I examine the performativity of 'wokeness' by music institutions and their leadership and then turn to what Sara Ahmed (2012) calls the 'non-performative' in order to examine the convergence of white interests with the interests of BIPOC communities. In conclusion, I propose ways to capitalize on this interest convergence and enact change in higher education music institutions.

Positioning Myself in Relation to This Work

I want to begin by interrogating my place in relation to this work. As a white, Jewish woman living in the United States, I benefit significantly from white privilege, and I recognize the injustice inherent therein. As a professor in music teacher education, I also match the dominant demographic in predominantly white music schools. I have always 'fit' in these spaces, which shapes my experience and what I notice. At the same time, early experiences of gender-based violence taught me intimately about injustice and I began critiquing the racism and whiteness of music education during my master's degree while attempting to enact an anti-racist praxis in my K-8 teaching position, sometimes more successfully than others. In this work, I position myself similarly to Amy Bergerson, a CRT scholar who writes: 'Our role [as white people] is to use our experiences as whites to increase awareness of how racist actions, words, policies, and structures damage the lives of our students, friends, and colleagues of color' (Bergerson, 2003: 59). I would add that it is also the responsibility of white people to take action after increasing awareness. Additionally, as a white scholar, I focus predominantly on issues of whiteness and white supremacy. Racism operates significantly in music education (see Bradley, 2015, for example), and white music educators must play a role in dismantling it.

Interest Convergence: A Tenet of Critical Race Theory

In this chapter, I bring forward a tenet of CRT: interest convergence. Interest convergence emerges from Derrick Bell's (1995) work on the legal case of *Brown v. Board of Education*. In 1954, this case ruled that racial segregation in public schools was unconstitutional and ordered states to desegregate their schools 'with all deliberate speed'. The *Brown* decision, which ruled that separate facilities were inherently unequal, was based on the conception of the United States on the world stage and accounted predominantly for the interests of white people. In the 1950s, declaring a commitment to equal rights during the Cold War tactically cemented the American dream in the eyes of people in the so-called Third World and simultaneously motivated African Americans to take up a position against Russia if that became necessary. The interest convergence principle thus crystallizes that white people are only interested in furthering the rights of Black people when it is in their own self-interest (Bell, 1995). Hiraldo (2010: 56) affirms that this 'tenet acknowledges white individuals as being the primary beneficiaries of civil rights legislation' (DeCuir and Dixson, 2004; Ladson-Billings, 1998; McCoy, 2006).

Scholars since Bell have added further complexity to interest convergence. Kenzo Sung (2017: 304) reminds readers that, according to Bell, interest convergence has a corollary – 'racial sacrifice' – 'a term to indicate the phenomenon of how U.S. courts are generally willing to sacrifice black interests over white interests if they are not aligned'. In theorizing interest convergence, it remains important to remember that when interests do not converge, it is the interests of BIPOC groups that will not be served. Thus, when the interests of BIPOC groups conflict with the interests of those in power, moving towards equity and racial justice becomes difficult (Leigh, 2003). Moreover, the speed at which society can move towards racial equity is dictated by the dominant group. Milner (2008: 334) observes that 'convergence and change are often at the moderately slow pace of those in power'. He continues: 'Change is often *purposefully* and *skillfully* slow and at the will and design of those in power' (p. 334; emphasis in original). When BIPOC groups have to wait for interests to converge with white people to make progress towards racial justice, progress happens at a glacial pace.

When interests between the dominant and minoritized groups are not aligned, finding ways to converge these interests may prove useful to accomplishing moves towards racial justice. Multiple scholars view interest convergence as a strategy for action. Gloria Ladson-Billings (1998: 12) reflects that CRT scholars have argued for a tactic that finds the 'place where the interests of Whites and people of color intersect'. Taking this approach, however, involves both benefits and drawbacks:

> On the one hand, the interest convergence principle exposes the selfishness behind many policies and practices that may advance greater racial equity – this is the bad news interest convergence analyses bring. On the other hand, perhaps some good news lies in the idea that if those of us working for greater social justice can convince those with power that certain policies and practices that bring about greater equity are *also* in their own best interests, then we may have found a promising strategy for social change. (Castagno and Lee, 2007: 10; emphasis in original)

Sung (2017) points to vigorous debate among scholars arguing as to whether interest convergence may offer a broader social justice strategy.

While such a tactic may ensure that racial progress occurs, it does so with considerable consequences to BIPOC groups. First, as noted previously, interest convergence as a social change strategy guarantees that change will occur at a glacial pace (Milner, 2008). This approach also centres white interests, as change or progress cannot occur until the interests of BIPOC groups align with the dominant white group. Thus, the priorities of BIPOC groups must bend and cater to white interests in order to advance racial justice. This approach leads BIPOC groups to centre issues that converge with dominant group interests, which may result in minimal focus on race and racism, as white people often diverge on those issues (Alemán Jr and Alemán, 2010). Moreover, Alemán and Alemán remind readers that incremental strategies are often not the best approach for transforming policies and institutions that oppress BIPOC groups. While a possible strategy for social change, for BIPOC groups, drawing on interest convergence requires caution.

In what follows, I critically examine interest convergence as a strategy for social action through exploring common interests in diversity. First, I address how 'wokeness' can be a form of social capital; second, building on Ahmed's notion of non-performativity, I explore how white interest in diversity does not necessary align with BIPOC interests. Finally, I offer some suggestions how interest in diversity can go beyond the performative and non-performative.

'Wokeness' as Social Capital

I would like to use the lens of interest convergence to consider the present interest that music schools are demonstrating in 'diversity'. I use the word 'diversity' deliberately, even though I do not believe it is helpful in equity work,[3] because this word is currently pervasive in music school discourse and in higher education (Ahmed, 2012). Music schools are predominantly white spaces.[4] Why this sudden interest in 'diversity'? The murder of George Floyd by police officer Derek Chauvin on 25 May 2020 prompted international outrage, which included national protests across the United States. In a hurry to be on the 'right side of history', organizations rushed to release statements affirming that Black Lives Matter, including the National Association for Music Education.[5] White people suddenly seemed eager to engage with racism, and many BIPOC folx challenged this newfound wokeness as performative.[6] White people performing themselves as woke seems to some to be a new way to accrue social capital, which may well lead to economic capital (Lubell, 2017). Leveraging wokeness provides some degree of social clout.

As a form of capital, performing wokeness bridges across categories. Pierre Bourdieu (1986) describes cultural, social and economic capital. While perhaps most obviously a form of social capital, performing wokeness does not align solely with Bourdieu's definition:

> Social capital is the aggregate of the actual or potential resources which are linked to possession of a durable network of more or less institutionalized relationships of mutual acquaintance and recognition – or in other words, to membership in a group – which provides each of its members with the backing of the collectively-owned capital, a "credential" which entitles them to credit, in the various senses of the word. (Bourdieu, 1986: 248–9)

Performing wokeness or performing oneself as 'good' certainly affects one's network. Being seen to be 'good' may widen one's network of recognition and credential. Part of the capital accrued from performing wokeness is social capital, one facet of which focuses on the 'value of resources accumulated through social relationships as useful capital for people' (Hwang and Kim, 2015: 480–1). This idea points readers' attention to how the resources forged through performing oneself as 'woke' can be mobilized through the resulting relationships or networks.

Bourdieu, however, argues that cultural capital exists in three forms:

> in the embodied state, i.e., in the form of long-lasting dispositions of the mind and body; in the objectified state, in the form of cultural goods (pictures, books, dictionaries, instruments, machines, etc.), which are the trace or realization of theories or critiques of these theories, problematics, etc.; and in the institutionalized state, a form of objectification which must be set apart because, as will be seen in the case of educational qualifications, it confers entirely original properties on the cultural capital which it is presumed to guarantee. (Bourdieu, 1986: 243)

Performing wokeness also aligns with the embodied state as a disposition and perhaps at times may also appear in the objectified or institutionalized state. Importantly, cultural capital leads to social mobility (e.g. cultural capital accrued from education – institutionalized capital – may allow a person to draw on this capital to advance their circumstances). Performing oneself as woke may lead to the kind of social mobility enabled by accruing cultural capital.

Perhaps most insidiously, performing wokeness may also lead to economic capital. The clout gained through performing oneself as woke may result in economic gains in various ways. Being seen as 'good' may ripple beyond accruing social and cultural capital, and these forms of capital may also be mobilized towards economic gains. How these gains occur is context-dependent but is perhaps the most significant form of capital accrued through this performance.

Like individuals, institutions too can perform wokeness and engage in virtue signalling. I specifically consider music schools in higher education. Institutions can engage in these practices through issuing policies about diversity, forming committees to enact these policies, including affirmative action protocols in search committees and so on. During the summer of 2020, many music schools signalled their commitment to matters of race and racism by issuing affirmations in support of Black Lives Matter and forming or reinvigorating committees on equity and diversity. Institutions engaging in these actions may be seen by their communities as 'woke' and supportive of their minoritized populations. Being perceived in this way might allow institutions to accrue social capital by extending their networks, cultural capital by enabling social mobility within the hierarchy of institutions and economic capital through the rewards that may come from grants and donors when the institution performs itself as woke.

Sara Ahmed's (2012) work is instructive for considering the effects of institutions being seen to do 'diversity work'. Ahmed interviewed diversity practitioners in the UK and Australia about their experiences of doing diversity work in higher education. She elucidates different ways that doing diversity work in an institution can be performative and suggests that this work can serve as a 'branding exercise' (Ahmed, 2012: 153). Institutions, she asserts, are deeply invested in how they are perceived and collect 'perception data' about these perceptions from external communities (p. 34). 'Diversity work becomes about generating the "right image" and correcting the wrong one' (p. 34). For example, an institution that the community perceives as predominantly white may be more interested in changing the perception of their whiteness than the whiteness itself (p. 34). In this way, an institution might project an 'appearance of valuing' (p. 59) diversity while actually engaging in a '"lip service" model of diversity' (p. 58). In this context, '[s]tatements like "we are diverse" or "we embrace diversity" might simply be what organizations say because that is what organizations are saying' (p. 57–8).

Ahmed explicitly examines the performative practices of institutions in regards to diversity work:

> Diversity thus participates in the creation of an illusion of equality, fitting in with the university's social mission: the idea the university has of itself as doing good ('the great benefactor'). Diversity can allow organizations to retain their good idea of themselves. (Ahmed, 2012: 71)

In engaging with diversity work, the institution and its leadership then get to understand themselves and be seen as 'good'. 'Doing well,' Ahmed argues, 'involves generating the *right kinds of appearance*' (p. 86; emphasis in original). As with perception data, generating the right appearance easily becomes more important than making systemic changes. 'Diversity becomes about "saying the right things"' (p. 59) or performing oneself in a particular way. Moreover, '[d]eclaring a commitment to opposing racism could even function as a form of institutional pride: antiracism, as a speech act, might then accumulate value for the organization, *as a sign of its own commitment*' (p. 116; emphasis in original). Being seen to be anti-racist may allow the institution to be perceived as 'good'. Ahmed suggests that diversity might 'accumulate commercial as well as affective value' (p. 78).

This commercial value translates to economic capital. When the university is perceived as having a commitment to diversity, certain financial possibilities may emerge. The affective value likely contributes to social and cultural capital, as being perceived as 'good' (which potentially generates good feeling in the institution) may allow an institution to achieve a high ranking and position it competitively among other institutions, which then generates economic capital.

I propose that music schools are now acting on diversity issues because interests have converged. It is now seemingly important for white people to be seen as interested in equity, and music schools are no exception to this trend. I argue that the people in the predominantly white spaces of higher music education, as well as the institutions themselves, have a desire to be seen as 'woke' and engage in self-congratulation. Institutions are 'virtue signalling' and have formulated committees to do so. White people want so desperately to be seen as good (Applebaum, 2010). Elsewhere I have written about 'the politics of self-congratulation' in relation to engagement with world music. I defined self-congratulation as 'the knowing of oneself through the assumption of the inferiority of the Other' and the applauding of oneself for being a 'culturally "tolerant" cosmopolitan' white subject (Hess, 2013: 71–2). I used scare quotes around the term 'tolerant' to indicate that tolerance, which implies putting up with something undesirable, is hardly a quality to aspire to and, yet, seemed to be exactly the quality desired. Ten years after that piece was published, white people are currently engaging in the politics of self-congratulation, now for performing themselves as 'woke' to racial justice issues. To return to the question of music schools engaging with 'diversity' issues, music schools that engage with racial justice can perform themselves as equitable spaces, which again benefits the white people who direct these institutions.

White people want to be perceived as 'good' (Applebaum, 2010), and this desire refracts in how predominantly white institutions (PWIs) wish to be perceived (Ahmed, 2012). White people engage in a 'race to innocence' – an avoidance of any complicity in the oppression of minoritized groups (Razack, 1998). Fearful of being perceived as racist (Watson and Thompson, 2015), being seen as 'good' becomes more important than engaging in the harder work of systemic change. Moreover, the capital gained from reflecting a positive image in relation to race and diversity ripples across social, cultural and perhaps, most significantly, economic capital. Projecting the *'right kinds of appearance'* (Ahmed, 2012: 86) results in gains for white people and for PWIs. Being seen as good or 'woke' results in social, cultural and economic capital. In this political moment, then, interests have converged. BIPOC groups are interested in advancing racial justice in a substantive way, while white people are interested in being seen to be committed to advancing racial justice in this way. Importantly, this interest convergence is not a full convergence. Being seen to be committed is not the same as being committed. I am interested, however, in how wanting to be seen to be committed may ultimately result in substantive change.

What Wokeness Does (or Doesn't Do)

I want to suggest that there is also a more insidious interest convergence at play in the performance of diversity work. Significantly, Ahmed (2012) contrasts performative speech acts to what she calls the non-performative. Here, she draws on John Austin's (1975) *How to Do Things with Words*. Austin distinguishes between utterances that report on something (descriptive or constative utterances) and utterances that do something (performative utterances). Performative utterances perform an action; they do what they say. In contrast, Ahmed proposes the 'non-performative': discourse that does not produce the effect it names (p. 117). 'In the world of the non-performative, to name is not to bring into effect' (p. 117). Ahmed argues:

> In my model of the non-performative, the failure of the speech act to do what it says is not a failure of intent or even circumstance, *but is actually what the speech act is doing*. Such speech acts are taken up *as if* they are performatives (as if they have brought about the effects they name), such that the names come to stand in for the effects. As a result, naming can be a way of not bringing something into effect. (Ahmed, 2012: 117; emphasis in original)

Doing diversity, Ahmed proposes, can be a way of not doing diversity:

> The ease or easiness in which diversity becomes description shows how diversity can be a way of not doing anything: if we take saying diversity *as if* it is doing diversity, then saying diversity can be a way of not doing diversity. (Ahmed, 2012: 121)

Simply saying 'diversity' is not a performative; it does not produce the effect it names. Ahmed's argument about non-performatives is complex and describes how doing diversity actually allows the maintenance of the status quo. 'Having an institutional aim to make diversity a goal can even be a sign that diversity is not an institutional goal' (p. 23). 'Succeeding' at equality may simply allow organizations to 'keep doing what they are doing' (p. 105). 'Doing diversity' becomes a way of avoiding change.

The word 'diversity' itself may be part of the problem. Somewhat of an empty signifier, 'diversity' lacks the directness of words like 'equity' and 'anti-racism' (Ahmed, 2012). The neutrality of 'diversity' and its detachment from power and inequality makes it difficult for diversity to effect change (Ahmed, 2012: 66). Moreover, the use of the word 'diversity' may also facilitate the concealment of systemic inequalities and racism (Ahmed, 2012). Significantly, there is a performative element to this non-performative:

> [D]iversity becomes a form of image management: diversity work creates a new image of the organization as being diverse. It might be image management – or perception management – that allows an organization to be judged as 'good at equality'. Just as changing the perception of an organization from being white to diverse can be a way of reproducing whiteness, so, too, being judged as good at equality can be a way of reproducing inequalities. (Ahmed, 2012: 102)

When institutions engage in virtue signalling in relation to diversity, that signalling may reproduce whiteness and inequalities. A commitment to anti-racism may in fact prevent the recognition of racism within institutions (Ahmed, 2012: 115).

'Doing diversity' may involve creating policies and forming committees, as many higher education institutions in music education have recently shown. Ahmed worries that 'while doing the document is doing something, it is also a way of not doing something: you do the document rather than "doing the doing," where this other sense of doing would require doing something more than the document' (p. 86). When policies are seen to be doing something unto themselves, these policies may allow institutions to understand themselves as having 'done diversity' – having succeeded at equality. Policies themselves may block those in institutions from recognizing the work there is to do. Ahmed writes: 'The more a document circulates, we might assume, the more it will do. But the circulation of the document can become *what it is doing*. Diversity work becomes moving documents around' (p. 97; emphasis in original). While institutions often deem policies as a place to begin, institutional change requires further action. When that action fails to occur, documents themselves make little difference. Importantly, '[t]he document becomes not only a form of compliance but of concealment, a way of presenting the university as being "good at this" despite not being "good at this" in ways that are apparent if you look around' (p. 102). A strong diversity policy may allow those in institutions to feel successful in their diversity efforts. Committees too may uphold the status quo:

> When the equality committee becomes a routine, it can provide a means of avoiding action as well as difficulties. To avoid a trap can be to avoid the situations in which you might be required to amend what is being done. Institutions can 'do committees' as a way of *not* being committed, of not following through. (Ahmed, 2012: 124)

When the university engages in diversity as a way of not doing diversity, the institution upholds the status quo. The virtue signalling that leads to being seen to be good at equity is a '"lip service" model of diversity' (Ahmed, 2012: 58). Turning to interest convergence, interests have aligned again, but in troubling ways. BIPOC groups have been pushing towards racial justice in higher education institutions. These institutions, including schools of music, have presented themselves as 'woke' to issues of racial justice and have enacted policies and struck committees to work on this issue. Ahmed's (2012) concept of non-performativity, however, leads to recognizing how this performance of wokeness or of diversity actually maintains the status quo. When doing diversity is a way of not doing diversity, the interests of white people are again served because maintaining the status quo allows white people to maintain their power and privilege. PWIs and the people within them then can perform themselves as 'good' while failing to cede any power or create institutional change.

Capitalizing on the Moment

I want to return now to the idea of interest convergence as a strategy for action. While waiting for moments when the interests of white and BIPOC groups align to advance racial justice is an injustice because it once again caters to white interests, this moment nonetheless feels as though change might be possible. BIPOC groups call for racial justice and white people, including those in predominantly white schools of music, are interested in being seen to be concerned about these matters. While doing diversity work may indeed serve as a non-performative – a way of not doing diversity work – perhaps this alignment of interests will become enough to motivate and effect meaningful change.

For right or wrong reasons, this appears to be a moment of change. Although I am deeply suspicious that the sudden movement is in the interests of white constituents, I am nonetheless wanting to capitalize on the moment to affect change of material relations. I am less concerned about the 'performative wokeness' that ensues, if the changes made actually move towards more just spaces for BIPOC groups. To do that, however, it is imperative to move far beyond conversations about recruitment and demographics to look critically at music school spaces, which are often violent places for BIPOC communities (Thomas-Durrell, 2022). Doing this work means taking a hard look at institutions and people in them. BIPOC colleagues and students have long found these spaces lacking, or worse.

I propose that predominantly white music schools that engage in virtue signalling their interests in racial justice should enact multiple changes at the curricular and policy level – the material changes that become necessary to making a meaningful difference. For solid or suspect reasons, interests have converged, and in this moment, institutions have an opportunity to shape curriculum and policy to match the wokeness they are performing.

In terms of curriculum, music schools can consider ways to broaden the musical practices studied at the institution. Presently, most music schools centre Western classical music and expanding this curriculum to include multiple musics produces other effects that include hiring individuals who can teach these musics, changing what ensembles are offered, honouring aurality and oral tradition and more. Professors can then approach the inclusion of multiple musics as integrative rather than additive (Hess, 2015). Rather than an 'add-and-stir' approach to incorporating multiple musics (Morton, 2003), a just approach to including a range of musics involves ensuring that professors and administration communicate their value. Pedagogues delivering curriculum in music schools can also actively interrogate how Western classical music came to be at the centre of the curriculum. Such interrogation may lead to important questions about power, colonialism and material relations. Challenging the centrality of classical music also perhaps allows other possibilities for curriculum to emerge. Once institutions have incorporated multiple musics, expanding theory and history offerings to reflect multiple histories and multiple theories, alongside aural and written traditions, becomes an important next step. Music history and music theory have long centred the canon, but, as Philip Ewell (2020) explicates, theory (and arguably history) operates from a 'white racial frame'. Expanding the racial frame of theory and history thus also makes a key contribution to systemic change in music schools. Institutions can also expand the types of ensembles offered and change ensemble requirements to open up possibilities for students to engage with different musics. Ensembles such as Ghanaian drumming ensembles or Gamelan centre entirely different principles from Western classical ensembles and students experiencing these musics have the opportunity to engage in diverse musical epistemologies (Hess, 2018). Finally, institutions can also address the racist repertoire that still pervades musical choices today. Songs rooted in blackface minstrelsy, for example, should no longer have a place in repertoire. These suggestions provide a mere beginning to curriculum reform in music schools.

From a policy perspective, music schools need to address their audition practices. As a gatekeeping exercise, auditions often successfully maintain the status quo of white, middle-class students. Koza (2008) calls this 'listening for whiteness' and encourages people conducting auditions to listen for whiteness in order to defund it. Changing audition practices may involve thinking through what it might mean for prospective students to have more choice about the genres with which they audition and widening audition expectations to embrace the multiplicity of musics students bring to the process. Institutional change also requires addressing hiring practices. In order to facilitate the teaching of multiple musics, schools of music require people who have expertise in these musics. Hiring these individuals at adjunct status, however, as institutions typically do, sends a clear message about the hierarchy of musics in the institutions. These hires must be on par with tenure-track faculty with opportunities for advancement. This type of hiring may also require reconsidering degree requirements, as a master tabla player, for example, would not be able to acquire a DMA or a master's degree in tabla given the classical focus of the current system. Changing hiring practices also must entail meaningful efforts to place BIPOC faculty in permanent positions in schools of music – not siloed in areas like jazz but integrated across all areas of the expanded curriculum envisioned earlier. The fact that many BIPOC students and faculty experience schools of music in PWIs to be violent spaces also requires addressing climate issues. Implementing mandatory education about whiteness, white supremacy, equity, racial bias and microaggressions then becomes part of the path forward. If predominantly white music schools want to signal that they are woke, they need to do the work towards becoming woke. Lastly, implementing these curricular and policy changes requires changes to the NASM accreditation process. Revisiting and revising NASM requirements is essential to this moment.

Conclusion

I have yet to see evidence that any of the virtue signalling going on presently will result in meaningful change, but I am hopeful that, at a time when institutions and their leaders seem to be so eager to perform themselves as 'woke', individuals interested in racial justice in schools of music might be able to implement meaningful change anyway. Effecting change requires pushing beyond the stubborn non-performativity embedded in current practices of diversity in higher education schools of music. Importantly, Ahmed (2012) asserts:

> The sentence [from the qualitative interview] 'commitments can't come without other actions' is instructive. It suggests that commitment is an action, but one that does not act on its own but depends on other actions: we might call these 'follow-up' actions. For a commitment to do something, you must do something 'with it'. (Ahmed, 2012: 120)

To avoid diversity work becoming a non-performative in which doing diversity work is a way of not doing diversity work, institutions must follow up their purported commitments with action.

In terms of interest convergence, Milner (2008) suggests the second facet of Martin Luther King, Jr.'s approach to a non-violent campaign – negotiation – aligns with Bell's (1995) concept of interest convergence. When interests are negotiated, he asserts, moving forward becomes possible:

> As is the case in teacher education, those in power sometimes 'speak', theorize, and philosophize about being committed to combating oppression, suppression, and marginalization yet sometimes do not follow through with their actions in their policies and practices. As a result, it will be difficult for those of us in teacher education to truly advance the field unless someone – some group, system, or institution – is willing to negotiate and give up some interest to benefit the 'other'. In this sense, giving up something and the gaining of something by the other result in benefits and gains of the masses (Hilliard, 1992); both the oppressor and the oppressed gain. (Milner, 2008: 342)

Milner points here to the performativity that sometimes occurs without the necessary actions to follow-up. He urges teacher educators to use interest convergence as a tactic – to find where the interests align and capitalize on it. In order to negotiate interests, however, dominant groups must come to the table in good faith. If PWIs and their leadership wish to be seen as woke, they must follow up with action. Moreover, the action needs to be substantive.

In this political moment, interests have converged, and while motivations may be suspect, predominantly white music schools have the opportunity to put action behind their performativity. Diversity work need not remain a non-performative – a way of not doing the work institutions say they do. Instead of institutions' virtue-signalling commitment, people within these institutions and the communities external to them can call for accountability. Accountability in this case, following Ahmed (2012), means that institutions enact their commitment rather than merely stating it. Signalling commitment is no longer sufficient. Predominantly white music schools have been and continue to be violent spaces for BIPOC students and colleagues. Changing that is crucial to how the field moves forward.

In the summer of 2020, many US music schools issued statements affirming that Black Lives Matter following the brutal murder of George Floyd. Yet Black lives must matter within music institutions as well as outside them. If music schools wish to be seen as anti-racist, they must enact the change their policies and committees describe. Being seen as 'woke' comes with particular responsibilities. Importantly, when it comes to racial allyship, allies do not get to claim they are 'woke'. They also do not get to claim they are allies. BIPOC groups determine that. If an institution engages in virtue signalling about their commitment to racial justice, it is their BIPOC community members who get to determine if they are living up to their mythology. If these community members find the institutions wanting, institutions must double down on their commitment and align their actions with their words. It is past time for music schools to live up to their mythology. Anything else is simply a non-performative.

Acknowledgements

A longer version of this chapter can be found here: Hess, J. (2022), The Surge Toward 'Diversity': Interest Convergence and Performative 'Wokeness' in Music Institutions. *Action, Criticism & Theory for Music Education*, 21 (2): 126–55. https://doi.org/10.22176/act21.2.126

Notes

1. See, for example, the College Music Society Conference in Fall 2020 entitled 'Fostering Equity and Opportunity in Music': https://www.music.org/index.php?option=com_eventbooking&view=event&id=90&Itemid=3524.
2. See https://mappingpoliceviolence.org.
3. See Hess (2018) – a YouTube video discussion on the difficulty of some of the words we use to talk about issues of race and racism: https://www.youtube.com/watch?v=9ytxe9YTyR8.
4. Brent Talbot and Roger Mantie (2015) describe the overwhelmingly Western European practices in music schools that facilitate the whiteness of these spaces.
5. See https://nafme.org/what-we-believe-black-lives-matter.
6. See, for example, https://www.adolescent.net/a/the-rise-of-performative-wokeness-.

References

Ahmed, S. (2012), *On Being Included: Racism and Diversity in Institutional Life*, London: Duke University Press.

Alemán Jr., E. and S. M. Alemán (2010), '"Do Latin@ Interests Always Have to 'Converge' with White interests?": (Re)claiming Racial Realism and Interest-convergence in Critical Race Theory Praxis', *Race Ethnicity and Education*, 13 (1): 1–21. Available online: https://doi.org/10.1080/13613320903549644

Applebaum, B. (2010), *Being White, Being Good: White Complicity, White Moral Responsibility, and Social Justice Pedagogy*, New York: Lexington Books.

Austin, J. L. (1975), *How to Do Things with Words*, Oxford: Oxford University Press.

Bell, D. (1995), 'Brown v. Board of Education and the Interest Convergence Dilemma', in K. Crenshaw, N. Gotanda, G. Peller and K. Thomas (eds), *Critical Race Theory: The Key Writings that Formed the Movement*, 20–29, New York: The New Press.

Bergerson, A. A. (2003), 'Critical Race Theory and White Racism: Is There Room for White Scholars in Fighting Racism in Education?', *International Journal of Qualitative Studies in Education*, 16 (1): 51–63. Available online: https://doi.org/10.1080/0951839032000033527

Bourdieu, P. (1986), 'The Forms of Capital', in J. G. Richardson (ed.), *Handbook of Theory and Research for the Sociology of Education*, 241–58, Westport: Greenwood.

Bradley, D. (2015), 'Hidden in Plain Sight: Race and Racism in Music Education', in C. Benedict, P. K. Schmidt, G. Spruce and P. G. Woodford (eds), *The Oxford Handbook of Social Justice in Music Education*, 190–203, New York: Oxford University Press.

Castagno, A. E. and S. J. Lee (2007), 'Native Mascots and Ethnic Fraud in Higher Education: Using Tribal Critical Race Theory and the Interest Convergence Principle as an Analytic Tool', *Equity & Excellence in Education*, 40 (1): 3–13. Available online: https://doi.org/10.1080/10665680601057288

DeCuir, J. T. and A. D. Dixson (2004), '"So When It Comes Out, They Aren't That Surprised That It Is There": Using Critical Race Theory as a Tool of Analysis of Race and Racism in Education', *Educational Researcher*, 33 (5): 26–31. Available online: https://doi.org/10.3102/0013189X033005026

DiAngelo, R. (2018), *White Fragility: Why It's So Hard for White People to Talk About Racism*, Boston: Beacon Press.

Ewell, P. A. (2020), 'Music Theory and the White Racial Frame', *Music Theory Online*, 26 (2). Available online: https://doi.org/10.30535/mto.26.2.4

Hess, J. (2013), 'Performing Tolerance and Curriculum: The Politics of Self-Congratulation, Identity Formation, and Pedagogy in World Music Education', *Philosophy of Music Education Review*, 21 (1): 66–91. Available online: https://doi.org/10.2979/philmusieducrevi.21.1.66

Hess, J. (2015), 'Upping the "Anti-": The Value of an Anti-Racist Theoretical Framework in Music Education', *Action, Criticism & Theory for Music Education*, 14 (1): 66–92.

Hess, J. (2018), 'A "Discomfortable" Approach to "World Music": Reenvisioning Contextualized "World Music Education"', *Philosophy of Music Education Review*, 26 (1): 24–45. Available online: https://doi.org/10.2979/philmusieducrevi.26.1.03

Hilliard, A. G. (1992), 'Behavioral Style, Culture, and Teaching and Learning', *Journal of Negro Education*, 61 (3): 370–7.

Hiraldo, P. (2010), 'The Role of Critical Race Theory in Higher Education', *The Vermont Connection*, 31: 53–59. Available online: https://scholarworks.uvm.edu/tvc/vol31/iss1/7

Hwang, H. and K.-O. Kim (2015), 'Social Media as a Tool for Social Movements: The Effect of Social Media Use and Social Capital on Intention to Participate in Social Movements', *International Journal of Consumer Studies*, 39: 478–88. Available online: https://doi.org/10.1111/ijcs.12221

Kendi, I. X. (2019), *How to be an Antiracist*, New York: One World.

Koza, J. E. (2008), 'Listening for Whiteness: Hearing Racial Politics in Undergraduate School Music', *Philosophy of Music Education Review*, 16 (2): 145–55. Available online: https://www.jstor.org/stable/40327298

Ladson-Billings, G. (1998), 'Just What Is Critical Race Theory and What's It Doing in a Nice Field Like Education?', *Qualitative Studies in Education*, 11 (1): 7–24. Available online: https://doi.org/10.1080/095183998236863

Leigh, P. R. (2003), 'Interest Convergence and Desegregation in the Ohio Valley', *The Journal of Negro Education*, 72 (3): 269–96. Available online: https://doi.org/10.2307/3211248

Lubell, M. (2017), 'Op-ed: Performing Wokeness', *The Michigan Daily*, 20 September. Available online: https://www.michigandaily.com/section/viewpoints/op-ed-performing-wokeness (accessed 27 March 2021).

McCoy, D. L. (2006), 'Entering the Academy: Exploring the Socialization Experiences of African American Male Faculty', PhD diss., Louisiana State University. https://digitalcommons.lsu.edu/gradschool_dissertations/3297

Milner IV, H. R. (2008), 'Critical Race Theory and Interest Convergence as Analytic Tools in Teacher Education Policies and Practices', *Journal of Teacher Education*, 59 (4): 332–46. Available online: https://doi.org/10.1177/0022487108321884

Morton, C. (2003), 'In the Meantime: Finding a Vision for Multicultural Music Education in Canada', in B. Hanley and B. A. Roberts (eds), *Looking Forward: Challenges to Canadian Music Education*, 251–72, Toronto: Irwin Publishing.

Razack, S. (1998), *Looking White People in the Eye: Gender, Race, and Culture in Courtrooms and Classrooms*, Toronto: University of Toronto Press.

Sung, K. K. (2017), '"Accentuate the Positive; Eliminate the Negative": Hegemonic Interest Convergence, Racialization of Latino Poverty, and the 1968 Bilingual Education Act', *Peabody Journal of Education*, 92 (3): 302–21. Available online: https://doi.org/10.1080/0161956X.2017.1324657

Talbot, B. C. and R. Mantie (2015), 'Vision and the Legitimate Order: Theorizing Today to Imagine Tomorrow', in S. W. Conkling (ed.), *Envisioning Teacher Education*, 155–80, Lanham: Rowman & Littlefield.

Thomas-Durrell, L. A. (2022), 'Unlearning Academic Music Education: How Music Education Erases Already-Present Musical Identities', in D. Bradley and J. Hess (eds), *Trauma and Resilience in Music Education: Haunted Melodies*, 110–24, New York: Routledge.

Watson, V. and B. Thompson (2015), 'Theorizing White Racial Trauma and its Remedies', in V. Watson, D. Howard-Wagner and L. Spanierman (eds), *Unveiling Whiteness in the Twenty-First Century: Global Manifestations, Transdisciplinary Interventions*, 247–66, Lanham: Lexington Books.

Part III

Transitions and Trajectories of Musicians

Chapter 12

Negotiating Pedagogical Cultures

Adaptive Challenges Facing Music Education
Graduates on Their Return to China

Elizabeth Haddon

Introduction

This study follows earlier research investigating Chinese students' reasons for studying music at master's level in the UK (Haddon, 2019). As programme creator and leader of the MA in Music Education: Instrumental and Vocal Teaching at the University of York, I have been privileged to witness and support the cultural and pedagogical adaptation processes of students progressing through this degree. Communication with returnees has revealed transitional challenges involving tensions between desired and required practices, however. While this should not be reduced to a binary opposition, desired learner-autonomy supportive practices may collide with hierarchical, goal-directed pedagogy expected within Chinese educational contexts (particularly in school and private or managed studio teaching). This qualitative study identifies pedagogical values developed during MA study and investigates how returnees negotiate these within their subsequent work as instrumental or vocal teachers in China. These mechanisms of re-immersion and re-engagement are potentially embedded in neoliberal constructs.

Both China and the UK exhibit forms of neoliberalism in regard to education. Pan (2021) articulates aspects of neoliberalism that can be related to the UK context, in which the legacies of various government White Papers and higher education acts have resulted in changes in institutional, academic and individual behaviours (McCaig, 2018). Higher education is defined as a 'cross-border' service, reliant on international students' tuition fees, operating within a state-supervised model in which governmental influence and control is strong despite reduced direct funding (Pan, 2021). Marketization and managerialism, defined as primary constructs of neoliberalism, result in a focus on metrics, performance, standardization, accountability and competition (Mullen, 2019). Despite the perceived benefits (including 'borderless' universities enabled through online tools, increased numbers of international students, cultural diversity, efficiency and knowledge transfer to industry), issues prevail relating to equality, academic standards, transparency of institutional budgetary and academic policy decisions, lessened autonomy and 'academic freedom', a 'cash cow' orientation towards international students and the deployment of their funding income to support managerial structures rather than pedagogy, as well as over-reliance on Chinese students (Pan, 2021). In higher music education, Ford (2020) argues that this dependence on international students is further problematized through the deployment of assimilationist values, whereby students are subjected to stereotypical objectification through cultural and racial prejudice.

In China, educational reforms have also led to an increased transnational focus for higher education, creating market diversification and competition, research capacity, variable state funding and regulation: 'centralized decentralisation' or 'regulated deregulation' (Mok, 2021: 7). In the school sector, Zhang and Bray (2017) identify intensified competition 'between families, teachers, schools, and governments' (Zhang and Bray, 2017: 67) as well as an audit culture focus on performance metrics, high-stakes testing, market metrics and monetization. Emphasis on competition within a growth market promotes extracurricular 'shadow education' (Chang and McLaren, 2018) and the state support of 'minban': privately owned schools offering extracurricular tuition (Mok, 2021). Within this context, instrumental music tuition is enmeshed in competitive and cultural values; pivotal components include the interrelationship between parental involvement, perceptions of the teacher's status and examination-focused pedagogy. As in other countries, instrumental learning often begins at a very early age, with considerable parental involvement (Bai, 2021); parents may deploy 'psychologically controlling' approaches involving strict discipline, pressure and progress monitoring (Kong, 2021: 289). Connecting to the authority of the teacher and associated respect and discipline (Li and Rivers, 2018), the combined power of parents and teachers may leave students with little agency.

Approaches to instrumental pedagogy in China have been described as utilizing memorization and rote learning within a master-apprentice relationship, prioritizing the acquisition of technical skill and emphasizing accurate realization/reproduction of musical notation (Zheng and Leung, 2021a). Problematic yet persistent views of Chinese performers as 'technicians' compared against emotionally expressive Westerners as highlighted by Yang (2007) indicate a predilection to a polarity of positioning of instrumental pedagogy and musicianship, depicting Chinese musicians as stereotypically limited in their engagement with the allegedly superior canon of Western repertoire. As discussed by Ford (2020) and Xu (2021), pervasive Western hegemony has been detrimental to the global understanding of Chinese social, educational and cultural perspectives. In advanced-level piano pedagogy, Zheng and Leung (2021a,b) encourage a reappraisal of purely reproductive pedagogy through the deployment of creative practices and expanded genres, supporting learner confidence, expressive autonomy and an awareness of the possibilities of player and instrument.

Despite these developments, examinations remain the prevalent mode of learning evaluation in China; students' results are also used by parents and schools to assess the performance of teachers, constraining pedagogical innovation (Wang, Liu and Zhang, 2018). Examination-driven pedagogy also connects to parental concerns about the comparative development of and opportunities for their offspring and to a target- and results-driven approach to instrumental music education: a focus on performance examinations and competitions involves rivalries among parents, learners and instrumental teachers (Bai, 2021). Guo and Cosaitis (2020) warn of negative consequences including learner attrition, mental ill-health and restricted musical development.

This competitive underpinning of pedagogy has been acknowledged as a consequence of the Chinese Communist Party's 'neo-liberal looking economic policies' (Duckett, 2020: 523); these have improved the quality of living but amplified regional and class inequalities, particularly concerning educational provision. While a 'collectivist ideology' is still apparent in China, the rise of individualism, entrepreneurship and status symbols indicates neoliberal values held by 'China's urban elite' (Duckett, 2020: 525). Despite possibilities afforded by the Chinese government's opening up of the education market to enable new structural, financial and management systems, operational autonomy for schools remains tightly regulated (Zhang and Bray, 2017), limiting pedagogical development and intensifying competition between providers, students and parents.

Pressure to succeed in the *Gaokao* (university entrance examination) has intensified, preceded by an ambition to achieve prior educational targets such as admission to elite secondary schools (Leung and McPherson, 2010) which may involve extra private tuition (Zhang and Bray, 2017). Instrumental music education is enmeshed in this construct, with many parents requiring children and teachers to pursue the rapid attainment of instrumental music certificates (Guo and Cosaitis, 2020). The narrow focus of the widely used Amateur Grading Tests (Bai, 2021) may have negative implications for the development of a rounded musical education due to undiversified repertoire (Bai, 2021) and the lack of assessment for skills such as sight-reading.

Many Chinese students choose overseas higher education: 143,820 Chinese mainland nationals studied at this level in the UK in 2020–1; of those, 74,045 studied postgraduate taught programmes (HESA, 2022). Career advancement is recognized as a primary aim among those pursuing international study (Hao, Wen and Welch, 2016); however, developments in the quality of Chinese higher education have increased the competitiveness of Chinese home-educated graduates (Hao, Wen and Welch, 2016). Research with Chinese music master's students studying in the UK has identified the desire for faster academic progression compared to that of peers remaining in China, the goal of building personal skills and independence, the perceived cultural legitimacy of studying Western music in the West and specific practical elements of master's courses as motivating their UK study (Haddon, 2019).

Overseas study has both positive and negative implications. While students may advance their educational and employability prospects and widen their cultural experience, they may be disadvantaged on return to China due to the limited '*guanxi*' (influential Chinese relationships) built during this time (Hao et al., 2017) despite their potential to have made international connections and to understand global practices (Gu and Schweisfurth, 2015). From a neoliberal perspective, they are exploited for their high fee-paying status (Xu, 2021); the high costs of overseas study may have repercussions for students and their families for some time prior to and after the actual duration of study. Although they may be viewed as 'instrumentalised as means for achieving China's modernisation' (Xu, 2021: 5), paradoxically, their progression and transformation of personal identity during their overseas study and/or employment may not align with the expectations and values of colleagues and employers on return to China (Hao, Wen and Welch, 2016). This particularly concerns the juxtaposition of a returnee's 'fluid identities' (Ai and Wang, 2017: 7) against more fixed identities as well as tensions in adopting discursive Western pedagogical approaches which may conflict with Chinese expectations of teacher-centred and exam-focused pedagogy (Ai and Wang, 2017). Within employment, differences may arise concerning work cultures (Hao et al., 2017), and in academia, difficulties relating to employers' understandings of academic standards, values and investment in facilities (Ai and Wang, 2017). Therefore, returnees may experience challenges of reverse 'culture shock' and reintegration. Despite the proliferation of research on returnees, understanding of the specific issues facing music returnees is lacking. This chapter illuminates the values developed during master's music study in the UK and the adaptive concerns of a sample of graduates post-return to China.

UK Study: MA Music Education: Instrumental and Vocal Teaching, University of York

In this one-year full-time taught master's programme, students gain knowledge of approaches to one-to-one and group teaching which include teacher-student relationship modes, pedagogical content knowledge, teacher and learner motivation, strategies to support instrumental and vocal practice and the development of skills such as sight-reading, memorization, working with learners of different ages, supporting physical and mental health, understanding different learning needs and inclusive practice. A blend of academic and practical work underpinned by reflection and critical thinking enables exploration of research-informed pedagogical approaches. The cohorts have always included home and international students, of whom the largest proportion have been from China. The programme welcomes a diversity of instruments and genres: Chinese traditional music as well as Western classical, jazz, popular and folk genres create the potential for rich knowledge exchange. Most international students subsequently return to their country of origin; many work as school classroom teachers or as instrumental teachers or in administrative roles; some pursue further study.

Method and Research Participants

A small-scale qualitative study was designed to explore the pedagogical experiences of Chinese returnees. Ethical approval was granted by the University of York's

Arts and Humanities Ethics Committee. Purposive sampling was deployed: Chinese alumni of the MA in Music Education: Instrumental and Vocal Teaching were contacted by email and informed of the aims and purpose of the study; respondents could either complete an anonymous survey or request an online or phone interview with the author. Difficulties with expired contact details meant that many alumni were unreachable; ten respondents (all female) completed the survey and one (Participant 7) additionally requested a phone interview, in which an unstructured format was deployed to enable in-depth elaboration of their survey answers. The survey utilized mostly open text boxes for respondents to answer items concerning their teaching experience and approach pre-/post-MA, focusing on changes and challenges, their work as returnees and observations of instrumental teaching in China. Table 12.1 presents the participants' demographic details relating to their involvement in teaching contexts prior to and after UK study.

All participants apart from P5 (Ehuang) had taught music before the MA. Four undertook school internships; the rest taught privately. On return, five taught in schools; one subsequently returned to the UK for a PhD; eight gave private lessons; two of these additionally worked in institutions as private teachers. One was also preparing students for university entry and one was job-seeking.

Data analysis utilized an interpretative approach, deploying an iterative process of thematic coding and inductive analysis (Braun and Clarke, 2006). The author was mindful to adopt a reflexive and neutral approach in order to limit potential bias arising from her involvement as creator and programme leader of the MA course. Due to the small sample size, findings cannot be generalized but nevertheless provide insights into the pedagogical adaptation of the returnees.

Instrumental Pedagogy Prior to and During the MA Year

All respondents delineated hierarchical instrumental pedagogy in China, identifying their pre-MA instrumental teaching as heavily conditioned by their learning experiences – 'teacher-dominated and exam-oriented' (P4: Dandan) – and describing their prior teaching as directive, critical, rarely asking questions or inviting students to engage in dialogue, which could lead to poor learner concentration, especially for younger pupils. Focusing on assessment outcomes obscured consideration of pedagogical change: 'My pupil's examination results were good, therefore I thought that approach was good enough' (P2: Baozhai). This respondent later realized that 'the result doesn't mean that I am a good teacher . . . my pupils didn't learn about music. They just copied my interpretation and suggestions.'

Respondents indicated that the MA facilitated pedagogical development through learning about new practical and theoretical perspectives and reflecting on teaching. P7 (Genji) observed that 'instead of focusing on "what's wrong with my student", I learned how to find out my own problem in order to improve the

Table 12.1 Demographic Information of Participants

Pseudonym, Year of UK Study, Instrument, Mode/s of Participation	Teaching Experience Prior to UK Study	Working Context(s) on Return to China
P1: Annchi 2015–16 Voice survey	Primary school class music teacher, Shanghai, internship	Private one-to-one vocal teacher and full-time class music teacher, international school, Shanghai
P2: Baozhai 2016–17 Piano survey	Private piano teaching, Hong Kong, four to five years	Private piano teaching, six days a week, Hong Kong
P3: Chunhua 2016–17 Erhu/piano survey	High school music teacher and college teaching, four months	Part-time school class music teacher, returned to UK for PhD
P4: Dandan 2016–17 Piano survey	Part-time piano teacher during undergraduate studies; three-month school internship	Private one-to-one teaching and classroom teaching, six days a week
P5: Ehuang 2017–18 Flute/piano survey	None	Private teaching, flute and piano in Hong Kong, four days a week in an education centre for children aged two to seventeen
P6: Fenfang 2017–18 Piano survey	Private piano teaching – five years	Opened a private piano studio; teaches piano, also involved in school class music teaching
P7: Genji 2017–18 Piano survey + interview	Private piano teaching – seven years, also helps students prepare for Chinese postgraduate entrance examinations	Private piano teaching; academic tutor for current and prospective university music students (two to four students per group). Works seven days a week during exam season; otherwise four days
P8: Huiqing 2017–18 Piano survey	Private piano teaching in primary school (group and one-to-one lessons)	Teaches piano in private studio and classroom music in primary school, five days a week
P9: Jilpa 2018–19 Piano/voice survey	Private piano and vocal teaching; high school internship – music theory and appreciation lessons	Not working at time of survey, seeking employment
P10: Luli 2018–19 Piano/theory survey	Music studio – piano and theory lessons	Employed by a piano teaching company in Beijing (required to use teaching materials provided by the company in one-to-one lessons); also gives private lessons

lessons and make the learning process interesting and suitable for each student'. The MA encourages the deployment of Socratic questioning in order to support learner metacognition, underpin positive student-teacher relationships and facilitate the teacher's understanding of the learner's reception of pedagogical processes and outcomes. P9 (Jilpa) felt that the biggest challenge was 'how to use different open questions to let the student find out their problem instead of telling

[them] their mistake immediately'. Respondents also became more conscious of learners' emotional responses during lessons and developed cultural awareness and sensitivity: 'Different languages . . . develop different mindset[s] and different ways of thinking' (P2: Baozhai); therefore, 'people from different countries will have different opinions on the method of education' (P6: Fenfang).

Observing course tutors giving one-to-one tuition led to awareness of the unexpected possibilities for student-teachers: 'In that lesson [tutor x] did not really tell [the pupil] what [they] expected, but let [the pupil] explore as far as she could. I started to realize that I cannot "steal" that experience from my pupil. I need to let them explore' (P8: Huiqing). P9 (Jilpa) also reconsidered the potential of a lesson: 'The most challenging part for me was how to teach in an innovative way . . . I was not taught in a creative way so I don't know what creative teaching looks like.' These realizations led to more collaborative and personal approaches:

> I am more flexible in teaching. I used to stick to my teaching plan, so if anything happened that was not in my plan, for example if my student responded to my questions with an answer I did not anticipate, I will panic and try to bring them back to the answer I wanted. But every student learns in their own ways, from then I would try to build on their thoughts and see how it goes. (P8: Huiqing)

Respondents indicated that the course developed their teaching in multiple dimensions, including knowledge of teaching theories and methods, promoting diversity and originality in teaching approaches that motivated their own further learning and supported enhanced student-teacher relationships. While these outcomes would be expected from all students, it is valuable to consider the challenges faced by Chinese returnees, who will re-immerse themselves in a country with different pedagogical and cultural norms.

Returnees: Pedagogical Aspirations and Realities

Several respondents had looked forward to deploying new teaching approaches in China. Educational developments in urban areas such as Shanghai were identified by P1 (Annchi) as potentially supportive of these due to increasing numbers of international and bilingual schools. P3 (Chunhua) was 'definitely excited . . . but also a bit worried':

> As a student, I really like to be taught in a student-centred way, I would love to be a student with a teacher who has these ideas. But I was not sure whether these ideas would be in conflict to the Chinese culture, as the old saying goes 'honour the teacher and respect his teaching'. (P3: Chunhua)

Most respondents identified concerns due to results-driven parental expectations: 'Chinese parents focus on the certificates and results, not on the actual improvement and keeping their children's learning motivation and happiness' (P7: Genji). While all returnees hoped to use strategies to promote student-teacher interaction, dialogue, learner motivation and autonomy, utilizing varied teaching materials from the UK and China, they also experienced pedagogical challenges, largely due to contradictions between their desire to implement new approaches and the expectations of parents or employers. These challenges are delineated later in the text in relation to parental expectations and examinations, the influence of educational conditioning on pupils, teacher flexibility and reflection, employers and families.

Parental Expectations and Examinations

Specific issues were identified in relation to parents of children taking one-to-one lessons. P5 (Ehuang) observed different expectations compared with the UK, where their pupils learned 'for entertainment and leisure purposes'. Almost all respondents mentioned the Chinese exam-focused culture as problematic in relation to parental expectations. P7 (Genji) felt that parents 'care about only one question, "when can my child pass ABRSM[1] Grade 8?"' as 'most parents want their kids to get the highest certification they can before 12 – the age they attend middle school'. P2 (Chunhua) identified even earlier pressures for obtaining 'more certificates for primary school interviews' in Hong Kong. Those working in institutions were obliged to deliver examination-focused teaching. P8 (Huiqing) felt this orientation was 'really hard for one teacher to change, the only thing I could do now is to try my best to make sure my students enjoyed each lesson'.

Creating additional tension for returnees were insights gained into UK performance examination syllabi, leading to a reappraisal of the Chinese system as less sophisticated: 'Local music exams don't have aural or sight-reading tests, and the standard of distinction, merit, and pass is not very clear. Teachers could be examiners at their own city, so these exams lose their authority throughout these years' (P8: Huiqing). Returnees may have therefore been required by parents or institutions to teach to a curriculum that they now consider inadequate for their students. Furthermore, pupils' parents influenced pedagogical practice by deeming approaches supporting pupil relaxation and learner enjoyment as unnecessary. While these issues are not exclusive to instrumental lessons in China, they indicated a disparity of pedagogical realities and ideals.

Influence of Educational Conditioning on Pupils, Teacher Flexibility and Reflection

Aspects of established roles and behaviours from the school context, particularly pupils' passive status and reliance on teachers, also affected one-to-one pedagogy: 'Teachers have to "feed" knowledge to pupils as much as possible in order to enable them to achieve the greatest results in the shortest time. This completely prevents pupils' ability to think independently' (P10: Luli). The limited verbal responses from subservient, passive pupils required modification of expectations and communication strategies such as reducing the number of questions asked by teachers, 'sharing opinions with pupils but without forcing them to follow' and giving 'more time for pupils to apply the playing techniques they have learned' (P2: Baozhai). Returnees responded with flexibility, adjusting teaching plans and considering motivational strategies which could involve 'more relaxed and fun materials such as duet exercises' (P5: Ehuang) if pupils and parents accepted this approach.

Some returnees continued their professional development through written reflection, observing other teachers, attending presentations on ABRSM exam pieces, Montessori training, reading pedagogy and psychology articles and watching masterclasses. Their continuation of the use of video as a reflective tool was variable, however: 'some parents cannot understand the purpose of doing this' (P6: Fenfang). While some returnees discussed their teaching with other teachers (including former classmates and their MA lecturers), P7 (Genji) found teachers in China to be disinterested in discussing professional pedagogical development as they interpreted employment and pay as indicative of successful teaching; this led to Genji's concern: 'if most of teachers here are lack of thirst of knowledge, what about their student's learning motivation?'

Employers and Families

Returnees indicated the power of employers (school heads of music/head teachers and those running private piano studios) to constrain the deployment of MA-informed pedagogical practices. School employers required teacher-centred approaches for large classes (up to fifty pupils per class), though those working in Shanghai and Beijing described employers as interested in hearing about teaching approaches from the MA. Nevertheless, P5 (Ehuang) in Hong Kong felt that employers were 'more or less neutral' about the application of new instrumental teaching ideas in an education centre, ascribing this to their own status: 'freshly graduated and lacking experience. The employers never really made a comment about my teaching, positive or negative.'

Four respondents mentioned that their current employers provided training and professional development. However, P5 (Ehuang), working in a music centre, stated, 'My employers didn't really train us, and mostly taught us things when we made a mistake ... I never really saw my boss ... and never really knew who to turn to when I had issues.' Ehuang was one of five participants grateful for input from their own parents: 'My family was supportive of me, listened when I needed to vent my frustrations from teaching. My mom gave me valuable advice as a teacher herself when I had to deal with issues I couldn't figure out.' The mother perspective was also appreciated in understanding the views of parents: P2 (Baozhai) valued seeing 'how a mother feels in some situations'. While training and support were mentioned, they were not delineated as focused to aid the specific issues faced by returnees; instead, they negotiated these challenges largely on their own, with some family or peer support.

Progressive Orientation

While most returnees seemed to be moving through an adaptive process of adjustment, reconciling ideals and realities through pedagogical flexibility, the situation seemed different for Genji (P7), who was the only returnee to refer to 'reverse culture shock', aligning more with UK educational and cultural values than Chinese ones. Genji operated selective processes as a private piano teacher, avoiding parents who were 'not interested in music or who do not care about their children's ideas', those who would 'try to control the teaching style' and those who blamed the child or pushed them to take exams beyond their ability, which would 'kill the learning motivation and all the fun'. Discussing her prior negative experiences of Chinese parents with MA tutors led Genji to realize: 'I do have a choice, if there is something beyond my ability, beyond my control, I can say no.' Reflecting on experiences with overcontrolling parents who destroyed their children's love of music, Genji observed that 'you can't save their children from the torture – at least you can save yourself'.

Genji applied a 'double-way selection' process: talking with parents and pupils prior to starting lessons, agreeing on learning goals and approaches, trialling these for three months and reviewing them, including the views of the students as well as the parents. Genji also created bespoke assessments, stating that existing music performance exams provided a flawed assessment due to the examiners' predilection for stopping candidates after only playing a minute or so of each piece, and the provision of a mark without feedback. Genji designed examinations not as a route to achieve credits or certificates but to support motivation and the adjustment of teaching approaches, following each exam with parent-student-teacher discussion of progress, learner support and ideas for developing her teaching. Genji, therefore, appears unique in working only with those who may be receptive to her particular teaching approach and philosophy.

Discussion

These views present a mixed picture of adaptation, teacher-parent-employer alignment and control. The pedagogical ideals created through the UK master's course continue to be held by these returnees; however, the strength of societal expectations, orientated towards a results-driven hierarchical pedagogy, generates ongoing challenges. These appear to align with a neoliberal focus on efficiency and effectiveness, particularly through the emphasis on performance examinations and, potentially, a focus on the examination repertoire as the sole curricular material in order to achieve required competitive targets. Such atomistic assessment, performativity and use of set material may reflect similar approaches in the Chinese school context. Mullen (2019) argues that 'pre-packaged curricula' may also position teachers as 'disposable labor – interchangeable workers' (p. 54); this could intensify the pressure on teachers to conform to expected norms in order to secure their livelihoods, particularly in a context where examination results define teachers' value.

The findings suggest variable pedagogical practice within China, which may impact teaching approaches and reception. Returnees teaching in international institutions in urban cities seemed to experience fewer difficulties than those working in music studios, teaching privately or in schools elsewhere. This aligns with employment reintegration being potentially easier in major urban cities than in rural areas (Hao, Wen and Welch, 2016). However, returnees working in private sector instrumental music education in first-tier cities were not immune to pressures created by the expected norm of master-apprentice, competitive and exam-focused pedagogy.

Deployment of returnees could be seen as a marker of progressive intentions by employers and by parents, who could view the returnee's UK qualification as an indicator of their own parental commitment to securing a competitive edge for their child's instrumental learning, a view that may align with neoliberal market-focused traits. This might go some way to explaining the finding that parents appear critical of the instrumental teacher, as they may have expected a UK-trained returnee to achieve extra competitive drive and faster progression for their child's learning. This perspective of critical and challenging parents seems at odds with literature proposing teachers as objects of reverence (Li and Rivers, 2018). However, in a hierarchical society such as China, parents may perhaps find it problematic to respect a teacher younger than themselves as it could weaken their parental authority. Parents may view themselves as the senior party in the parent-pupil-teacher triangle and therefore feel emboldened to express criticism of the returnee teacher. Furthermore, parents may feel justified in intervention if cultural norms such as 'children are spoiled if praised' and 'no pain, no gain' (Watkins, 2003: 246) are undermined by returnees' methods involving praise, encouragement and practical measures to avoid pain. If parents still expect teachers to embody the attributes of a 'good moral role model' (Watkins, 2003: 247), any divergence from expected practices may be viewed as potentially disruptive and deserving of corrective parental measures. Furthermore, from a neoliberal perspective, surveillance of the teacher links to conformity (Mullen, 2019); therefore, private sector teaching may involve parental monitoring of the teacher to align with perceived norms to achieve pupil progression.

In addition, the returnee occupies a position where expectations of themselves and from others of them may be significant, yet they appear to lack formal support structures: addressing resultant cognitive dissonance is their own responsibility. Two returnees discussed pedagogical problems with their mothers; several mentioned family support and talking to others, yet P7 (Genji) felt that many teachers regarded professional development as irrelevant: pay and status affirmed their value. Faced with pedagogical infrastructures expressed as problematic in terms of their educational value and enactment (such as music performance examinations), societal expectations and educational conditioning, it is in many ways unsurprising to read of these challenges. This suggests that the varied employment contexts of these returnees may, to some extent, mirror neoliberal developments in China, which determine and restrict returnees' agency in relation to the application of new pedagogical approaches, their relationship with traditional educational structures and assessment and with parents. From a global pedagogical neoliberal perspective, institutional support for students' adjustment to study in the UK is not counterbalanced by support for returnees; this compounds the issues discussed in this chapter's introduction concerning the reliance of UK institutions on Chinese students' fee income, related perceptions of hegemonic Western views of Chinese students and investment in dialogic, collaborative work to support cross-cultural pedagogy.

Conclusion

This study creates a starting point for future music returnee research. The findings indicate challenges related to pedagogical expectations, approaches, aims and beliefs that concern the parent-teacher-pupil relationship and exam-driven culture and which connect to neoliberal values – in particular, competition and performativity. Tensions arising from the extent to which the knowledge from the master's course can be utilized and accepted within their instrumental teaching in China indicate that returnees attach value to the pedagogical outcomes of their MA study. Chinese contexts for teaching afford varying amounts of agency for returnees, affecting the implementation of new ideas and the potential development of instrumental pedagogy in China.

The limitations of this research include the small number of respondents and the lack of impartial teaching observation. Implications for assimilation of values from overseas study may also benefit from consideration in relation to the increased provision of remote study online options during and following the Covid-19 pandemic. These could limit opportunities for immersion in overseas culture during the period of study, which could potentially dilute the influence of the programme. Conversely, remote study might facilitate the smoother integration of practice if students can apply concepts within their home context throughout the duration of the programme. Further research could usefully explore this in relation to instrumental pedagogy, neoliberal positioning and returnee agency. Finally, the relative values of the overseas programme as understood by returnees warrant further investigation, particularly in regard to aspects of practical, cultural and educational understanding relating to instrumental learning in China, the relationship between neoliberal and traditional values and support for the development of instrumental and vocal pedagogy within China.

Note

1 Associated Board of the Royal Schools of Music – a UK-based music performance and theory examination system available in some urban areas of China.

References

Ai, B. and L. Wang (2017), 'Homeland Integration: An Academic Returnee's Experiences in Chinese Universities', *International Journal of Qualitative Methods*, 16: 1–9.

Bai, B. (2021), 'Piano Learning in the Context of Schooling during China's "Piano Craze" and Beyond: Motivations and Pathways', *Music Education Research*, 23 (4): 512–26.

Braun, V. and V. Clarke (2006), 'Using Thematic Analysis in Psychology', *Qualitative Research in Psychology*, 3 (2): 77–101.

Chang, B. and P. McLaren (2018), 'Emerging Issues of Teaching and Social Justice in Greater China: Neoliberalism and Critical Pedagogy in Hong Kong', *Policy Futures in Education*, 16 (6): 781–803.

Duckett, J. (2020), 'Neoliberalism, Authoritarian Politics and Social Policy in China', *Development and Change*, 51 (2): 523–39.

Ford, B. (2020), 'Can Culturally Specific Perspectives to Teaching Western Classical Music Benefit International Students? A Call to Re-examine "What the Teacher Does"', *Frontiers in Education*, 5: 113. Available online: https://doi.org/10.3389/feduc.2020.00113

Gu, Q. and M. Schweisfurth (2015), 'Transnational Connections, Competences and Identities: Experiences of Chinese International Students after their Return "Home"', *British Educational Research Journal*, 41 (6): 947–70.

Guo, W. and L. J. Cosaitis (2020), 'A Cutting Edge Method in Chinese Piano Education: The Xindi Applied Piano Pedagogy', *Higher Education Studies*, 10 (1): 7–15.

Haddon, E. (2019), 'Perspectives of Chinese Students on Studying MA Music Programmes in a UK University', *ORFEU*, 4 (2): 30–58.

Hao, J., W. Wen and A. Welch (2016), 'When Sojourners Return: Employment Opportunities and Challenges facing High-skilled Chinese Returnees', *Asian and Pacific Migration Journal*, 25 (1): 22–40.

Hao, X., K. Yan, S. Guo and M. Wang (2017), 'Chinese Returnees' Motivation, Post Return Status and Impact of Return: A Systematic Review', *Asian and Pacific Migration Journal*, 26 (1): 143–57.

HESA (2022), 'Higher Education Student Statistics: UK, 2020/21 – Where Students Come From and Go To Study'. Available online: https://www.hesa.ac.uk/data-and-analysis/students/where-from (accessed 12 May 2022).

Kong, S. H. (2021), 'A Study of Students' Perceptions of Parental Influence on Students' Musical Instrument Learning in Beijing, China', *Music Education Research*, 23 (3): 287–99.

Leung, B. W. and G. E. McPherson (2010), 'Students' Motivation in Studying Music: The Hong Kong Context', *Research Studies in Music Education*, 32 (2): 155–68.

Li, L. and G. J. Rivers (2018), 'An Inquiry into the Delivering of a British Curriculum in China', *Teaching in Higher Education*, 23 (7): 785–801.

McCaig, C. (2018), *The Marketisation of English Higher Education*, Bingley: Emerald Publishing.

Mok, K. H. (2021), 'Managing Neo-liberalism with Chinese Characteristics: The Rise of Education Markets and Higher Education Governance in China', *International Journal of Educational Development*, 84: 102401.

Mullen, J. (2019), 'Music Education for Some: Music Standards at the Nexus of Neoliberal Reforms and Conservative Values', *Action, Criticism, and Theory for Music Education*, 18 (1): 44–7.

Pan, S. (2021), 'Covid-19 and the Neo-liberal Paradigm in Higher Education: Changing Landscape', *Asian Education and Development Studies*, 10 (2): 322–35.

Wang, Y., X. Liu and Z. Zhang (2018), 'An Overview of E-learning in China: History, Challenges and Opportunities', *Research in Comparative and International Education*, 13 (1): 195–210.

Watkins, D. (2003), 'Teacher Thinking and Practice from a Chinese Cultural Perspective: Lessons for East and West', in F. Salili and R. Hoosain (eds), *Teaching, Learning, and Motivation in a Multicultural Context*, 243–58, Charlotte: Information Age Publishing.

Xu, C. L. (2021), 'Portraying the "Chinese International Students": A Review of English-language and Chinese-language Literature on Chinese International Students (2015–2020)', *Asia Pacific Education Review*. Available online: https://doi.org/10.1007/s12564-021-09731-8

Yang, M. (2007), 'East Meets West in the Concert Hall: Asians and Classical Music in the Century of Imperialism, Post-Colonialism, and Multiculturalism', *Asian Music*, 38 (1): 1–30.

Zhang, W. and M. Bray (2017), 'Micro-neoliberalism in China: Public-private Interactions at the Confluence of Mainstream and Shadow Education', *Journal of Education Policy*, 32 (1): 63–81.

Zheng, Y. and B.-W. Leung (2021a), 'Cultivating Music Students' Creativity in Piano Performance: A Multiple-case Study in China', *Music Education Research*, 23 (5): 594–608.

Zheng, Y. and B.-W. Leung (2021b), 'Perceptions of Developing Creativity in Piano Performance and Pedagogy: An Interview Study from the Chinese Perspective', *Research Studies in Music Education*. Available online: https://doi.org/10.1177/1321103X211033473

Chapter 13

Swedish Dance Music Scenes, Female Career Trajectories and the Neoliberal Shift

Anna Gavanas

Introduction

This chapter examines the effects of neoliberalism on electronic dance music (EDM) scenes in Sweden and shows how female participants who were active as club organizers, designers and decorators in the 1980s and early 1990s underground club scenes used their skills to advance a do-it-yourself (DIY) career as (sub)cultural entrepreneurs from the mid-1990s onwards. While the overwhelming majority of the literature on gender and EDM culture highlights the experiences of DJs or club audiences (e.g. Farrugia, 2012; Gavanas and Reitsamer, 2013; Pini, 2001), this chapter widens the focus by including 'support personnel' (Becker, 1982). The alternative perspectives of these (sub)cultural entrepreneurs bring new light to the gendered working conditions under neoliberalism as their career trajectories differ significantly from those of (male) DJs.

Entrepreneurship in the context of underground music scenes has negative connotations. It tends to evoke commercialization and purely profit-driven purposes, thus being associated with notions of inauthenticity and 'selling out' (Gavanas, 2009; Trondman, Lekberg and Bjälesjö, 2022). However, subcultural entrepreneurs involved in small-scale businesses in local scenes are driven by a DIY ethos to create spaces for people with similar experiences and a passion for subcultural music and alternative politics who are aiming to make a living as cultural workers (e.g. Reitsamer, 2023). According to Haenfler's (2018) study on creative workers in Straight Edge scenes in the United States, DIY is characterized by a prioritization of creative control, authenticity and community over mass appeal, individualized notions of musicianship and economic profit. Similarly, Bennett and Guerra (2019) argue that DIY has contributed significantly to articulations of resistance to capitalism and has more recently become 'a counter-force to neoliberalism' (p. 12). The DIY dispositions and communal values appropriated by participants in youth-oriented post-punk scenes and rave subcultures in the 1980s and early 1990s have lived on as they move into their adult lives and forge their DIY careers by transforming their 'subcultural capital' (Thornton, 1995) into cultural and economic capital (Bennett and Hodkinson, 2012; Haenfler, 2018; McRobbie, 2016).

Taking female pioneers in the early Swedish EDM scene as example, this chapter shows how young women acquired their DIY skills and became (sub)cultural entrepreneurs as they grew older. The chapter is based on an interview study with male and female participants in the early Swedish underground EDM scene of the 1980s and 1990s (Gavanas and Öström, 2023). Between 2018 and 2022, 100 interviews were conducted with DJs, MCs, decorators, organizers, dancers and other creative participants in the rare groove, warehouse, rave/acid house and jungle/reggae scenes in the Swedish cities of Gothenburg, Malmö/Lund and Stockholm. Among these interviewees, thirty were female participants, which reflects the significant underrepresentation of women at all levels of the EDM scenes (female:pressure, 2022; Wolfe, 2021). The majority of these interviewees had white middle-class backgrounds and higher education in cultural industry professions.

The chapter begins with a brief description of the DIY EDM club culture of the 1980s and early 1990s in Sweden as an illuminating example of the impact of neoliberal cultural policies on cultural entrepreneurship (part one). In the second part of the chapter, I discuss the gendered division of labour in music scenes and the career paths of female DIY pioneers that emerged in the EDM context. The chapter concludes with the observation that the early EDM underground scene in Sweden underwent a neoliberal restructuring, following the neoliberal restructuring of Swedish cultural policy in the early 1990s. As a result, like all sectors of the cultural industries (e.g. Hesmondhalgh and Baker, 2011; McRobbie, 2016; Standing, 2011), the EDM club economy is characterized by precarious working conditions and stark patterns of social inequality. Although the gendered division of labour assigned female participants to less prestigious 'supportive' roles, some female pioneers in the early Swedish EDM scene who worked as decorators, fashion designers and/or club organizers were able to cultivate skills, knowledge and abilities to forge a DIY career with small businesses. Thus, despite an unfavourable gendered division of labour, female pioneers were part of the neoliberal restructuring of EDM club culture and the commercialization of that culture could even operate as a stepping stone to remain sustainably within Sweden's cultural industries.

The Swedish Case: From Anti-commercialism to 'Entrepreneurial' Sweden

Swedish cultural policy has been a major factor in providing, as well as in restricting, space for a broad variety of cultural expressions. Music schools, youth recreation centres and immigrant and cultural associations have operated as state- and municipal-funded sites for fostering youth development (Björk, 2009; Gavanas, 2018; Håkansson, Lundin and Nilsson, 2009). Simultaneously, the cultural and creative industries are dependent on the supply of appropriate and low-cost spaces facilitating socially embedded processes of creativity and valuation (Jansson and Gavanas, 2022). In EDM underground culture, the demand for cheap and functional premises is partly due to the inability to pay high rents and partly due to the need for spaces that do not disturb neighbours and other ongoing activities.

Against the background of its anti-commercial leftist cultural policies in the 1970s and 1980s, Sweden is an interesting case in Western Europe for examining the effects of neoliberalism on creative work using DIY EDM scenes as an example.

The introduction of neoliberal cultural policies occurred during the peak of the 'people's home' (*folkhemmet*) movement of social democracy, when cultural policies prioritized state-funded associations (*föreningssverige*) that provided infrastructure and venues for cultural life as an alternative to the commercial sector (Jansson and Gavanas, 2022). These cultural policies also became (indirectly) beneficial to underground club culture in the 1970s, 1980s and early 1990s. For instance, when DIY pioneers looked for inexpensive spaces (where strict alcohol licensing laws could also be circumvented), they found venues through state-funded migrant cultural associations that were open to new international musical influences (Gavanas and Öström, 2023). Many EDM pioneers in rare groove, house, techno and jungle/drum and bass music had migrant backgrounds and were connected to migrant associations through their parents. State-funded immigrant associations thus indirectly became platforms for early underground EDM clubs, such as Gambian, Yugoslavian and French associations. In addition, state-funded cultural associations and spaces (including carnival, jazz and art associations) founded by underground pioneers also became platforms for early EDM scenes.

When disco music came to Stockholm in the 1970s via soul and funk music, it was played not only at discotheques and nightclubs but also at municipal youth recreation centres. Many legendary DJs in Sweden from the 1960s onwards started their careers at youth recreation centres. One of them was DJ René Hedemyr, who later became one of the best-known pioneers on the house music scene in Sweden as a member of the DJ/studio collective and record label Swemix, founded in 1986, and a co-founder of the legendary Bat Club in 1988 (Gavanas, 2020).

However, the first EDM waves from disco to house/techno and jungle/drum and bass were introduced to Stockholm through translocal flows of traveling pioneers, music (via radio, magazines and vinyl records) and styles (dances, aesthetics and fashions) (Gavanas, 2020). Pioneering Swedish DJs and club promoters travelled mainly to the United States and the United Kingdom and were inspired by the new sounds, styles and dance cultures. Commonly, these pioneers came from resourceful contexts with the means and time to travel or connect through networks. The DJ and club promoter Claes Hedberg, for example, worked on various ships between the UK and the Swedish west coast from the late 1960s onwards, and his uncle, who was an airline pilot, brought records from the United States that had not yet been released in Sweden. Claes also gained interest and knowledge in EDM culture by visiting the famous club Studio 54 in New York and started DJing at nightclubs in Stockholm and other cities in Sweden. In the 1980s, the popularity of disco faded and mutated into house music scenes where similar developments can be discerned, with transnational pioneers 'importing' the new sounds and styles to nightclubs in Sweden (Gavanas, 2020).

Rave culture, and the preceding warehouse culture, differentiated themselves from this nightclub culture in terms of space and infrastructure (Melville, 2020). Rave and warehouse parties were located in unconventional outdoor or industrial settings anywhere inside and outside the city centres, and participants made a point of claiming previously 'un-danced' spaces. Moreover, with their DIY approach, warehouse and rave organizers were able to build sound, lighting and decoration from scratch. In other words, while disco was part of the public and formalized discotheque/nightclub industry, warehouse parties and raves were partly introduced as informal alternatives to this industry in terms of space and organization by loosely organized networks of supporters – as opposed to employees in discotheques and nightclubs. Underground EDM pioneers, influenced by trips to London, involved themselves in organizing underground DIY warehouse and rave parties in Stockholm and Gothenburg that were advertised to those 'in the know', aiming to attract a diverse mix of music fans, musicians, artists, fashionistas, designers and other young creative individuals (Gavanas, 2020; Gavanas and Öström, 2023). Per Sandström, a DJ and club organizer who was one of the pioneering actors on Stockholm's EDM club scene, told us in our conversation about the transformation that the club economy had undergone in the early 1990s:

> [In the 1980s] it was exhausting to run underground warehouse parties. One needed to build everything from scratch. There were no bars, but there was also an artistic freedom to create whatever one wanted. [. . .] It took about a week to prepare [a party] and then afterwards one had to do the cleaning. But we were young and in shape with the energy to pull it off. It was a hell of a grind, but it was fun! Later on [in the 1990s] it became more practical to promote clubs in existing commercial venues where one could just show up. In the 1990s, everything became sponsored and one could get pre-paid and it was much easier to organize clubs. [. . .] During the 1990s, the traditional venues [the night clubs] realized their mode of operation was no longer working and people [cultural entrepreneurs] started to promote clubs in various spaces. And companies started to sponsor club organizers [. . .] and there was a lot more money [in the commercial club industry].

As this quote illustrates, DJ crews in the 1980s organized underground club events according to the DIY principle, which meant that they did everything out of their own pocket and with their own hands. According to Sandström, this situation changed in the early 1990s: Commercial companies discovered their interest in the emerging club culture and began sponsoring club nights, which, in turn, allowed club hosts to offer free drinks and organize parties and fashion shows that were advertised with luxurious flyers with the logos of the respective companies. However, in the early 1990s, there was also an economic crisis in Sweden that affected the conditions for commercial actors and highlighted the precariousness of a cultural life depending on the volatile marketplace.

In the 1990s, Swedish cultural policies shifted away from a focus on anti-commercialism, socio-economic redistribution and social issues towards neoliberalism. As in other countries, such as the UK, this shift included a repositioning of the creative and cultural industries as sectors promising urban regeneration, economic growth and future employment, a promotion of entrepreneurialism and a focus on competitive international business models as well as a strengthening of collaboration between the public and commercial sectors in order to compete globally in media, IT and entertainment (Elmhorn, 2013; Gavanas, 2020; Nilsson, 2003). Consequently, state-funded cultural associations, which provided the spaces for the early EDM scene in Stockholm, Gothenburg and other Swedish cities, were replaced by commercial bars and nightclubs (Gavanas and Öström, 2023), and DJs and club organizers became ambulating promoters and multitasking freelancers who eliminated the nightclub owners' needs to employ resident DJs. This change corresponds to the shifting positions of DJs to cultural entrepreneurs in (trans)local EDM scenes in the late 1980s and early 1990s, marking a break with the previous employment practices of DJs.

In the 1970s and 1980s, many DJs in Sweden held 'residencies' at local clubs, where they played music several times a week to entertain particular audiences, with some of them even being employed by club owners, entertainment companies or other management. Similarly, in his study on the white gay club scene at the club The Saint, operating from 1980 to 1988 in New York City, Tim Lawrence (2013) illustrates how neoliberal shifts in employment practices in the 1980s were embedded into a more general shift towards one-off, flexible 'freelance' contracts that has become the hallmark of market-driven neoliberalism and employment practices in the cultural industries. These developments can also be observed in Swedish EDM scenes: From the 1990s onwards, DJs became self-employed entrepreneurs, combining DJing with other activities such as producing music, running record or clothing labels and organizing club nights (Gavanas, 2020). Participants in the DIY underground of the 1980s and early 1990s thus became part of the media, design and fashion industries. As the neoliberal shift took hold in cultural life, creativity became the key source of prosperity in post-industrial cities (Hesmondhalgh and Baker, 2011: 3), and Swedish DIY pioneers of the EDM underground club scene became multitasking entrepreneurs in overlapping creative sectors.

Compared to the previous working conditions where cultural workers held employment contracts, freelancing entrepreneurs became part of the generally precarious conditions in the cultural sector, driven by neoliberal 'flexploitation' (Gray, 2004). Precarity (Standing, 2011) is a hallmark of the cultural industries internationally, driven by economic, technological and sociocultural changes, such as the increasing importance of intellectual property and the development of urban property markets through the dynamics of gentrification (Hesmondhalgh and Baker, 2011: 4). Numerous scholars have explored the working conditions of musicians in diverse musical scenes by highlighting the endemic features of creative labour: precarious employment, low and sometimes non-existent wages, dense social networking, the holding of multiple jobs to sustain livelihoods and music--making and the blurring of work and leisure that often leads to self-exploitation (e.g. Banks, 2007; Hesmondhalgh and Baker, 2011). Moreover, in cultural production, the lines between paid and unpaid work and between professionals and amateurs are often blurred. It is not unusual for unpaid work to provide the basis for a reputation that allows cultural producers to turn professional, such as a fanzine writer or a musician who pays for their own recordings (Hesmondhalgh and Baker, 2011: 13). The underground EDM scene is a clear example of this sort of self-generated economic activity, which often involves self-exploitation, and the ways in which DIY activity and the skills acquired through its 'dance-party-rave' organization facilitate the careers of cultural entrepreneurs in creative work (McRobbie, 2016: 21).

Female Pioneers of the Early Swedish Club Scenes

Female pioneers of the Swedish EDM scenes in the late 1980s and early 1990s were part of the changing relationships internationally between culture and society associated with neoliberal economics in post-Fordist models of industry, which increasingly pushed cultural producers to adopt an entrepreneurial position (Gavanas, 2009; Gavanas and Öström, 2016; Gavanas and Reitsamer, 2013; Reitsamer, 2011, 2012, 2013). At the same time, these pioneers faced similar obstacles as female musicians in various other musical 'worlds' (Becker, 1982), such as jazz, rock, pop, rap, electronic music and Western art music, when seeking recognition as legitimate professionals (e.g. Buscatto, 2007; Cohen, 1997; Gavanas and Reitsamer, 2013; Hutton, 2006, Rodgers, 2010; Scharff, 2015; Whiteley, 2000). Numerous feminist studies conclude that female musicians face barriers to developing a sustainable career due to male homosocial network dynamics, genre-specific gendered practices and gendered representations in the media, including various forms of sexualization and racialization, as well as the 'burden of representation' (Puwar, 2004) placed on women and minorities working in white cis male-dominated professions. Moreover, the music industries continue to favour white cis men as normative figures in positions of power, while women are 'ghettoized' in PR work (Farrugia, 2012: 138). Gendered ideals and social network dynamics are consequently instrumental to accessing resources, gaining recognition and being able to make a living from music-making, but they are also part of wider economic and technological shifts, including digitalization and the emergence of the internet and social media.

In Sweden, as elsewhere in Europe, gendered practices in DIY underground club culture in the 1980s and 1990s constituted barriers to female career trajectories in musical worlds when it came to prestigious positions such as DJs. There are some notable exceptions, such as DJ Pamela Leal Viñals, who has been a house DJ mainly in the lesbian and gay/queer scene since 1993 and is still working (Gavanas and Öström, 2016). Through the early history of DJing in Sweden, we have been able to trace a handful of forgotten but important female DJs, such as Eva Carlsson, Inger Flyckt and Birgitta Söderberg, who worked as DJs as early as the 1960s and 1970s (Gavanas, 2020). However, the same skill sets that were expected from the majority of female pioneers within the gendered division of labour (i.e. women taking on a wide array of organizational, promotional, clerical, social, administrative and aesthetic tasks) were simultaneously instrumental to their (self-)employability in other areas of the cultural industries. When Swedish dance music scenes entered the neoliberal era, some actors, including women, were in a position to launch DIY careers in the cultural industries out of their previous unpaid or low-paid work in design, fashion, media, retail and club promotion. It is important to keep in mind, however, that all these cultural sectors are characterized by precarious working conditions. For instance, DJs who remained active in EDM culture after the 1990s faced precarious conditions when payment levels dropped and digitalization made DJs more dispensable to club owners (Gavanas, 2020; Gavanas and Öström, 2016).

In Sweden, women played an important role for the development of club culture and EDM scenes in the 1980s and 1990s, not primarily as DJs but as decorators, promoters, clubwear importers, shop owners, dancers, costume and outfit designers, writers, photographers, door staff and other forgotten and low-status but indispensable supportive roles. 'Support personnel', as Becker argues in his seminal book *Art Worlds (1982)*, is fundamental for the creation of artistic works because they are a product of the cooperative activity of many people. Becker's sociological understanding of artistic works is useful because it focuses on the complexity of the cooperative networks through which the arts happen and points to the importance of conventions and the division of labour that are gendered and racialized in art words (e.g. Bourdieu, 2019 [1998]).

Drawing upon Becker's (1982) conception of art world, Lund and Trondman (2022) discuss in the book *The Hultsfred Festival: Punk Ethos, Festival Spirit and Entrepreneurship* the female participants who were part of the organization of this DIY-driven festival that took place in the Swedish town Hultsfred from 1986 to 2017. They found that despite the DIY punk ethos that informed the festival organization, the male organizers had prestigious visionary roles as the curators of the festival line-up, while the female organizers tended to work in administration, food services and other supporting functions. The organization of the festival was thus based on a gendered division of labour which reproduced the historically established distinction between 'male creativity' and 'female support'.

In our research on the development of club culture and EDM scenes in Sweden (Gavanas and Öström, 2016, 2023), we found similar patterns to those identified by Lund and Trondman in the DIY punk scene: male participants took the front positions as DJs and club organizers, while female participants often worked as support personnel and their creative activities were considered as less important compared to those of the male DJs, music producers and club organizers. However, some of today's celebrities in the Swedish music scene owe their careers to supporting and forgotten female and migrant underground pioneers and subcultural entrepreneurs, since they enabled the spaces where alternative music could be played at a time when the Swedish popular music scene was dominated by pop and rock music. Before techno and house music became mainstream in Sweden, underground participants from a range of socio-economic and ethnic backgrounds built the infrastructure for the EDM scene where later male DJs like Avicii and the Swedish House Mafia became international mega stars.

Malena, Elinor and Kajsa

The early pioneers of the underground EDM club scene were driven by DIY ethos, collectively creating new dance music experiences and aesthetics in unconventional spaces. These underground EDM events also became a breeding ground for women to forge a DIY career in music, fashion and media because, as Pini (2001) argues, the collectivist DIY rave culture of the 1990s, the non-commercial and transgressive dance floor and the PLUR aesthetic, which included rave culture's crucial ideals of Peace, Love, Unity and Respect, were liberating for female participants and opened up an opportunity to successfully challenge and transcend gendered barriers and ideals. Among the thirty female study participants, about a handful left the cultural industries to work in, for example, social services, medical professions and government work or are barely getting by working in different jobs, but most earn their living in creative professions in the media, design or fashion industries. In the following, I will describe the career trajectories of three women whose trajectories correspond with a majority of the stories told by interviewees who participated in supporting roles in the early DIY underground EDM music scenes where men represented the scene in the public eye as DJs and curators of club nights.

At the end of the 1980s, Malena studied fashion design at a garment-making school in Gothenburg and got to know a gay man who worked in the coat check of a queer club in Gothenburg. Together, they started a pioneering queer underground club, for which Malena created decorations and party costumes such as hotpants, cat suits and wings from plastic, sequins, PVC, vinyl and feathers, and inspired by Paris's club culture, she booked pioneering male house/techno DJs. The queer underground club was inclusive, since Malena and her friend charged only a symbolic entrance fee, and by welcoming everybody interested in extravagant and transgressive clubbing experiences, the club became a haven for transvestites, queers and acid house freaks. In 1993, Malena moved to Stockholm and continued to organize gay club nights for a few years and continues to work as a designer, decorator and tailor with her own company. The skills she acquired during her studies, working life and on the early underground EDM scenes became crucial for both the success of the queer club nights that Malena and her friend pioneered in Gothenburg and subsequently in her professional working life presumably furthering the development of her design and fashion company.

Elinor participated in the early Swedish rave scene as a dancer and decorator and later moved on to higher education in trade and graphic design at a number of different universities in Sweden. As part of various rave collective and club crews, she began making backdrops for DIY clubs and festivals in Gothenburg and Stockholm in the early 1990s and started a decoration collective with a female friend, while their boyfriends at the time were pioneering DJs and rave organizers in the trance scene. With their DIY crew, Elinor and her female friend toured Sweden and Europe making backdrops for the Boone festival in Portugal, the VOOV festival in Germany and parties in Copenhagen, Paris and Prague. In 1996, Elinor opened a rave fashion shop in Gothenburg, supported by another female rave fashion entrepreneur in Stockholm. Elinor imported clubwear from Bali and India (fractal and tie-dye wear) as well as the UK (e.g. the label Cyberdog) and kept a close connection to the rave and EDM scene. After closing her shop in 2003, Elinor moved on to work first in sales at a major clothing company, then as a decorator and, since 2009, as a graphic designer with her own design company. Her aesthetic skills have thus transferred to a career in the cultural industries.

In the early 1990s, Kajsa lived in London and participated in the early jungle scene by working as a journalist, mainly on a volunteer basis, for a music magazine for which she interviewed artists and wrote about jungle events. However, the male jungle DJs and music producers Kajsa supported did not take her to the clubs because, as she told us in the interview, they felt that 'these clubs are not good places for a girl like you' and that 'you are too white and naïve to make it there' (quotes from Kajsa). Since Kajsa was not paid for her work as a journalist, she eventually had to return to Sweden. In Gothenburg, she started importing jungle records and opened a jungle club with a male and a female friend, where the male friend was a DJ. In addition, Kajsa booked male jungle artists from London and introduced the style to a Swedish audience. In 1997, Kajsa moved to Stockholm and started working as a television journalist for a music channel, for which she did music features. Today, she still works as a journalist. The skills and knowledge she acquired in the jungle scene, combined with her education at the Gothenburg University school of journalism and her previous university studies in international relations in Switzerland and the UK, were probably conducive to her DIY career in the media industries.

As the stories told by Malena, Elinor and Kajsa demonstrate, many female pioneers started out as contributors to early DIY underground scenes in their twenties, which together with higher education could be described as a stepping stone for DIY careers in the cultural industries. In contrast, with a few exceptions, DJing has not been a sustainable way to make a living in Sweden from the 1990s onwards, and up until that time, it was mainly a male profession. In the 1970s and 1980s, when DJing was professionalized in Sweden, DJs could earn a full-time living, employed by discotheques and entertainment companies. In the late 1980s, club culture slowly became a mass phenomenon and as a result, DJs also started to work as promoters running mobile club concepts. This emerging type of entrepreneurship, which combines DJing with promoting clubs, getting sponsorship/PR deals and running record labels and shops, has become a precondition to survive economically in the club scene, but technological and economic factors keep making the conditions volatile and precarious. Thus, transitioning and working in adjacent creative sectors such as media, fashion, design and PR became viable career trajectories for some female pioneers who helped to build the infrastructure of the DIY club scenes of the 1980s and early 1990s.

Conclusion

This chapter has shown that the underground EDM club scene that emerged in Sweden in the 1980s and early 1990s was inspired by a DIY ethos and went on to be captured by neoliberalism and the corresponding cultural policies that promoted cultural entrepreneurship from the mid-1990s onwards. In this context, subcultural capital was transferred from cultural producers into careers in the cultural industries. I have also shown that there was a gendered division of labour within the early underground EDM scenes, where men (with a few exceptions) took the prestigious roles of DJs and club organizers, while women often performed more anonymous aesthetic tasks, such as decoration and design. Female pioneers who worked as 'support personnel' were able to use their subcultural and trained skills as they continued as cultural entrepreneurs in the media, PR and fashion industries (see Bennett and Guerra, 2019; Haenfler, 2018; McRobbie, 2016). Some of these DIY skills, which also required higher education, proved marketable, while sustainable careers in DJing have been the privilege of a few (male) exceptions. All these choices are of course embedded in larger political, economic and class structures that create differing opportunities and hinderances to transitioning successfully from DIY volunteer work and (higher) education to a professional working life and that favour the white middle class, which possesses cultural capital and economic resources and has access to higher education and family support (Haenfler, 2018).

Since the late 1980s, female participants in the Swedish EDM scenes have founded support networks such as Gloria Ladies, Sister Sthlm, Yoko DJs, Femtastic, Grupp 13 and Radical Love Crew, which actively seek to change the gendered division of labour in the EDM club scenes (Gavanas and Öström, 2016, 2023). As a result, women, non-binary and trans* cultural producers have become more widely represented and visible as DJs, visual artists, curators and club promoters as well as in the media. At the same time, however, the working conditions in the Swedish cultural industries – and especially in the music sector – have become increasingly precarious because of neoliberalism. DJs and club organizers have become increasingly dispensable due to big-tech (post-)capitalist developments in digitalization, streaming platforms and social media. Moreover, there are fewer and fewer club venues available for club organizers with an interest in creating alternative cultural spaces, since gentrification is driven by commercial interests and cultural policies by market liberalism. In order to change this situation, the Swedish state would need to reinvigorate cultural policies by prioritizing state- and municipality-funded venues, gender equality and ethnic and class inclusivity over the commercialization of cultural life.

References

Banks, M. (2007), *The Politics of Cultural Work*, Basingstoke: Palgrave.
Becker, H. (1982), *Art Worlds*, Berkeley: University of California Press.

Bennett, A and P. Guerra (2019), *DIY Cultures and Underground Music Scenes*, London: Routledge.
Bennett, A. and P. Hodkinson, eds (2012), *Ageing and Youth Cultures. Music, Style and Identity*, Oxford: Bloomsbury.
Björk, F. (2009), 'Gitarrsolon som folkbildning och hantverk: Bland proffs och amatörer på musikhus och folkhögskolor', in L. Berggren, M. Greiff and B. Horgby (eds), *Populärmusik, uppror och samhälle*, Skrifter med historiska perspektiv, 8, Malmö: Malmö högskola.
Bourdieu, P. (2019), *Den Manliga Dominansen*, trans. B. Englund, Stockholm: Daidalos [originally published as *La domination masculine*, 1998].
Buscatto, M. (2007), 'Women in Artistic Profession. An Emblematic Paradigm for Gender Studies', *Social Cohesion and Development*, 2 (1): 69–77.
Cohen, S. (1997), 'Men Making a Scene: Rock Music and the Production of Gender', in S. Whitley (ed.), *Sexing the Groove: Popular Music and Gender*, 17–36, New York: Routledge.
Elmhorn, C. (2013), *Från hot till löfte: Stockholms ekonomiska omvandling 1945-2010*, Stockholm: Stockholmia förlag.
Farrugia, R. (2012), *Beyond the Dance Floor. Female DJs, Technology and Electronic Dance Music Culture*, Chicago: Intellect, The University of Chicago Press.
female:pressure (2022), 'FACTS 2022'. Available online: https://femalepressure.wordpress.com (accessed 13 April 2023).
Gavanas, A. (2009), '"You Better be Listening to My Fucking Music You Bastard!" Teknologi, genusifiering och andlighet bland DJs på elektroniska dansmusikscener i Berlin, London och Stockholm', in H. Ganetz, A. Gavanas, H. Huss and A. Werner (eds), *Rundgång: genus och populärmusik*, 77–120, Stockholm: Makadam.
Gavanas, A. (2018), 'Klubbkuturens värde i den politiska ekonomin. Disco och rave i Stockholms dansmusikhistoria', in J. Björkman and A. Jarrick (eds), *Musikens Makt*, 249–64, Göteborg: Makadam.
Gavanas, A. (2020), *Från Diskofeber till Rejvhysteri i den svenska dansmusikhistorien*, Stockholm: Stockholmia.
Gavanas, A. and A. Öström (2016), *DJ-liv. Historien om hur DJn erövrade Stockholm*, Möklinta: Gidlunds.
Gavanas, A. and A. Öström (2023), *Tillbaka till underjorden. 80/90talens klubbrevolution i Sverige*, Möklinta: Gidlunds.
Gavanas, A. and R. Reitsamer (2013), 'DJ Technologies, Social Networks and Gendered Trajectories in European DJ Cultures', in B. Attias, A. Gavanas and H. Rietveld (eds), *DJ Culture in the Mix. Power, Technology, and Social Change in Electronic Dance Music*, 51–78, London: Bloomsbury.
Gray, A. (2004), *Unsocial Europe. Social Protection or Flexploitation?*, London: Pluto Press.
Haenfler, R. (2018), 'The Entrepreneurial (Straight) Edge: How Participation in DIY Music Cultures Translates to Work and Careers', *Cultural Sociology*, 12 (2): 174–92.
Håkansson, P., J. Lundin and F. Nilsson (2009), 'Rock'n'roll och folkbildarnas gränser', in L. Berggren, M. Greiff and B. Horgby (eds), *Populärmusik, uppror och samhälle*, Skrifter med historiska perspektiv, 8, Malmö: Malmö högskola.
Hesmondhalgh, D. and S. Baker (2011), *Creative Labour. Media Work in Three Cultural Industries*, London: Routledge.
Hutton, F. (2006), *Risky Pleasures? Club Cultures and Feminine Identities*, Burlington: Ashgate.

Jansson, J. and A. Gavanas (2022), 'Curated by Pioneers, Spaces and Resistance. The Development of Electronic Dance Music in Stockholm', in B. J. Hracs, T. Brydges, T. Haisch, A. Hauge, J. Jansson and J. Sjoholm (eds), *Culture, Creativity and Economy: Collaborative Practices, Value Creation and Spaces of Creativity*, 124–38, London: Routledge.

Lawrence, T. (2013), 'The Forging of a White Gay Aesthetic at the Saint, 1980-4', in B. Attias, A. Gavanas and H. Rietveld (eds), *DJ Culture in the Mix. Power, Technology, and Social Change in Electronic Dance Music*, 219–46, London: Bloomsbury.

Lund, A. and M. Trondman (2022), 'Så småningom lossnar det. Hultsfredsfestivalen och kvinnornas entreprenörskap', in M. Trondman, R. Lekberg and J. Bjälesjö (eds), *Hultsfredsfestivalen: punkens etos, festivalens anda och entreprenörskapets vara*, 274–317, Stockholm: Carlssons förlag.

McRobbie, A. (2016), *Be Creative*, Cambridge: Polity Press.

Melville, C. (2020), *It's a London Thing. How Rare Groove, Acid House and Jungle Remapped the City*, Manchester: Manchester University Press.

Nilsson, S. (2003), *Kulturens nya vågor. Kultur, kulturpolitik och kulturutveckling i Sverige*, Malmö: Polyvalent.

Pini, M. (2001), *Club Cultures and Female Subjectivity: The Move from House to House*, Basingstoke: Palgrave.

Puwar, N. (2004), *Space Invaders. Race, Gender and Bodies Out of Place*, Oxford: Berg.

Reitsamer, R. (2011), 'The DIY Careers of Techno and Drum'n'Bass DJs in Vienna', *Dancecult: Journal of Electronic Dance Music Culture*, 3 (1): 28–43.

Reitsamer, R. (2012), 'Female Pressure: A Translocal Feminist Youth-oriented Cultural Network', *Continuum: Journal of Media & Cultural Studies*, 26 (3): 399–408.

Reitsamer, R. (2013), *Die Do-it-yourself-Karrieren der DJs. Über die Arbeit in elektronischen Musikszenen*, Bielefeld: Transcript.

Reitsamer, R. (2023), 'Youth and DIY Music and Media-making', in A. Bennett (ed.), *The Bloomsbury Handbook of Popular Music and Youth Culture*, 595–614, New York: Bloomsbury Academic.

Rodgers, T. (2010), *Pink Noises: Women on Electronic Music and Sound*, Durham: Duke University Press.

Scharff, C. (2015), 'Blowing Your Own Trumpet: Exploring the Gendered Dynamics of Selfpromotion in the Classical Music Profession', *The Sociological Review*, 63 (S1): 97–112.

Standing, G. (2011), *The Precariat: The New Dangerous Class*, London: Bloomsbury.

Thornton, S. (1995), *Club Cultures: Music, Media and Subcultural Capital*, Cambridge: Polity Press.

Trondman, M., R. Lekberg and J. Bjälesjö, eds (2022), *Hultsfredsfestivalen. Punkens etos, festivalens anda, entreprenörskapets vara*, Stockholm: Carlssons bokförlag.

Whiteley, S. (2000), *Women and Popular Music. Sexuality, Identity and Subjectivity*, London: Routledge.

Wolfe, P. (2021), *Women in the Studio. Creativity, Control and Gender in Popular Music Sound Production*, London: Routledge.

Chapter 14

The Unstable Lightness of Rock Once Again

Careers, Trajectories and DIY Cultures in Portuguese Indie Rock

Paula Guerra, Ana Oliveira and Andy Bennett

DIY Music Careers in a Neoliberal Atmosphere[1]

In the early twentieth century, do-it-yourself (DIY) referred to creating, repairing and/or modifying something without using an experienced craftsman or professional. It later came to encompass a wide range of cultural and creative practices (Bennett and Guerra, 2019a; Guerra, 2017, 2018). While its musical roots date back to the 1950s and the rock 'n' roll era, DIY gained greater prominence with the emergence of punk from the mid-1970s. Based on a logic of empowerment and musicians' ownership of the means of production as an alternative to the traditional and mainstream production and promotion circuits, several punk bands created their production platforms and organized themselves into networks, fostering the emergence of alternative distribution circuits to those dominating the music-cultural industries. During the 1980s and 1990s, the DIY ethos remained strongly linked to the punk aesthetic but extended to other music genres and spheres of alternative cultural production (Bennett, 2018) as well as to other sociocultural domains, including environment/climate change, animal rights, veganism and the fight against poverty and racism (Haenfler, 2018; McKay, 1998). Once the different genres and music scenes, such as punk, metal and electronic dance music, expanded beyond the Anglo-Saxon context, DIY culture followed and now manifests in various local cultures globally, including the Global South (Guerra, 2020). Despite local specificities, music scenes and DIY cultures are now a transglobal phenomenon. At the same time, they occur at the intersections between art and economics, resistance and subsistence and/or existence, ethos and praxis (Guerra, 2021):

> While by no means eschewing anti-hegemonic concerns, this transformation of DIY into what might reasonably be termed a global 'alternative culture' has also seen it evolve to a level of professionalism that is aimed towards ensuring aesthetic and, where possible, economic sustainability of cultural production practices. (Bennett and Guerra, 2019: 7)

The conceptualization of a DIY career requires understanding it as a professional trajectory that stems from the need to manage the 'pathological effects', both political and economic, of post-industrialization and the risk and uncertainty that characterize contemporary societies. In the risk society of late modernity (Beck, 1992; Giddens, 2002), guided by neoliberal configurations, ideals and narratives, not only are biographical trajectories more uncertain and unpredictable, but processes are also becoming increasingly individualized and/or atomized (Chapman, 2013; Dale, 2016; Everts, Hitters and Berkers, 2021; Gavanas and Reitsamer, 2016).

DIY careers have emerged as a response to this context, asserting themselves as cultural-creative expression, materialized in economic practices and assuming themselves as viable professional occupations (Bennett, 2018; Bennett and Guerra, 2019; Guerra, 2018; Oliveira, 2020). Technological innovations and the internet have made a decisive contribution to this through the emergence of a platform economy (YouTube, TikTok, Instagram) that makes uploading and publishing content extremely simple and capitalizes on content created by independent cultural creators. Although they do not provide a total democratization of cultural-creative production processes, the role of DIY careers in enabling more people to produce and disseminate their own cultural products is transforming cultural production practices into professional careers.

Yet if a DIY career remains linked to the original DIY ethos and independence, there is now recognition of the need to achieve a sustainable lifestyle in which notions such as lifelong employment or a regular salary no longer hold (Bennett, 2018; Threadgold, 2018). Considering the uncertainty in employment trajectories over the last twenty years, led by the Global North and replicated in the Global South, Standing (2011) argues that such changes have created a new type of social category: the *precariat*, comprising those who live and work in precarious conditions because they are dependent on short-term employment opportunities with little prospect for stable career development; moreover, they are at the mercy of market fluctuations and the cyclical crises of capitalism. When building artistic and creative careers, it is common to navigate between different part-time and short-term jobs to earn an income, leading many people to mobilize their often informally acquired skills to manage their professional trajectories. This is the re-conversion of 'subcultural capital' (Thornton, 1995) and the activation of DIY skills, of resistance, of achievement, of freedom and of collective action, to manage the uncertainty and precariousness that currently characterize the labour market and society (Haenfler, 2018).

This chapter is concerned with DIY careers as an employability pattern (Guerra, 2010, 2016; Oliveira, 2020) affected by the impact of the neoliberal world view on the trajectories of Portuguese indie rock scene participants. We first examine the social positions of the protagonists of the Portuguese indie rock scene, focusing on gender and social class and highlighting the sociopolitical and economic changes that occurred between 2010 and 2020, marked by the economic and financial crisis that impacted Portugal between 2011 and 2014. We seek to understand how these social actors have built their professional creative DIY careers in terms of their different positions within the indie rock scene, the crossings or contamination with other artistic domains, their tacit and formal competencies, their school, professional and informal qualifications and their promotion, dissemination, communication and agency networks. We then propose a typology synthesis for reading these careers in the Portuguese context, based on the most extensive and intensive research carried out on the sociology of Portuguese culture. This exercise of constant combination between DIY and do-it-together (DIT) creation and production questions the boundaries between the professional and the amateur, and the artistic contaminations between both arts and music, and between music and the 'lifeworld'.

The data were collected in the periods 2005–10[2] and 2015–20.[3] Using a mixed-methods approach (Crossley and Edwards, 2016), we conducted 273 in-depth and semi-structured interviews (202 interviews in the first study and 71 in the second) with individuals involved in the production and mediation of Portuguese indie rock, including musicians, promoters, record label heads, music venue programmers, managers and journalists. In both cases, we used snowball sampling to achieve an extensive territorial coverage of the indie rock scenes. All interviews were audio-recorded and fully transcribed. The analysis was carried out by building key categories for data interpretation, based on the interview scripts. The interviews were subjected to a thematic content analysis. Multiple correspondence analysis was used for the construction of the typology.

The Social Space of Portuguese Indie Rock

As in other music scenes and other geographical contexts (Berkers and Schaap, 2018; Gavanas and Reitsamer, 2016; Guerra, 2016; Guerra and Oliveira, 2019; Leonard, 2017; Reddington, 2021; Reitsamer, 2012), male hegemony is a defining feature of the Portuguese indie rock scene. This is particularly visible in our 2010 research, where 89 per cent of our sample was male. The underrepresentation of women was mainly evident among the older generations, where there was an almost exclusive male presence. The difficulties in advancing a music career expressed by the few active women included exclusion from scene networks; gender stereotypes of supposed female characteristics, their interests, abilities, skills and roles assigned to them by society; horizontal and vertical segregation, which relegates women to less favourable employment conditions, income, power and recognition in the field of popular music production; difficulties in balancing professional and family life, especially with children; and objectification and sexual harassment. These experiences are in line with other research (Richards, 2016; Smith et al., 2019). Ten years later, we still had a mainly male group of interview partners, but the proportion of women had increased to 21 per cent. Indeed, as expressed in the interviews, greater problematization of gender inequalities and prevailing heteronormative constructions of gender and sexuality in the wake of feminist-queer movements and #MeToo have created more awareness of and engagement with gender issues, especially among younger generations. This is shown in the recognition of the underrepresentation of women and the need to change the current configuration of the indie rock scene. We found that the greater problematization of gender inequalities has been translated into promoting the reduction of differences between men and women when composing festival line-ups and programming music venues, so music becomes a space for acceptance and tolerance. The collective and promoter Maternidade,[4] formed in 2014 in Lisbon, and its transdisciplinary, feminist and queer festival Rama em Flor[5] are examples. They want to counteract the marginalization of women in concert line-ups as well as the *machismo* and paternalism they consider institutionalized in Portuguese society. It also manifests in more recent musical projects, through the themes addressed in the lyrics and how the artists present themselves, questioning gender stereotypes and criticizing discrimination. This is the case for artists such as Vaiapraia and Filipe Sambado.[6]

In terms of age, we are facing a relational space marked by people aged between thirty and forty (43 per cent of the sample in 2010; 56 per cent in 2020). These data suggest both continuity and a generational renewal of the Portuguese indie rock scene, although the continuity does not mean music careers are viewed and experienced in the same way by the younger generations.

In both moments, our respondents had a high level of education compared with the average Portuguese population. In 2010, 55 per cent of the interview partners had a higher education; in 2020, this figure was 69 per cent. In 2020, the percentage of the resident population in Portugal aged fifteen and over with a higher education was 21.2. Yet few interview partners had a formal higher education in music, and this was mainly in the fields of music production and sound engineering. This does not mean a total rejection of musical education: among the interview partners from the first moment, 19 per cent took singing and instrumental lessons; in the second, 38 per cent had similar 'private' music learning experiences. Seventeen of the latter respondents had attended a music conservatory, while others had rock and jazz lessons in institutions accredited by the Portuguese Ministry of Education. However, these classes were generally a means to acquire basic knowledge for a later self-taught DIY evolution, where freedom and experimentation contrasted with the rigidity of Portuguese music education.

DIY practices were important to most actors from the beginning of their cultural activities. They manifested in different learnings: singing and playing instruments; recording, producing, distributing, booking and organizing concerts and tours; and elaborating/planning choreographies/performances on stage, making clothes and aesthetic artefacts, scenography and videography. In these three learning axes, we speak of informal learning processes and contexts characterized by trial and error and the sharing of information and skills based on belonging to creative artistic communities and local music scenes, facilitated by digital technologies.

In 2010, only 21 per cent of the respondents were professionally involved in music and 44 per cent were amateurs. Due to the small Portuguese music industries, which makes it difficult to earn a living from music, the main professional activity of this group was outside of these industries and music happened in their free time. The remaining 35 per cent combined music-making with other activities in fields such as design, architecture and illustration to ensure their economic survival and to achieve social and personal fulfilment. All research participants felt the profession of a musician was practised in a precarious environment due to the low and unstable income.

In 2020, although musicians (like other creative workers – see e.g. Bennett, 2018; Guerra, 2016, 2020; Hesmondhalgh and Baker, 2011; McRobbie, 2016) face increased precariousness and insecurity, we have seen an increase in those who describe their musical and/or music-related activities as professional (49 per cent) and a marked decrease in those considering themselves amateurs (14 per cent). These data include interview partners working as mediators, such as journalists/music critics, programmers, promoters or agents for record labels – areas where professionalization is easier.

Despite this change, in 2010 and in 2020, most interview partners belonged to the middle classes associated with liberal professions (58 per cent in 2010 and 66 per cent in 2020) in artistic, intellectual and scientific areas.[7] These data are in line with what several authors (Bennett, 2018; Friedman, O'Brien and Laurison, 2016; Threadgold, 2018) have shown about the importance of socio-economic background in the creation of conditions for building DIY careers in the creative and cultural industries.

Most research participants lived in the municipalities of Lisbon and Porto. This geographical distribution closely follows the distribution of social agents of the artistic field generally, as well as of culture more broadly, denoting the structural asymmetries and dualisms of Portugal. The markedly urban configuration of the Lisbon and Porto music scenes is unsurprising: it is easier to find more diverse lifestyles in the larger cities as well as more and bigger circuits of production and circulation of different forms of artistic expression (Guerra, 2010, 2016).

A Typology of Portuguese DIY Indie Music Careers

Aiming to better understand the construction of DIY music careers, we conducted a typological reading of these careers to identify different career profiles according to the main strategies mobilized in the current neoliberal context and the intensity and forms of manifestation of DIY among these social actors. To define the career profiles, we considered two analytical dimensions: The first captures the strategies adopted by social actors to ensure the sustainability and economic viability of their careers, including continuous musical activity (i.e. always being in a phase of the production cycle), networking, the capacity for reinvention, a concert circuit, regularly publishing albums and other artistic materials and using copyright and related rights. The second dimension describes a combination of music-related activities with other activities in non-musical/artistic fields to earn a living. Based on these dimensions, we were able to identify seven ideal-typical career profiles in music: catch-all musicians, non-stop musicians, mediator musicians, author musicians, mediators, non-musicians and weekend musicians. They are fluid ideal types since, due to the precariousness and uncertainty in their trajectories, it is usual to pass from one to another ideal type throughout their musical careers. Sometimes abrupt, these transitions are the result of the state of the music industries and the cultural industries, on the basis of precarious contracts, or even external factors such as the economic situation of the country, for example, the effects of the Covid-19 pandemic and the subsequent restructuring.

'Catch-all musicians' comprise 8 per cent of respondents in 2010 and 27 per cent in 2020. This profile includes musicians who mostly combine their music careers with other music-related activities to overcome the instability and uncertainty of a music career, such as writing and playing for other musicians and working as producers and composers for cinema, television and advertising. Their own music-making is not their primary source of income. We have designated this career profile as 'catch-all musicians' because such a music career involves greater versatility. This capacity for adaptation and multiplication of projects and roles is also their main strategy for dealing with an uncertain artistic trajectory. This occurs in a markedly DIY way, but it is also DIT because it is anchored in relational networks.

'Non-stop musicians' included 6 per cent of respondents in 2010 and 10 per cent in 2020. Finding a balance between music-making and other professional activities is a reality for these individuals, but the connection between the day job and the artistic sphere is more evident. The defining element is maintaining a continuous musical activity by planning the whole creative process and its phases as well as by defining the objectives to be achieved and a work methodology. These actors are able to reinvent themselves as musicians and artists, which translates into the development of various musical projects, not only enabling musicians to express their creativity in different musical styles but also broadening the possibilities of playing live and finding sources of income. This means ensuring that their cycle of creation–performance–dissemination is never interrupted, requiring regular releases of albums, EPs, singles and videos. In this career profile, music takes on a professional character, with planning, dedication to work, perseverance and the capacity to multiply roles in the music scene. It is in this and the previous category that a highly professional perception of music-making prevails and DIY practices take on a more professional dimension.

'Mediator musicians' encompassed 6 per cent of respondents in 2010 and 31 per cent in 2020. Unlike the two previous career profiles, these actors do not combine music-making with other professions outside the music industries. However, a split still exists: they work as promoters, editors, agents or music venue creators – professions that allow for creativity but are focused on 'mediation' activities. This reflects DIY ethics and praxis due to the lack of channels for publicizing and promoting their musical work. At the same time, DIY labels and promoters act as important creative agents, fostering collaborative practices to maintain and consolidate musical careers. The development of several musical projects is not an option for this career profile because the focus is on the multiplication of roles rather than the realization of musical projects. The musicians in this career profile tend to be younger, particularly in 2020. This is also the only career profile in which most members understand music as being only one of the channels and possible languages to share their vision of the world. We find a sceptical perspective towards living solely as musicians in Portugal, with the interviewees stating the virtual impossibility of being a full-time musician in the country, let alone an independent one. Together, they reveal the will to express themselves through artistic languages besides music, including video, poetry, urban art, comics, cinema and dance. They see the possibility of eventually combining music with other artistic activities and playing other roles in the independent music scene, more related to mediation than creation. Involvement in the world of music tends to be seen as a cyclical form of experimentation with diverse artistic languages.

'Author musicians' made up 6 per cent of respondents in 2010 and 7 per cent in 2020. This is the only career profile whose members live exclusively from the music they create for themselves. In other words, they do not need to create music for other people or be involved in mediating activities. This implies a diversified set of strategies. First, in line with several studies that have identified networking and the acquisition of social capital as crucial for advancing a music career (Becker, 1982; Guerra, 2016; Reitsamer and Prokop, 2018), these interviewees referred to the mobilization of networking and the establishment of relationships in the musical environment. However, like the 'mediator musicians', the reduction of the size of musical projects (solo projects or projects with two or three people) was also a career management option, making it easier and cheaper to book bands and allowing salaries to be divided among fewer people. This denotes the influence and impact of neoliberal ideals and their individualization logics on the trajectories of musicians. The same happens with the planning and definition of a work methodology, the maintenance of continuous musical activity and the realization of a concert circuit. Still, within the scope of strategies mobilized by these musicians, it is important to mention the copyrights from the works they create, which enable them to generate income from their music, often an essential supplement in periods when income from other sources is scarce. This is the only career profile in which this option is so significant.[8] This leads us to an authorial vision of the artistic work, as for most of these interview partners, music has a professional dimension. Consequently, as with the 'non-stop musicians', planning and dedication to work and a persistent posture are their main ways of managing the uncertainties associated with a professional trajectory in music. Most also face trajectories explicitly marked by DIY, leading them to seek control over the different phases of the processes of creation, production and dissemination of music, often adding technical and management tasks to creative activities.

'Mediators' included an extensive set of interviewees, especially in 2010 (51 per cent in 2010, 25 per cent in 2020). These heterogenous social actors play crucial roles in the indie rock music scene but are not musicians, distinguishing this from the other career profiles. They are journalists/music critics, radio broadcasters, promoters, agents, managers, label managers, music venue owners and/or programmers and record store owners. Almost all of them could make a living exclusively from their activity in the music field in both 2010 and 2020. They therefore had a professional perception of music, with the exception of those in charge of record labels, especially in 2010. At that time, about half had another job that was their main source of income, while their publishing activity was a hobby, reflecting a strong passion for music. Ten years later, this was the reality for only one of the record label heads who worked as an office clerk in a textile company during the day. In the remaining cases, the economic sustainability of their careers was entirely anchored in the musical sphere, often combining editorial activity with promotion or management. Nevertheless, except for the journalists, who mostly had higher professional education, professional trajectories were developed on a DIY basis. This means that learning was based on learning by doing and trial and error as their involvement in music grew. It is in this career profile, as well as among the 'mediator musicians', that we find more women in the two moments.[9] A music career for women continues to pass essentially through the sphere of mediation.

The last two career profiles concern only the first period of analysis.[10] We have designated one as 'non-musicians', comprising 7 per cent of the interviewees. Their main characteristic is that they have built musical trajectories without considering music as a professional option. They never lived (or considered living) from their activity as musicians and have never been economically dependent on music as they forge their careers in non-musical fields. It has always been a space of freedom and passion. For many, their involvement in music goes back more than thirty years and DIY logics and practices have prevailed in how they acquired their musical skills, their attitude to the musical field and the self-taught way they have managed their careers. This career profile brings together the founders of Portuguese indie rock who have marked – and continue to mark – the history of popular music. This is related to them being young during the dictatorship and/or immediately after 25 April 1974, being the pioneers of the break with a traditional, closed, rural Portugal.

The last career profile, 'weekend musicians', encompasses 16 per cent of the 2010 respondents. Unlike the previous career profile, for whom involvement in music is a constant, their connection to and involvement in the world of music is intermittent. They are essentially DJs and bloggers who, like the interviewees from the previous career profile, never envisaged their musical activity as a profession. It occupies their free time, but their professional daily life is filled with other professional activity. It is also a career profile where the configuration of musical trajectories is marked by a DIY ethos and praxis, prefigured in the dispositions of assumed 'music lovers'. Their designation as 'weekend musicians' is not stigmatizing: it reveals a vibrant and cosmopolitan urban culture at the dawn of the 2010s in the cities of Coimbra, Lisbon and Porto that has allowed more people to combine art with life.[11] This occurred in the 1990s with UK club culture but could only emerge in Portugal recently, given the particularities of its semi-peripheral sociohistorical development and dictatorship.

Conclusion

We have read DIY careers as a pattern of promoting employability within the framework of the effects of neoliberalism on the trajectories of the musicians and other creatives who make up the Portuguese indie rock scene. Based on a pioneering empirical study on the Portuguese and European scales, our investigations over a ten-year period led to two main conclusions. The first conclusion is that the protagonists of these music scenes have not changed much in terms of their main socio-demographic characteristics. However, within this framework of continuity, two relevant changes have occurred: Although the Portuguese indie rock scene remains predominantly male, there is increased participation of women and a greater awareness of and concern with gender issues – especially among the younger generations. Nevertheless, we should highlight that women continue to develop careers mainly as 'mediators' and 'mediator musicians', so differences remain in the types of music careers women pursue. At the same time, there has been a significant increase in the number of people who represent their involvement in music as professionals, accompanied by a sharp reduction in those who consider themselves amateurs. This is most clearly expressed through a decrease in 'mediators' and an increase in 'mediator musicians'. This is due to the fact that, by 2020, improved access to digital technologies for music led to an increasing number of mediators who are also active as musicians, as well as to the increase in the DIY *ethos* and *praxis*. It has become more and more common to see the formation of collectives of musicians who share mediation activities related to the music they create, due to a lack of channels for publicizing and promoting their musical work. In recent years, even if developed precariously, a career in indie rock music has become an increasingly viable and sustainable option from both the professional and financial perspectives. As McRobbie (2016) argues, for middle-class youth, it has become important to forge 'affective attachments' with employment and to develop careers for satisfaction. Over the past decade, there have thus been both continuities and discontinuities.

The second conclusion refers to the common denominator of these careers: although DIY ethics and praxis can be seen as intertwined with neoliberal values and ideas in modern capitalism, for our interviewees, they also represent an essential strategy for pursuing their music careers in the context of neoliberal working conditions. In their differences, the trajectories of these social actors have been marked by DIY from their beginnings to the present day. Whether it manifests itself in the processes of learning and acquiring skills, in their stance within the musical field or in the self-taught way they manage their careers, this DIY ethos has allowed these actors to deal with precariousness and with the impacts that result from a neoliberal paradigm in the trajectories of creative workers. This seems to be intensified in Portugal, where, due to sociohistorical circumstances, the weaknesses of the cultural and creative industries are accentuated and the effects of the cyclical financial crises of capitalism are felt very intensely – a situation that is shared with Spain, Greece and Italy.

Finally, we wish to examine what could be done to improve the situation of DIY musicians in Portugal. Both investigations made it clear that these DIY careers are also DIT. They imply a strong involvement in collaborative and co-creation networks. One way to improve the situation of these musicians may be to promote the creation and consolidation of networks for sharing information, resources and coping strategies. These careers could also be developed in line with public policies specifically oriented towards popular music, as occurs in other countries.

Acknowledgements

This publication was supported by FCT – Foundation for Science and Technology, Portugal, within the scope of UIDB/00727/2020. We must give special thanks to Susan Jarvis and Michael Fix for their copy-editing and proofreading.

Notes

1. This title refers to Guerra's (2010) PhD thesis, which inspired this chapter. It launched a 'research programme' in Portugal on the sociology of music, DIY cultures and underground music scenes, in which the authors of this chapter have participated since 2010. For more details, see https://www.kismifcommunity.com.
2. We refer to 'Urban Cultures and the Youth Ways of Living: Scenarios, Sonorities and Aesthetics in Portuguese Contemporaneity' (funded by the Portuguese Foundation for Science and Technology), which supported Guerra's 2010 PhD thesis, 'The Unstable Lightness of Rock: Genesis, Dynamics and Consolidation of the Alternative Rock Scene in Portugal' (1980–2010) at the University of Porto. The interviews were conducted between 2005 and 2010.
3. We refer to the research project 'Do It Together Again: Networks, flows and spaces in the construction of careers in the Portuguese independent scene' (funded by the Portuguese Foundation for Science and Technology), which supported Oliveira's PhD thesis in Urban Studies at Iscte – University Institute of Lisbon, presented in 2021. The interviews were conducted between 2016 and 2019.
4. More details at https://www.facebook.com/maternidade2014.
5. Additional details at https://ramaemflor.com.
6. Further details at https://www.facebook.com/Vaiapraia and https://www.facebook.com/ofilipesambado.
7. In the Portuguese context, this refers to people who occupy professional management positions, who are integrated within the so-called intellectual jobs or who are highly specialized. In the case of the younger generations, it means highly educated people such as senior managers, administrative or directorate workers, knowledge professionals or professionals such as doctors, lawyers and economists.
8. Musicians in other career profiles also use copyright, but this is less significant for them.
9. In the case of mediators, in 2010, the proportion of women was 11 per cent and in 2020 it was 24 per cent. In the case of mediator musicians, in 2010 the proportion of women was 10 per cent and in 2020 it was 32 per cent.
10. This is due to the objectives of the doctoral thesis that supports the second moment of analysis considered in this chapter. In this case, only people who make their living from music creation or other activities within the music industries were considered for the sample. DJs were also excluded from the analysis.

11 In the same sense, it should be made clear that this does not mean musicians in the other career profiles do not play at the weekend. Our point is that for the musicians who are part of this career profile (essentially DJs), their involvement with music only happens in their leisure time.

References

Beck, U. (1992), *The Risk Society: Towards a New Modernity*, London: Sage.
Becker, H. S. (1982), *Art Worlds*, Berkeley: University of California Press.
Bennett, A. (2018), 'Conceptualising the Relationship between Youth, Music and DIY Careers: A Critical Overview', *Cultural Sociology*, 12 (2): 140–55.
Bennett, A. and P. Guerra, eds (2019a), *DIY Cultures and Underground Music Scenes*, London: Routledge.
Bennett, A. and P. Guerra (2019b), 'Rethinking DIY Culture in a Post-industrial and Global Context', in A. Bennett and P. Guerra (eds), *DIY Cultures and Underground Music Scenes. Collection Routledge Advances in Sociology*, 7–18, London: Routledge.
Berkers P. and J. Schaap (2018), *Gender Inequality in Metal Music Production*, Bingley: Emerald.
Chapman, D. (2013), 'The "One-man Band" and Entrepreneurial Selfhood in Neoliberal Culture', *Popular Music*, 32 (3): 451–70.
Crossley, N. and G. Edwards (2016), 'Cases, Mechanisms and the Real: The Theory and Methodology of Mixed-Method Social Network Analysis', *Sociological Research Online*, 21 (2): 217–85.
Dale, P. (2016), *Anyone Can Do It: Empowerment, Tradition and the Punk Underground*, Farnham: Ashgate.
Everts, R., E. Hitters and P. Berkers (2021), 'The Working Life of Musicians: Mapping the Work Activities and Values of Early-career Pop Musicians in the Dutch Music Industry', *Creative Industries Journal*, 15 (1): 97–117.
Friedman, S., D. O'Brien and D. Laurison (2016), '"Like Skydiving Without a Parachute": How Class Origin Shapes Occupational Trajectories in British Acting', *Sociology*, 51 (5): 992–1010.
Gavanas, A. and R. Reitsamer (2016), *Neoliberal Working Conditions, Self-promotion and DJ Trajectories: A Gendered Minefield, PopScriptum, 12. Online*, Berlin: Humboldt-Universität zu Berlin.
Giddens, A. (2002), *Runaway World: How Globalisation is Reshaping Our Lives*, London: Routledge.
Guerra, P. (2010), *A instável leveza do rock: génese, dinâmica e consolidação do rock alternativo em Portugal 1980-2010* [The unstable lightness of rock: Genesis, dynamics and consolidation of alternative rock in Portugal 1980–2010], Porto: University of Porto.
Guerra, P. (2016), 'Keep it Rocking: The Social Space of Portuguese Alternative Rock (1980–2010)', *Journal of Sociology*, 52 (4): 615–30.
Guerra, P. (2017), '"Just Can't Go to Sleep": DIY Cultures and Alternative Economies from the Perspective of Social Theory', *Portuguese Journal of Social Science*, 16 (3): 283–303.
Guerra, P. (2018), 'Raw Power: Punk, DIY and Underground Cultures as Spaces of Resistance in Contemporary Portugal', *Cultural Sociology*, 12 (2): 241–59.
Guerra, P. (2020), 'Other Scenes, Other Cities and Other Sounds in the Global South: DIY Music Scenes Beyond the Creative City', *Journal of Arts Management and Cultural Policy*, 1: 55–75.

Guerra, P. (2021), 'So Close Yet So Far: DIY Cultures in Portugal and Brazil', *Cultural Trends*, 30 (2): 122–38.

Guerra, P. and A. Oliveira (2019), 'Heart of Glass: Gender and Domination in the Early Days of Punk in Portugal', in D. Vilotijevic and M. I. Medic (eds), *Contemporary Popular Music Studies: Proceedings of the International Association for the Study of Popular Music 2017*, 127–36, Dordrecht: Springer.

Haenfler, R. (2018), 'The Entrepreneurial (Straight) Edge: How Participation in DIY Music Cultures Translates to Work and Careers', *Cultural Sociology*, 12 (2): 174–92.

Hesmondhalgh, D. and S. Baker (2011), *Creative Labour: Media Work in Three Cultural Industries*, London: Routledge.

Leonard, M. (2017), *Gender in the Music Industry: Rock Discourse and Girl Power*, Aldershot: Ashgate.

McKay, G. (1998), *DIY Culture: Party and Protest in Nineties Britain*, New York: Verso.

McRobbie, A. (2016), *Be Creative: Making a Living in the New Culture Industries*, Cambridge: Polity Press.

Oliveira, A. (2020), 'Do It Together Again: Redes, fluxos e espaços na construção de carreiras na cena independente portuguesa [Do It Together Again: Networks, Flows and Spaces in the Construction of Careers in the Portuguese Independent Scene]', PhD diss., Instituto Universitário de Lisboa.

Reddington, H. (2021), *She's at the Controls: Sound Engineering, Production and Gender Ventriloquism in the 21st Century*, Sheffield: Equinox.

Reitsamer, R. (2012), 'Female Pressure: A Translocal Feminist Youth-oriented Cultural Network', *Continuum: Journal of Media & Cultural Studies*, 26 (3): 399–408.

Reitsamer, R. and R. Prokop (2018), 'Keepin' It Real in Central Europe: The DIY Rap Music Careers of Male Hip Hop Artists in Austria', *Cultural Sociology*, 12 (2): 193–207.

Richards, J. (2016), 'Shifting Gender in Electronic Music: DIY and Maker Communities', *Contemporary Music Review*, 35 (1): 40–52.

Smith, S., M. Choueiti, K. Pieper, H. Clark, A. Case and S. Villanueva (2019), *Inclusion in the Recording Studio? Gender & Race/Ethnicity of Artists, Songwriters, & Producers across 700 Popular Songs from 2012–2018*, Los Angeles: USC Annenberg.

Standing, G. (2011), *The Precariat: The New Dangerous Class*, London: Bloomsbury.

Threadgold, S. (2018), 'Creativity, Precarity and Illusio: DIY Cultures and "Choosing Poverty"', *Cultural Sociology*, 12 (2): 156–73.

Thornton, S. (1995), *Club Cultures: Music, Media and Subcultural Capital*, Cambridge: Polity Press.

Chapter 15

Music Therapy as Profession and Practice

The Shifting Interrelationship of Precarity and Entrepreneurialism

Simon Procter

Setting the Scene

Sarah and Linda sit together at a keyboard, intensely making music characterized by a wide dynamic range, harmonic direction and a sense of each moment being keenly anticipated. Sarah seems to be the director-soloist, indicating downbeats with her gestures and with loud clusters of notes as her right hand sometimes strikes the keyboard. Linda accompanies her, using her voice and the keyboard.

This example illustrates music therapy in action as situated shared musical work. It is happening in a school for children with complex needs. Sarah, age twelve, has no language and no movement below the waist: she sits at the keyboard in a complex wheelchair. Her cognitive ability is unclear, but her contributions are evidently engaged with and celebrated by a skilled musician. These music therapy sessions offer her an opportunity to experience a very different kind of relating to the people around her. Rather than primarily being dependent on adults, in music, Sarah can take control, be aesthetically imaginative, share humour and revel in her own ability. Over time, these interactions will impact on her own experience of herself as well as on the expectations of people around her.

Linda is a newly qualified music therapist in her early thirties – a skilled musician responding to all Sarah offers as intentional contributions to the music-making, which can then be structured and collaboratively developed. Her attention to detail enables Sarah to experience creativity, leadership and co-sculpting of the musical experience. Linda is a pianist and singer with a music degree and some experience working musically with people via a 'music in the community' module at her university, before she enrolled in a two-year full-time master's training programme in the UK, during which she experienced placements in a hospital, a school and a care home. Since graduation, Linda spends a day each week in a school for children with complex needs, working with children individually and in small groups. She also works on other days in a school for children with sensory difficulties, a care home for older people living with dementia and a psychiatric hospital. At the heart of this music therapeutic work is a practical understanding of music as something that is both personal and social and the co-cultivation of a craft that is as broad as music itself and simultaneously aesthetic and focused on each person's thriving, development and well-being.

Music therapy is an example of musical work. It is framed by contrasting social and economic forces, including the state imperative for control via regulation (powerful in the UK until the change of government in 2010), the neoliberal push towards increased precarity (increasingly prevalent in the UK since 2010) and the urge towards entrepreneurialism, which, as we shall see later in the chapter, can be understood both as something developed internally, personally or professionally as a means of delivering work that is relevant and acknowledged as useful and else as something imposed externally as a means of adapting to the strictures of precarity. In this chapter, I therefore consider how precarization (Alberti et al., 2018) may affect not only music therapists' careers, but also the ways in which the affordances of music can be made available to people, places and communities via music therapy and related professionalized practices. Taking the UK as my example, I first consider access to training, then outline three shifts in the landscape: the arrival of regulation, a new-found entrepreneurialism of practice and precarity resulting from economic and policy shifts. I tell this story from the perspective of a music therapist who has worked across public and charitable sectors for the last twenty-five years.

Access to the Profession and the Role of Regulation

Music has been made with the intention of improving health or well-being in some way or other for many centuries (Hordern, 2000) and is observable around the world in various forms (Gouk, 2000). Various professional iterations of this are currently practised: in the UK, for example, we see musicians earning their living from activities described variously as community music, music for health and music therapy. Of these, music therapy is the most clearly defined, as it is regulated by the Health and Care Professions Council (HCPC), the government-mandated organization overseeing allied health professions. Thus, music therapy finds itself in the company of more recognizable professions such as physiotherapy, occupational therapy, radiography or dietetics. The HCPC sets entry levels, approves training programmes and imposes requirements for therapists to remain registered, such as Continuing Professional Development (CPD). This state regulation of music therapy in 1999 was part of a broader trend towards increased regulation of work related to healthcare (see Saks and Allsop, 2007, on the regulation of health support workers).

Various definitions of music therapy are offered by professional bodies around the world. There are national traditions as well as particular approaches or methods practised to different extents in different places. In practical terms, most music therapy work in the UK could be described as co-improvisational in that the music is generally co-created in sessions by therapist and client(s) together, rather than there being any attempt to 'dispense' music by the therapist to the client. In this sense the work is more 'co-created' than most paramedical work. Nevertheless, there is generally also an expectation that the therapist will be 'curating' the work in some way that ensures it addresses the reasons why people are attending.

While most professionals might recognize a personal identification with their professional work, at the heart of music therapy is a putting of oneself at another person's disposal, musically and personally, moment by moment. This is demanding, skilful work that involves emotional labour in ways comparable to, but distinctive from, the situation that is well mapped in nursing or care work (Theodosius, 2008). It is also identity work, both for the client and for the therapist (Amir, 2012; Ruud, 1997).

Music therapists work in a wide variety of settings, including special and mainstream education, care settings of various kinds (including dementia care homes as well as neurological and social care services), palliative care in and around hospices, psychiatric and other mental health services as well as a range of other medical and community settings. It is for this range of musical work in this range of settings that training programmes endeavour to prepare their students.

There are currently eight HCPC-approved master's training programmes in the UK – six run by universities, one run by a music academy and one run by a music therapy specialist charity – in three geographically distinct teaching sites. In different ways, all the training programmes emphasize both musical skills and personal qualities in addition to the ability to work academically at the master's level.

However, the fact that all UK music therapy trainings are at the master's level, whereas most HCPC-regulated professions have a bachelor's entry level, restricts access to music therapy training (and its co-bracketed arts therapy professions of art therapy and drama therapy) for musicians who might be very suited to such work on a practical and personal level but who might struggle with the academic demands of a master's programme or whose previous trajectory through education means they have neither a bachelor's degree nor alternative evidence of an ability to work at the master's level.

Other obstacles to training need to be briefly considered, since they set the scene for experiences of precarity after graduation. Perhaps most obvious is the financial obstacle. Students on some courses are able to access a government-backed master's loan but, even where this is available, it can be experienced as a gateway to long-term debt, something that is off-putting to many on lower incomes (Blackburn, 2016). In addition, the availability of music teaching in secondary education in the UK is increasingly variable and associated with social privilege (Bath et al., 2020) and the number of university courses in music is now also declining. The current government actively discourages students from pursuing arts degrees, cutting the core funding for such courses and valuing degrees purely in terms of their capacity to lead to high salaries – part of the neoliberalization of education.

Thus, the music therapy profession is likely to be populated by people who have already enjoyed some degree of privilege, since achieving entry is associated with having already completed a degree and having had access to music education. It would be fair to describe the UK profession as currently predominantly female (80 per cent), white (72 per cent) and at least anecdotally middle class (figures from BAMT, 2020). This may make it seem unlikely for a case study in precarity. Nevertheless, as Standing (2011) makes clear, precarity is by no means simply descriptive of the situations of what has traditionally been seen as unskilled labour. Let us therefore now consider the working world in which these students find themselves after graduation and how this world has evolved since the 1990s.

Changing Landscapes of Practice – 1. The Optimism of the Dawn of Regulation

In the mid-1990s, music therapy was already well established, with four training programmes in the UK. Although there were almost no full-time posts, music therapists found work in schools, care homes, hospitals and community settings, typically for a day per week in each place, with therapists building up portfolios of employed work, sometimes combining this with other musical work such as teaching, performing or composing. It was quite usual for newly qualified therapists to set up new posts, persuading a school or a care home to employ them on a trial basis and then to make the arrangement permanent once they had seen the value of the work in action.

There was real excitement around the coming of state registration, which was perceived as a gateway to a new era of expansion and security. It was anticipated that music therapy would become a core part of National Health Service (NHS) provision, with music therapists embedded within medical multidisciplinary teams. This should be understood in the context of the election of a Labour government (albeit with neoliberalizing tendencies) in 1997, which seemed to assure continuing investment in public services: a credentialed career within health or education seemed to be a safe and reliable way of contributing to society.

In retrospect, however, the perceived need to earn registration by emphasizing music therapy's legitimacy as a paramedical discipline led the profession to consider itself narrowly, emphasizing medical rhetoric. This new 'modern' rhetoric was also influential internally. The music therapy literature increasingly emulated medical literature by focusing on individual 'cases', sending a message that working in this way was the pinnacle of practice. Music therapists likewise sought to be professional by focusing on one-to-one sessions conducted in private, downplaying or avoiding many of the social and collaborative aspects of music-making (such as performance), which had attracted them into music therapy in the first place.

On a theoretical level, the profession increasingly adopted non-Indigenous theory as a legitimizing tool, particularly psychodynamic or psychoanalytic theory. While this theory was no doubt assuring and helpful for some music therapists, for those who had trained on the basis of their experiences of musicking to enable people to thrive, this could also be experienced as alienating, creating a gap between theory and practice. The new 'modern' rhetoric also focused attention on certain kinds of work, in particular that which pursued apparently transformative or curative effects, neglecting work that was more about companionship and care. This shift tended to give the impression that music therapy was located within the clinic, whereas it has always been diversely located in a wide range of settings, most of which (schools, care homes, etc.) are not primarily 'clinical'. It also came with an overlay of pseudo-ethical stricture: certain activities (such as working towards performance or working outside the usual therapeutic space) were frowned upon not simply as unconventional but actually as unethical.

I now consider two ways in which entrepreneurialism can be seen as a response to this situation within the first two decades of the twenty-first century.

Changing Landscapes of Practice – 2. Entrepreneurialism from within: The Emergence of Community Music Therapy

In the early 2000s, a flurry of publications outlined an attitude to working in music therapy that is less rooted in medical or psychotherapeutic conformity and instead more concerned with advocacy and situated musical responses to people's situations. It regarded people not just as individuals but also as part of their wider communities. This became known as Community Music Therapy. One of its protagonists, Ansdell (2002), describes this shift as an anti-model, opposing authoritarian attempts to confine music therapy to medical or psychotherapeutic rules. Advocates of Community Music Therapy (Pavlicevic and Ansdell, 2004; Stige and Aarø, 2011) called for the restoration of the full range of possibilities of what music-making had to offer to people.

However, it can also be read as an expression of entrepreneurialism within the community. Indeed, entrepreneurial spirit is often invoked in the tradition of Community Music Therapy, not referring to commercial activities but rather to an encouragement of music therapists to recognize that their musical responsibility in a community setting is to be whatever kind of musician is required by those people in that place at that time in order to enable them to flourish and to live as well as possible given the constraints that they are experiencing. Such an approach contrasts with the more psychotherapeutic idea of clients coming to appointments with their therapists, much as ill patients go to an expert doctor, and suggests a different way of valuing music therapy within the institutions where music therapists work. In practice, this meant an acknowledgement of the need for therapists to work flexibly and for the use of a wide diversity of formats of work across contexts. Entrepreneurialism therefore becomes an attitude aimed at the engagement of people and places and associated with an expectation of imagination, flexibility and responsiveness as well as a rejection of any attitude of 'one size fits all'. Given the obvious importance of play within music therapy, this kind of entrepreneurialism can be seen as a playful response to the (sometimes necessary) containment imposed by state regulation and professional norms.

This provoked a variety of responses. Many music therapists expressed relief that Community Music Therapy legitimated the range of their practice, including work that happened outside a private space or which aimed to benefit places or communities rather than individuals. They were liberated to discuss the work they did between sessions, in corridors and in unplanned ways – matters that until then had perhaps seemed little valued or even disapproved of. This discourse has resituated music therapy as musical-psychosocial work rather than merely as a clinical intervention and invites a potential political discourse around the valuing of people and the role of music in society. It has also provoked a turning to sociological rather than medical or psychological ways of theorizing the work of music therapists, with a particular influence being DeNora's (2003) discussions of 'musical affordances'.

Proponents of psychodynamic approaches, however, were less impressed by the articulation of Community Music Therapy and its social framing. They felt that this undermined their hard-won professional position highly associated with clinical expertise and professional regulation, and that in this sense, it took the profession into reverse (e.g. Barrington, 2008).

Changing Landscapes of Practice – 3. Entrepreneurialism from without: Precarity and the New Therapy Industry

The UK has in recent decades moved significantly away from its post-war socially minded consensus (Addison, 1994) or social contract (Heldring, Robinson and Whitfill, 2022). Two ways in which music therapy has been impacted by this shift are the systematic disintegration for commercial exploitation of the NHS, albeit disguised beneath apparently unified branding (Brookes and Harvey, 2016; Davis and Tallis, 2013), and the steady decline of musical opportunities for less privileged school students. Whereas proponents of Community Music Therapy committed themselves to a view of their work as psychosocial, valuing the individual in the context of the communal, something to be offered in order to make society better and in particular to benefit the most vulnerable in society, a new wave of business-minded people began to carve out opportunities for monetizing the growth of music therapy. This development coincided with the closing years of the new Labour administration, paving the way for the Conservative-Liberal Democrat alliance from 2010 that would introduce searing levels of austerity to the UK and particularly to UK public services (Stuckler et al., 2017). The era of growth of music therapy in public services was clearly at an end. Since then, there has been an overall decline in music therapy within the NHS, although this has been compensated for by growth in other sectors, particularly within charities and (more or less) commercialized chains of schools (such as multi-academy trusts) and care homes, most of which are run for profit, in some cases even by private equity groups (Horton, 2021).

Of particular interest here is the rise of private companies that work to varying degrees as agencies. These agencies seek out systematized contracts with NHS trusts and other publicly funded providers and also with national commercial providers of education, health and care services. Once a contract is secured, agencies then employ therapists, predominantly on sessional rates, to fulfil those contracts. They also pursue short-term pots of money for work with particular individuals, for example, via the government's Adoption Fund, which provides funding for professionals to work with particular adopted children. Such sources of funding can be lucrative for the agency but result in a therapist being recruited to work temporarily with one child, not with a school or community in the long term. Indeed, therapists are often required to travel long distances to a school to work with one child; they may well be paid only for the session they deliver, whereas the usual practice has been for the therapist to be employed by the school for a full day to work with whichever children are thought most likely to benefit. The fee paid to the agency for that one session may be comparable to what a therapist employed for a whole day would have been paid, but the agency's cut means the therapist earns significantly less while fewer children within the school also have access to music therapy.

In this way, neoliberal policies have three privatizing effects at once for music therapy. Firstly, the work becomes privatized in the sense that it once again reverts to being a 'treatment' for an individual client whose 'problem' is private to them, as is their therapy. Thus, the work of music therapy is de-socialized, once again taking little or no account of the person's context and making no attempt to engage with it. Secondly, the relationship between setting and therapist is disrupted by the intrusion of a mediating profit-making and economically controlling interest in the form of the agency. Traditionally a music therapist who has found work in a particular setting will gradually grow to understand its culture and ethos and will become an increasingly valued member of staff there as they learn to tailor their work in ways that clearly have an impact on life within the setting, including on the work of other staff. This relationship is particularly valued by proponents of Community Music Therapy, not least because of the evidently situated nature of the ways in which people engage with each other musically and the inherently social nature of music-making. An intervening agency means therapists no longer have this direct embeddedness in the setting, since their work there is always likely to be temporary in nature. Thirdly, by 're-sessionalizing' the work, a greater degree of risk is transferred to the therapist, who in many cases is essentially on a zero-hours contract. This passing of risk to the end workers is characteristic of the precarity seen under neoliberalism (Moore and Newsome, 2018; Ravenelle, 2017) as it puts the music therapist in a different situation from that of the other people working in the same place (and working to the same ends with the same clients), who are more likely to be on full-time assured permanent contracts directly paid by the workplace. It is also an example of the degradation of the employment relationship under neoliberalism (Thomas, McArdle and Saundry, 2020) – affecting not only legal aspects such as contracts but also people's experiences of the quality of the work they are able to do, with systemic social consequences.

These developments bring with them not only privatization but also precarity, with a slice of the available funding being diverted from the therapist to the agency. On the other hand, the agencies claim to be making music therapy more available and often use the rhetoric of entrepreneurialism not simply to describe what they do but also to describe what they see themselves as enabling music therapists to do – effectively running their own business as a subcontractor for the agency. This phenomenon is not unique to music therapy: the wider and more disparate world of psychotherapy and counselling has been undergoing a well-documented transformation into a 'gig economy' of its own in recent years (Jones, 2016).

Precarity and the New Music Therapy Industry

As Hassard and Morris (2018) note, people at work are aware of their precarity, particularly in circumstances of 'manufactured uncertainty'. There is therefore perhaps also a 'coming to terms' founded on what Carfagna describes as 'entrepreneurial vagueness', which 'works to buffer subjective status aspirations amidst dwindling objective life chances in the new economy' (Carfagna, 2017: ii). Manolchev (2020) describes 'soft resistance' and the potential for enjoyment and sensemaking as key resources for people who find themselves in precarious employment. Within music therapy, there is ample scope for such enjoyment and sensemaking in the sensorial play of the work itself as well as in the sense of connection and intimacy that nevertheless emerges in the making of music with people – regardless of the disconnect underlying the contractual arrangements. So how does this play out in the new music therapy industry?

The best remunerated working opportunities are within the NHS, although these form a small proportion of the available work. The 'Agenda for Change' salary review process that took place within the NHS in the early 2000s (Buchan and Evans, 2008) banded existing music therapy positions comparably to those of psychologists and other paramedical therapists. These posts continue to be well paid, but their number is declining as funding wanes. Even newer posts, which tend to be introduced at lower banding levels, usually bring with them permanent contracts and access to all the benefits of working for an NHS trust. In particular, NHS employees have access to potentially lucrative promotion prospects, some of which will entail leaving music therapy practice behind either entirely or partially in order to join the ranks of NHS management.

Elsewhere, some music therapists are paid much less as social care workers or classroom assistants, while others are paid on alternate professional scales. Another variation concerns the permanence of work: some organizations pay sessionally, while others offer the full benefits of permanent employment. Meanwhile, the new agencies seek to employ many of their therapists on zero-hours contracts in order to meet the requirements of short-term contracts.

The British Association for Music Therapy (BAMT), once seen as something of a union, now liaises with these agencies as industry leaders, while occasionally lamenting the loss of substantive posts. BAMT's publicly disseminated information about the profession continues to primarily showcase work within the NHS, even though this is a small and declining part of music therapy work. The 'job list' issued to its members by BAMT now routinely features 'calls for expressions of interest', whereby agencies seek to sign up music therapists to deliver for them without committing to provide any work for them.

For some music therapists, the lurch towards precarity is not only unwelcome in the sense of bringing challenge and insecurity but also oppositional to the reasons why they may have come to music therapy in the first place: social solidarity, radical views about the role of music in society or the quest for a secure musical career. Working sessionally for an agency may not present satisfying opportunities to care for people, to establish meaningful therapeutic relationships or to impact significantly on the settings where they work. Disillusionment may mean these therapists reduce their focus on music therapy or even leave the profession entirely.

On the other hand, some music therapists seem to thrive on this – they embrace the challenge of navigating earning a living as an 'entrepreneur'. Especially for younger therapists who do not yet have financial responsibilities for others, this may fit with a world view they have been educated or encultured into. Many training courses now include elements of 'entrepreneurialism training', an example of the cultivation of a habitus of trainability (Bourdieu, 1984).

Masquelier (2019) debates Bourdieu's and Foucault's approaches to precarity, highlighting Bourdieu's insistence on the relevance of a person's social position to their experience of precarity. This is clearly reflected in the range of music therapists' responses to the emerging situation within their profession: where they locate themselves in the spectrum of reactions noted above may well be connected with previous experiences of precarity, of social background, of existential security and of the perceived need to support oneself (and others) financially.

Implications for Profession and Practice

These three phases of regulation, disciplinary entrepreneurialism and economically enforced entrepreneurialism have brought us to a position where the profession is increasingly subject to precarity. It also threatens music therapy's attempts to shed its socially privileged profile by actively seeking to attract entrants who are currently less represented in the workforce. There is clearly a danger that precarity may deter some potential entrants and restrict the kinds of work that music therapists do (and hence the range of people that music therapy ultimately reaches). There is also a danger of the profession becoming dominated by 'entrepreneurialists' whose eager embrace of commercialized opportunity might detract from the music-therapeutic imperative of waiting, accompanying another person unconditionally and being led into uncharted creative-relational waters. A more precarious working environment may also deter older musicians from changing careers into music therapy – a real loss to the richness of the profession as well as to the wider working world of music.

However, alternative employment models are now emerging, particularly in the charitable sector. Two examples will suffice here. Firstly, MHA, a not-for-profit chain of care homes with its roots in Methodism,[1] has established a national network of music therapists, each of whom works across several of their care homes within a geographical area. Therapists are employed on permanent contracts and offered opportunities for relevant development and support. Secondly, the music therapy charity Nordoff Robbins, which runs one of the HCPC-approved training programmes in three locations across England, has launched a national Graduate Employment Scheme to ease its graduates into the world of work, after which they are offered permanent employment for three to five days per week. Some of its work is done in its own dedicated music therapy centres, but mostly this consists of supplying music therapists to work within other organizations that either contribute towards the costs in yearly contracts or else open their facilities for no charge to other people in their local area so that they, too, can freely access music therapy. Nordoff Robbins will redeploy the therapist elsewhere if the arrangement comes to an end but mitigates against this by encouraging therapists to become well embedded into the organizations in which they work, in accordance with the principles of Community Music Therapy. In this way, risk to the therapists is minimized and a greater diversity of work is enabled than would be possible commercially, including with refugee communities and others who are socially excluded.

Ours is an era of change: our experience is highly moulded by macroeconomic forces imposing commodification as well as the neoliberal political shift. That precarity is on the rise within music therapy, recasting its nature as a profession for many, is clear. That this will deter some musicians from putting their musicianship at the disposal of the most sidelined members of our society is inevitable. But what is also evident is that, in entrepreneurialism, we encounter not simply a capitalizing response but also a means of achieving creativity and effective engagement within communities and hence of generating satisfaction for some therapists, too. It is in the practice of music therapy, rather than in its status as a profession, that entrepreneurialism can be exercised in the most creative and communally productive ways. Perhaps for further encouragement, we can turn to McRobbie (2016), who, in her survey of the new culture industries, looks forward to a solidarity-based, intergenerational 'familial/community' ethos underpinned by shared experiences of working life. Amidst these challenges – economic, political and cultural – the need for the communal has never been greater.

Note

1 Methodism started as a movement within the UK's Anglican church in the eighteenth century, led by John Wesley, and later became a separate non-conformist denomination. The principles of the 'Social Gospel' underpin its ongoing commitment to social justice and the meeting of social need.

References

Addison, P. (1994), *The Road to 1945: British Politics and the Second World War*, London: Pimlico.

Alberti, G., I. Bessa, K. Hardy, V. Trappmann and C. Umney (2018), 'In, Against and Beyond Precarity: Work in Insecure Times', *Work, Employment and Society*, 32 (3): 447–57.

Amir, D. (2012), '"My Music is Me": Musical Presentation as a Way of Forming and Sharing Identity in Music Therapy Group', *Nordic Journal of Music Therapy*, 21 (2): 176–93.

Ansdell, G. (2002), 'Community Music Therapy and the Winds of Change', *Voices: A World Forum for Music Therapy*, 2 (2): n.p.

BAMT (2020), *Diversity Report*, London: British Association for Music Therapy. Available online: https://www.bamt.org/resources/diversity-report (accessed 31 March 2023).

Barrington, A. (2008), 'Challenging the Profession', *British Journal of Music Therapy*, 22 (2): 65–72.

Bath, N., A. Daubney, D. Mackrill and G. Spruce (2020), 'The Declining Place of Music Education in Schools in England', *Children and Society*, 34 (5): 443–57.

Blackburn, L. H. (2016), 'Equity in Student Finance: Cross-UK Comparisons', *Scottish Educational Review*, 48 (1): 30–47.

Bourdieu, P. (1984), *Distinction: A Social Critique of the Judgment of Taste*, trans. R. Nice, Cambridge, MA: Harvard University Press.

Brookes, G. and K. Harvey (2016), 'Opening up the NHS to Market: Using Multimodal Critical Discourse Analysis to Examine the Ongoing Commercialisation of Health Care', *Journal of Language and Politics*, 15 (3): 288–302.

Buchan, J. and D. Evans (2008), 'Assessing the Impact of a New Health Sector Pay System upon NHS Staff in England', *Human Resources for Health*, 6 (12): n.p.

Carfagna, L. B. (2017), 'The Pedagogy of Precarity: Laboring to Learn in the New Economy', PhD diss., Boston College. Available online: https://dlib.bc.edu/islandora/object/bc-ir%3A107564/datastream/PDF/download/citation.pdf (accessed 31 March 2023).

Davis, J. and R. Tallis, eds (2013), *NHS SOS: How the NHS was Betrayed – And How We Can Save It*, London: Oneworld.

DeNora, T. (2003), 'Music Sociology: Getting the Music into the Action', *British Journal of Music Education*, 20 (2): 165–77.

Gouk, P., ed. (2000), *Musical Healing in Cultural Contexts*, Aldershot: Ashgate.

Hassard, J. and J. Morris (2018), 'Contrived Competition and Manufactured Uncertainty: Understanding Managerial Job Insecurity Narratives in Large Corporations', *Work, Employment and Society*, 32 (3): 564–80.

Heldring, L., J. A. Robinson and P. J. Whitfill (2022), *The Second World War, Inequality and the Social Contract in England*, Cambridge, MA: National Bureau of Economic Research.

Horden, P., ed. (2000), *Music as Medicine: The History of Music Therapy since Antiquity*, Aldershot: Ashgate.

Horton, A. (2021), 'Liquid Home? Financialisation of the Built Environment in the UK's "Hotel-Style" Care Homes', *Transactions of the Institute of British Geographers*, 46: 179–92.

Jones, R. E. (2016), 'In the Absence of Proper Jobs, Therapists Turn to Precarious Work', *LSE Business Review*, London: LSE. Available online: https://blogs.lse.ac.uk/businessreview/2016/11/21/in-the-absence-of-proper-jobs-therapists-turn-to-precarious-work (accessed 27 May 2022).

Manolchev, C. (2020), 'Sensemaking as Self-defence: Investigating Spaces of Resistance in Precarious Work', *Competition and Change*, 24 (2): 154–77.

Masquelier, C. (2019), 'Bourdieu, Foucault and the Politics of Precarity', *Distinktion: Journal of Social Theory*, 20 (2): 135–55.
McRobbie, A. (2016), *Be Creative: Making a Living in the New Culture Industries*, Oxford: Polity Press.
Moore, S. and K. Newsome (2018), 'Paying for Free Delivery: Dependent Self-employment as a Measure of Precarity in Parcel Delivery', *Work, Employment and Society*, 32 (3): 475–92.
Pavlicevic, M. and G. Ansdell, eds (2004), *Community Music Therapy*, London: Jessica Kingsley Publishers.
Ravenelle, A. J. (2017), 'Sharing Economy Workers: Selling, not Sharing', *Cambridge Journal of Regions, Economy and Society*, 10 (2): 281–95.
Ruud, E. (1997), 'Music and Identity', *Nordisk Tidsskrift for Musikkterapi*, 6 (1): 3–13.
Saks, M. and J. Allsop (2007), 'Social Policy, Professional Regulation and Health Support Work in the United Kingdom', *Social Policy & Society*, 6 (2): 165–77.
Standing, G. (2011), *The Precariat: The New Dangerous Class*, London: Bloomsbury Academic.
Stige, B. and L. E. Aarø (2011), *Invitation to Community Music Therapy*, New York: Routledge.
Stuckler, D., A. Reeves, R. Loopstra, M. Karanikolos and M. McKee (2017), 'Austerity and Health: The Impact in the UK and EUROPE', *European Journal of Public Health*, 27 (Suppl 4): 18–21.
Theodosius, C. (2008), *Emotional Labour in Health Care: The Unmanaged Heart of Nursing*, London: Routledge.
Thomas, P., L. McArdle and R. Saundry (2020), 'Introduction to the Special Issue: The Enactment of Neoliberalism in the Workplace: The Degradation of the Employment Relationship', *Competition & Change*, 24 (2): 105–13.

Epilogue

Neoliberalism's Others

Imperatives of Activism in Portland, Oregon

Elizabeth Gould

Introduction

The May 2020 murder of George Floyd at the knee of police in Minneapolis, Minnesota, exposed white supremacy and a historical amnesia of slavery in every aspect of US society, including higher (music) education. The public protests it ignited worldwide in the context of Black Lives Matter were larger and more persistent than any that had occurred previously in twentieth- and twenty-first century neoliberal societies. That these protests in Portland, Oregon, continued more than a year later, 'with no end in sight' (Gaitán, 2021), even as music education responds (only) as necessary, underscores the urgency of activating anti-racism (Kendi, 2019) to defund higher education's investments in the neoliberalism-effacing sources of difference – race, class, gender, sexuality, (dis)ability – rendering them infinitely fungible and the groups and individuals they represent radically precarious. In this philosophical essay, I take up Judith Butler's (2015) 'performative theory of assembly' in my Deleuzian analysis of the Portland protestors' transmogrifying tactics, in counterpoint with the potentialities of music education, to argue that both the Portland protesters and higher education hold potentialities for functioning as Deleuzian collective assemblages of enunciation. Instantiating 'incorporeal transformations' (Deleuze and Guattari, 1987), the protestors and higher (music) education become catalysts of anti-racist responses, expressed in my concept of *assembl(y)age*.

Following a brief discussion of the context of my argument and (neo)liberal democracy, I review Butler's theory of gender performativity in relationship to her concepts of precarity, Foucauldian biopolitics and racism, particularly as they work in the United States with regard to incarceration and capital punishment. I also link the existential threats (im)posed by neoliberalism to higher education institutions and music programmes. Framed by Black Lives Matter and Ibram X. Kendi's (2019) concept of anti-racism, my analysis of public assemblies focuses on tactics (notably singing) used by protesters in Portland, intensified by the insertion of weaponized anonymous federal agents. In conclusion, I theorize this edited book and music education in general as a Deleuzian collective assemblage of enunciation, inciting potentialities for music education's plural performativity to articulate and catalyse anti-racist activism.

Some years ago, I wrote a critique of liberal democracy(ies) that called upon normatively white, male, cisgender, heterosexual music education to engage in 'outrageous' acts expressing 'utter contempt' for 'this empty form of democracy, a simulacrum, the ultimate bait and switch, as it promises what – by its very definition – it cannot deliver [. . . and] engag[e] the Other in terms of her anger, rage, and fury' (Gould, 2008: 40–1). How naïve and stupid, frankly, that seems now – contempt for a form of democracy that even then was an empty signifier to the extent that it no longer existed in any substantive way. With neoliberal forms of government and capitalism already entrenched worldwide by 2011, tens of thousands of people took to the street in protest during what came to be known as the Arab Spring and the Occupy movement. These and other large public protests after 9/11 compelled Judith Butler to extend and re-conceive her theory of gender performativity in terms of 'plural forms of agency and social practices of resistances', where 'acting in concert can be an embodied form' of political protest, calling into question dominant concepts of the political (Butler, 2015: 9).

Gender Performativity in/as Precarity

Repurposing John Austin's (1975) performative verbal speech act as a gestural speech act, Butler (1993) theorizes how, and the power with which, language acts and acts upon us, engaging Gilles Deleuze's (1988) assertion (via Spinoza) that we can never know ahead of time what a body can do. As a condition of possibility for human existence, gender is an ontological effect produced by compulsory iterations of coercive norms that signify on the skin through one's corporeal gender presentation. Rather than evidence of 'an internal or inherent truth', or essence about the subject, compelled gender performance is 'a certain kind of enactment' by which the gendered subject appears (Butler, 2015: 32) – not just normatively but in ways that may resist and re-signify constraining norms, disrupting their citational chains. The subject's vulnerability to the action of norms is where agency may be found and to the extent that gender 'performance' is read in terms of fealty to authoritative and obligatory norms; individuals who present otherwise are at risk – even and especially unto death.

Inasmuch as everyone is liable to illness, injury and death, all subjects are precarious, but racialized groups produced as less-than-human live in conditions of precarity, 'that [neo]politically induced condition in which certain populations suffer from failing social and economic networks of support more than others, and become differentially exposed to injury, violence, and death' (Butler, 2015: 33), based on their 'value and utility' (Foucault, 1978/1990: 144) to society. In Foucauldian terms, this expresses neoliberal biopower which 'qualif[ies], measure[s], appraise[s], and hierarchize[s]' (Foucault, 1978/1990: 144) groups in relationship to norms that form the basis for their regulation in ways that have the potential to threaten their existence as 'living beings'. In addition to 'indirect murder' (Foucault, 2003) carried out by withholding, through 'systematic negligence', the conditions necessary to thrive politically, socially and economically (Butler, 2015) is the very real threat of actual murder.

Racism, 'the break between what must live and what must die', is the 'precondition for exercising the right to kill' (Foucault, 2003: 254, 256), directly or indirectly. Far removed from 'ordinary racism', expressed as animus between racial groups, 'modern racism [. . .] is bound up [. . .] with the technology of power' that enables biopower (Foucault, 2003: 258). The most racist states are 'murderous' in that they carry out capital punishment with impunity, as Nazis did during the Holocaust. With Black people in the United States, this is abhorrently demonstrated through the effects of white supremacy manifesting in actual murder carried out by state actors embodied as law enforcement officers. Their rates of killing 'disproportionately Black and other people of color civilians' in prison executions as well as on the streets far outpace 'other wealthy countries' (Jones and Sawyer, 2020: para 1).

To the extent that bodily appearance is a performative claim to public recognition, 'a public insistence on existing and mattering' (Butler, 2015: 37), individuals assert their status as human in stark relief to the ways they are produced by widespread and ubiquitous neoliberal discourses as non-human. This obtains uniquely dissonant resonance in the United States due to 'historically entrenched forms of racism [that] rely on bestial constructions of [B]lackness' (Butler, 2015: 36) produced by the country's centuries-long trafficking in chattel slavery which morphed into 'Jim Crow' laws enacted across the US south in the latter half of the nineteenth century as well as the mass incarceration of Black bodies in the twentieth and twenty-first centuries (Alexander, 2020). Consequently,

> all public assembly is haunted by the police and the prison. And every public square is defined in part by the population that could not possibly arrive there; either they are detained at the border, or they have no freedom of movement and assembly, or they are denied or imprisoned. In other words, the freedom to gather as a people is always haunted by the imprisonment of those who exercised that freedom and were taken to prison. (Butler, 2016: 20)

Moreover, all forms of appearance are possible only insofar as they are tangibly and intangibly supported. Indeed, every body requires material, social and emotional infrastructures to act and appear (Butler, 2015), making all of us radically dependent on each other and, most notably here, on governments and institutions such as universities that provide for the safety and flourishing of all those within their purview.

Neoliberalism and the Academy

Even as they failed in fulfilling their obligations to the very people who depended on and protected them, too often with their very lives, liberal democracies were ostensibly committed to act in the interest of the people for the public good. By contrast, neoliberal democracies place 'the state in [. . .] direct service to the economy' (Brown, 2005: 44), severely debilitating the 'essential *conditions* of democratic existence' (Brown, 2011: 21; emphasis in original): equal opportunity, minimal economic disparities, citizenship as and for the public good. The fourth condition, 'citizens modestly discerning about the ways of power, history, representation, and justice' (Brown, 2011: 21), necessitates substantive and reflective public education that is now increasingly inaccessible due to punishing tuition increases necessitated in part by exploding administrative costs justified as 'rational entrepreneurial action' (Brown, 2005: 40) that constrain the curriculum to vocational training, interpellating all those who study and work in higher education as 'entrepreneurial actors' (Brown, 2005: 42). Rather than 'teachers and thinkers', graduate students are 'professionalized' as entrepreneurs who 'network', 'go on the market', 'shop', 'workshop', 'game their Google Scholar counts and "impact factors," [to] follow the money' (Brown, 2011: 32). For their part, faculty 'are generally unable to grasp, let alone resist, what is happening in postsecondary education', distracted as we are by our own 'research, publications, invitations, prizes, fellowships, rankings, offers and counter-offers' (Brown, 2011: 34). Meanwhile, both groups – students who have never known the academy any other way and faculty who are too disempowered and/or demoralized to recall or reimagine it any other way – are acculturated through processes of precaritization to academic life consumed by the demands of the market requiring our writing and/or editing articles, chapters, single-authored and edited books.

Music programmes in higher education are doubly impacted by governmental economic policy driving both cultural and education policy. Existing in a liminal space of a neoliberal rationality that systematically defunds public art as well as public education, contingent faculty positions replace tenure-track positions at the very moment faculty duties and obligations exceed the time and resources required to carry them out. Considerations of equity and diversity associated with liberal democracies are the first casualty of budgetary constraints, producing non-normative bodies as exceptions or disappearing them altogether under the crushing weight of fulfilling impossible demands marginalizing and isolating faculties of music within universities as well as individual faculty members – both contingent and (previously) stable – within music faculties. Our efforts to chase the money/prestige so that we may 'maximize [our] own market value' (Butler, 2015: 15) demonstrate a form of 'cruel optimism' (Berlant, 2011). Playing a game that we 'have no chance to win' (Atari Teenage Riot, 1995), shrinking music faculties in North America and Europe, can only become less equitable and more normatively white, cisgender, male and heterosexual, as anxiety overwrites optimism itself – for everyone. Awash in neoliberal capitalism, economic force capitalizes everything, remaking universities as corporations. Higher education, increasingly self-defined as creative, flexible and entrepreneurial, is an ends-focused commodity that faculty produce and students consume.

But bigger issues are at stake now; larger issues have overrun the academy – not only precaritized institutions and precaritized employment but also precaritized lives. Several students and faculty members from Al-Beroni University in Afghanistan were killed or injured by a roadside bomb while traveling in a minibus on 29 May 2021 (Scholars at Risk Network, 2021), presaging the current Taliban takeover shuttering Afghanistan's National Institute of Music. Ahmed Tohamy of Egypt's Alexandria University was arrested at his home in Cairo on 3 June 2020 and remains in unlawful pretrial detention (DAWN, 2021). Held in solitary confinement in Tehran's notorious Evin prison for 125 days in 2006, Iranian scholar Ramin Jahanbegloo poses a question to US and Canadian academics that would be rhetorical in other circumstances but, at this critical time, is existential: 'Where do you stand when basic liberties are in danger? Moreover, what will the academy be – a class of arm-chaired professionals or guardians of the democratic soul?' (Jahanbegloo, 2017: para 5).

Black Lives Matter: Portland, Oregon

Like virtually every protest staged against the murder of George Floyd by Minneapolis police, those in Portland were organized around Black Lives Matter. Founded in 2013 by three radical Black organizers, Alicia Garza, Patrisse Cullors and Opal Tometi, Black Lives Matter is committed to an 'inclusive and spacious movement [that] affirm[s] the lives of Black queer and trans folks' (Black Lives Matter/About, n.d.: para 2, para 3). Since then, the organization has established dozens of chapters worldwide in addition to a 'philanthropic arm', the Black Lives Matter Global Network, which raised over $90 million in 2020 (Morrison, 2021). The implications of a radical activist organization becoming affiliated with a registered charitable non-profit are as complicated to parse as the plethora of Black-led organizations in Portland (Blaec, 2020b).

The day after video evidence of George Floyd's murder was posted online, protests were staged in cities internationally and across the United States, including in Portland on May 28, when protesters first took to the streets. Over a year later, they were still there – with 'no end in sight' (Gaitán, 2021). During the day, they disrupted traffic, marched on highways and in neighbourhoods throughout the city, lined streets while holding signs supporting Black Lives Matter and listened to Black speakers at rallies held in city parks. That the demonstrators are overwhelmingly white is consistent with the city's history and racial demographics: 70.6 per cent white, 6.8 per cent Black (United States Census Bureau, 2020) – a legacy of white Oregonians' historical animus towards Black people. Determined to keep white Oregon white, a Black exclusion clause written into the 1857 state constitution was belatedly rescinded in 1926 (Nokes, 2013).

What started out peacefully in Portland almost immediately devolved into violence. Following a rally and vigil organized by the local chapter of the National Association for the Advancement of Colored People (NAACP) in Portland's Peninsula Park on 29 May, protesters marched downtown where a small group broke away, igniting a fire at the Multnomah County Justice Center, breaking windows and looting local businesses (KGW Staff, n.d.). Federal law enforcement officers under the auspices of the Department of Homeland Security (DHS) began arriving in Portland on 4 June in what would become a huge operation. By the end of August, 755 people were deployed, including Customs and Border Protection (CBP) agents and Immigration and Customs Enforcement (ICE) officers, virtually all of whom had little or no training in crowd control, riots and the use of so-called less lethal weapons (Wilson, 2021). Wearing two different militarized uniforms without proper identification, their very presence exacerbated tensions.

Throughout July, peaceful protests in support of mutual aid and defunding the police were met with 'extreme violence' by DHS forces augmenting the Portland Police Bureau (PPB), which has a documented pattern of brutality (Physicians for Human Rights, 2020). The less lethal weapons that law enforcement officers used included chemical irritants, batons and kinetic impact projectiles (KIPs), such as pepper balls, flash grenades and tear gas cannisters fired directly at protesters at point-blank range, resulting in dozens of injuries, many serious. For their part, DHS personnel claimed nearly 700 injuries, complaining that protesters used unusual 'techniques' involving 'lasers and fireworks' (Wilson, 2021). Injured and incapacitated protesters were treated by volunteer medics because medical services and ambulances connected to PBB and the Portland Fire Department were barred from the immediate area. Amidst the ensuing chaos, civilian medics and protesters independently reached the same conclusion: Law enforcement officers were there to hurt them (Physicians for Human Rights, 2020).

Protesters responded to this aggression and outsized use of force in several ways. To protect themselves from chemical irritants, they wore safety goggles or face masks with respirators, using leaf blowers to direct noxious gas back towards law enforcement. To protect themselves from munitions, they wore snowboarding helmets and goggles, using garbage can lids and open umbrellas as shields. Despite, and in some cases, because of the violence directed at them, protesters participated in increasingly large numbers, growing quickly from hundreds in early June to over 5,000 in July. Organizing themselves and marching in occupation-based groups (health professionals, lawyers, teachers, firefighters) offered another layer of protection. Groups such as Disabled Comrade Collective and Wall of Vets linked arms to form a physical barrier shielding protesters from harm. The most controversial of these groups was Wall of Moms, later renamed Moms United for Black Lives.

Evoking the women who weaponized motherhood by protesting human rights violations in Chile and governmental 'disappearances' in Argentina during the 1970s and 1980s (Krause, 2004; Mooney and Pieper, 2007), a group of white women chanting 'Feds stay clear, the Moms are here!' (Conley, 2020) marched into downtown Portland the night of July 18. The unintended and unwanted effect of this was that they visually and aurally displaced Black mothers in Portland and, by extension, those who have protested and mourned their murdered Black children in the United States for centuries. Videos were posted two days later of the (white) Moms singing, 'Hands up, please don't shoot me', characterized by bystanders as a lullaby. The appellation of this apparently impromptu song may be attributed to the singers defining themselves in terms of motherhood and the slow tempo and even rhythm (four eighth notes, two quarter notes) they used to sing it. The melody – rendered in solfege as sol-sol-mi-la-sol-mi – is not a lullaby, however. It outlines the first phrase of 'Ring Around the Rosie', a children's game song from England that US children, Black and white, have historically learned in elementary school music programmes and/or on the playground (Winick, 2014). The game involves holding hands and skipping in a circle while singing the lyrics in an uneven (long-short) rhythm at a relatively fast tempo. Coinciding with the song's last line, the singers 'all fall down'. As sung by Portland's white Moms, the misremembered and misidentified song lulled no one. Excoriated for organizing and acting without Black leadership, representation or collaboration (Blaec, 2020a), the race and class privilege enabling their actions did not protect them. Law enforcement officers attacked a few nights later with tear gas triggering vomiting, and batons and KIPS breaking bones, disassembling their right to assembly (Physicians for Human Rights, 2020).

Singing is historically associated with large public gatherings and social movements from the 1950s and 1960s US Civil Rights Movement to peace and labour movements worldwide. This singing constitutes a performative effect of appearance by which the singers are produced as 'the people' (Butler, 2015), claiming recognition not only for their existence and their humanness but also for their status within society, their status of belonging. Collective assemblies enact plural performativity as a function of their spontaneous gathering – in the street – in assemblies that are transitory, forming and re-forming in resistance to processes of precaritarization. In this way, precarity itself functions as a site of alliance, a site of possibility for resistance. Asking who 'the people' are establishes lines that demarcate who is and is not recognizable as human. The issue is not simply that people sing together, but that 'singing is a plural act, an articulation of plurality' (Butler and Spivak, 2010: 59), which is to say, the act of collective singing performatively produces the 'we' and the 'our'. Anti-racism expressed in terms of equality (Kendi, 2019) and inclusion is at stake in collective singing, without which the 'we' of any performative assembly, including those in higher education, 'is not speakable' (Butler and Spivak, 2010: 60).

Imperatives of Activism

Public assemblies of bodies become political when they theorize themselves, where theory involves reflection (Butler, 2015), comparing and relating to others in a form of 'travel' by which we 'leave home' (Clifford, 1989) and encounter our other(s) – on their terms (Gould, 2008). Theorizing in this way distinguishes political public assemblies from 'joyous forms of cruelty' (Butler, 2015: 13) first associated with the US Tea Party rallies organized in opposition to former US president Barack Obama's Affordable Care Act, enacting a necropolitics (Mbembe, 2003) celebrating the 'death' of impoverished and/or medically uninsured others. Joyous cruelty was similarly demonstrated after the 2020 US presidential election when throngs of Donald Trump supporters chanted in reference to the former

US vice president, 'Hang Mike Pence!' Promising him death metaphorically and literally for certifying results of the 2020 election that Joe Biden won, the crowd was eager to act as executioner, perhaps literally but certainly through their chant, the 'indirect discourse' of a collective assemblage of enunciation that 'explains all the voices present within a single voice [. . .] the languages in a language' (Deleuze and Guattari, 1987: 80) – implied discourses, claims, myths embedded in language; in this case, pervasive racism and white supremacy underscored by a noose attached to makeshift gallows erected during the insurrection at the US capitol on 6 January 2021, enacting a Deleuzian 'instantaneous incorporeal transformation'.

Constituted by 'no individual [or] subject of enunciation' (Deleuze and Guattari, 1987: 79), Deleuze's performative speech act is not uttered by a singular subject. Instead, language itself speaks in and through subjects as it acts on them, shaping and ordering bodies in the social-political world by expressing and enacting incorporeal transformations that occur upon their utterance. In this case, a state official transforms into condemned political prisoner, convicted – repeatedly – by false claims issued by the defeated incumbent and his lawyers, right-wing media and conservative members of congress – through the illocutionary force of the 'assemblages of enunciation in society' (Deleuze and Guattari, 1987: 81) expressing race and class ressentiment motivated by hatred, as it/they delight in the execution of Pence's political life and the peaceful transfer of power, evoking the past in the present, lynching Black, Indigenous and all transgressive bodies from edifices of white supremacy.

Julia Koza (2007) defines politics in terms of relations of power in every social interaction. Arguing that we – music educators – are necessarily politically engaged in 'every sound and silence' (Koza, 2007: 172), she troubles us with a 'thorny question: "What are the effects and consequences of the recent forms of political engagement we individually and collectively have chosen?"' (Koza, 2007: 173). Again, this question is not rhetorical. Based in part, perhaps, on long-held assumptions that music and the aesthetic are, by definition, not political, that education carried out by teachers with students is not political, that music education only occurs (as music education) outside politics, we have – at least as a profession – hesitated to engage in and with politics except through apolitical discourses of 'social justice'. To the extent that the political potentialities of performativity are located when and how it intersects with precarity, itself a function of politics, we are inextricably linked to each other, our communities and the world – in music education expressed as shifting sites of alliance, consisting not only of compassion and aspiration but also art independent of aesthetics, art that does things, moving people with its 'aesthetic force' (Lewis, 2017) resonating throughout the cosmos. Compelled by the power relations of this political moment in this political space, we speak/enact/sing collectively as a Deleuzian performative assembl(y)age.

The inserted y-in-parentheses in my concept, *assembl(y)age*, acknowledges our assembly-ness, in that collectively we are constituted in this edited book as an assembly, and by appearing here, we are assembled. Deleuze's concept, assemblage, tucked before and after our assembly-ness, signifies the transitory machinic connections formed and broken through our activism beyond the book. Rather than acting through filiation, 'starting or beginning' our activism, we proceed rhizomatically, which is to say, through the 'conjunction, and . . . and . . . and . . . ' in and as shifting alliances, between our writing and readers' reading. This is the middle where, Deleuze and Guattari (1987) insist, 'things pick up speed'. It is where we/they exhort us and readers, 'Don't have just ideas, just have an idea' (25); in other words, have an idea that does something, changes something, moves something – and someone.

The form this avowedly political work takes cannot be known ahead of time as our collective body affects and is affected by other bodies. Queer theorist Jasbir Puar (2008) argues this is not so much a matter of forming assemblages but of acting in and with local circumstances, activisms and bodies, as we encounter them, in 'a reading practice [to] open up new avenues of thinking, speaking, organizing' (Puar, 2008: para 15). The plural performativity of our assembl(y)age is a function of the enunciative force of our speaking/acting/singing by which what we say/do/musick enacts – in Butlerian terms, materializes; in Deleuzian terms, actualizes – what it names, as well as the incorporeal transformations that the collective assemblage of enunciation incites. Acting collectively as public intellectuals in our (Christopher) Smallian musicking (1998), as well as in our scholarship, which is musicking, too, we reject what separates and 'modulates' us (Deleuze, 1995), 'set[ting] individuals against one another [. . . while] dividing each within' (Deleuze, 1995: 179), through so-called merit systems that require international impact achieved through constant travel to present research, endless writing to publish conclusions, cascading grant applications to pay for it all – even when they don't – in what Deleuze describes as '*continuing education* [and] continuous assessment' (Deleuze, 1995: 179; emphasis in original) that is never, ever finished.

Deleuze published these comments on 'control societies' in a collection of essays, letters and conversations spanning nearly twenty years. In the context of his definition of philosophy as a practice of creating concepts, Deleuze specifies in a prefatory paragraph to the collection that instead of communication, philosophy is a matter of negotiation. Moreover, philosophy is not a power, so it cannot 'battle with the powers that be, [but instead] fights a war without battles, a guerrilla campaign against them' (Deleuze, 1995: n.p.). To the extent that these powers that are power-full 'permeate each of us, philosophy throws us into constant negotiations with, and a guerrilla campaign against, ourselves' (Deleuze, 1995: n.p.).

And so, here we are, collected in an edited volume, its very existence speaking volumes about battles that are not battles, guerrilla campaigns against each other and ourselves – all before we can manage any action, in the middle or otherwise, against the powers implicated in 'generating human misery', the 'compromised [. . .] democratic states' (Deleuze, 1995: 173) in which we are citizens and 'the people' (Butler, 2015). Deleuze's insistence that 'all philosophy is political' (Deleuze, 1995: 175) propels us to act as Deleuzian war machines and incorporeally transform from a book *about* responses into a catalyst *of* responses. Negotiating philosophy as public intellectuals, we are mindful that the 'lifestyle [enabling us to travel, write and read chapters in edited books] relies on intensive environmental degradation and untold oppression' (Strouse, 2017: para 19). To divest from the predatory capitalism that funds not only our writing, reading and travel but also ecological catastrophe, plagues, endless war and every imaginable human indignity, music education refuses to 'let our educational institutions make [us] into something that [we] will be ashamed of' (Edwards, quoted in Kolowich 2016: para38), and becomes-political by moving in place with an idea of anti-racism based on equality between and among racial groups, interrogating racist ideas that 'substantiate' and sustain racist policies written in law and lived on the street (Kendi, 2019), even as late capitalist democratic governments devolve into fascism by first disempowering and then disenfranchising their citizens, the people, rending the collective good. Working from and with the world, we extend an idea of research and teaching beyond curricular requirements and higher education institutions, physical and virtual, and align with assemblages of resistance to neoliberalism itself in and with communities where and how they are, in terms of their priorities instead of our own. With teach-ins and lea(r)n-ins committed to embodied intersectional antiracism, we performatively appear to and with each other and our communities. Theorizing bold new and different responses we engage – at last – our Deleuzian performative assembl(y)age of connections, encounters and movement.

References

Alexander, M. (2020), *The New Jim Crow: Mass Incarceration in the Age of Colorblindness*, 2nd edn, New York and London: The New Press.
Austin, J. L. (1975), *How to Do Things with Words*, ed. J. O. Urmson and M. Sbisà, 2nd edn, Cambridge, MA: Harvard University Press.
Berlant, L. (2011), *Cruel Optimism*, Durham and London: Duke University Press.
Black Lives Matter (n.d.), 'About', Black Lives Matter. Available online: https://blacklivesmatter.com/about (accessed 14 August 2021).
Blaec, J. (2020a), 'The Complicated Rise and Swift Fall of Portland's Wall of Moms Protest Group', *Portland Monthly*, 3 August. Available online: https://www.pdxmonthly.com/news-and-city-life/2020/08/the-complicated-rise-and-swift-fall-of-portland-s-wall-of-moms-protest-group (accessed 9 July 2021).
Blaec, J. (2020b), 'Who Speaks for the Black Lives Matter Movement in Portland? It's Complicated', *Portland Monthly*, 19 December. Available online: https://www.pdxmonthly.com/news-and-city-life/2020/12/who-speaks-for-the-black-lives-matter-movement-in-portland-it-s-complicated (accessed 14 August 2021).
Brown, W. (2005), *Edgework: Critical Essays on Knowledge and Politics*, Princeton and Oxford: Princeton University Press.
Brown, W. (2011), 'The End of Educated Democracy', *Representations*, 110: 19–41.
Butler, J. (1993), *Bodies That Matter: On the Discursive Limits of 'Sex'*, New York and London: Routledge.
Butler, J. (2015), *Notes toward a Performative Theory of Assembly*, Cambridge, MA: Harvard University Press.

Butler, J (2016), 'Rethinking Vulnerability and Resistance', in J. Butler, Z. Gambetti and L. Sabsay (eds), *Vulnerability in Resistance*, 12–27, Durham: Duke University Press.

Butler, J. and G. C. Spivak (2010), *Who Sings the Nation-State? Language, Politics, Belonging*, London, New York, Calcutta: Seagull Books.

Clifford, J. (1989), 'Notes on Travel and Theory', *Inscriptions*, 5: 177–88.

Conley, J. (2020), '"Feds Stay Clear, Moms are Here": Portland Mothers form Human Shield to Protect Protesters from Federal Agents', *Common Dreams*, 20 July. Available online: https://www.commondreams.org/news/2020/07/20/feds-stay-clear-moms-are-here-portland-mothers-form-human-shield-protect-protesters (accessed 13 August 2020).

DAWN: Democracy for the Arab World Now (2021), 'Academic Freedom under Fire: Egyptian Government Jails Ahmed Tohamy', 3 June. Available online: https://dawnmena.org/academic-freedom-under-fire-egyptian-government-jails-ahmed-tohamy (accessed 12 July 2021).

Delete Yourself: You Have No Chance to Win (1995), [CD] Atari Teenage Riot, A. Empire and D. Harrow, producers, UK: Digital Hardcore Records.

Deleuze, G. (1988), *Spinoza: Practical Philosophy*, trans. R. Hurley, San Francisco: City Lights Books.

Deleuze, G. (1995), *Negotiations*, trans. M. Joughin, New York: Columbia University Press.

Deleuze, G. and F. Guattari (1987), *A Thousand Plateaus: Capitalism and Schizophrenia*, trans. B. Mussumi, Minneapolis and London: University of Minnesota Press.

Foucault, M. (1978/1990), *The History of Sexuality, Volume 1: An Introduction*, trans. R. Hurley, New York: Vintage Books.

Foucault, M. (2003), *Society Must Be Defended: Lectures at the Collège de France, 1975–76*, trans. D. Macey, New York: Picador.

Gaitán, C. (2021), 'After a Year of Portland Protests, Activists See No End in Sight', *The Oregonian/OregonLive*, 28 May, updated 9 June. Available online: https://www.oregonlive.com/portland/2021/05/after-a-year-of-portland-protests-activists-see-no-end-in-sight.html (accessed 10 July 2021).

Gould, E. (2008), 'Devouring the Other: Democracy and Music Education', *Action, Criticism, and Theory for Music Education*, 7 (1): 29–44.

Jahanbegloo, R. (2017), 'Why the Academy Must Protect America's Democratic Soul', *The Chronicle of Higher Education*, 31 January. Available online: http://www.chronicle.com/article/Why-the-Academy-Must-Protect/239051?cid=at&utm_source=at&utm_medium=en&elqTrackId=c8521654025041a49f7472f572fc93ae&elq=481ba479f6c44fd9a6f4f92446cf1eb4&elqaid=12364&elqat=1&elqCampaignId=5024 (accessed 31 January 2022).

Jones, A. and W. Sawyer (2020), 'Not just "a Few Bad Apples": US Police Kill Civilians at Much Higher Rate than Other Countries', *Prison Policy Initiative*, 5 June. Available online: https://www.prisonpolicy.org/blog/2020/06/05/policekillings (accessed 13 April 2023).

Kendi, I. X. (2019), *How to Be an Antiracist*, New York: One World Books.

KGW Staff (2020), 'Portland Protests: Nonviolent Gatherings and Unlawful Assemblies in the Wake of George Floyd's Death', *KGW8*, 1 June, updated 15 June. Available online: https://www.kgw.com/article/news/local/protests/protests-in-portland/283-21d67e10-4b33-46d4-a81e-7d3b437a7519 (accessed 9 July 2021).

Kolowich, S. (2016), 'The Water Next Time: Professor Who Helped Expose Crisis in Flint Says Public Science is Broken', *The Chronicle of Higher Education*, 2 February. Available online: https://www.chronicle.com/article/the-water-next-time-professor-who-helped-expose-crisis-in-flint-says-public-science-is-broken/?cid2=gen_login_refresh&cid=gen_sign_in (accessed 25 July 2021).

Koza, J. (2007), 'In Sounds and Silences: Acknowledging Political Engagement', *Philosophy of Music Education Review*, 15 (2): 168–76.

Krause, W. C. (2004), 'The Role and Example of Chilean and Argentinian Mothers in Democratization', *Development in Practice*, 14 (3): 366–80.

Lewis, S. E. (2017), 'How Artists Push Social Change', *The Chronicle of Higher Education*, 18 April. Available online: https://www.chronicle.com/article/how-artists-push-social-change (accessed 6 July 2021).

Mbembe, A. (2003), 'Necropolitics', trans. L. Meintjes, *Public Culture*, 15 (1): 11–40.

Mooney, J. and E. Pieper (2007), 'Militant Motherhood Re-Visited: Women's Participation and Political Power in Argentina and Chile', *History Compass*, 5 (3): 975–94.

Morrison, A. (2021), 'Exclusive: Black Lives Matter Opens Up about Its Finances', *Los Angeles Times*, 23 February. Available online: https://www.latimes.com/world-nation/story/2021-02-23/ap-exclusive-black-lives-matter-opens-up-about-its-finances (accessed 13 April 2023).

Nokes, G. R. (2013), *Breaking Chains: Slavery on Trial in the Oregon Territory*, Corvallis: Oregon State University Press.

Physicians for Human Rights (2020), '"Now They Seem to Just Want to Hurt Us": Dangerous Use of Crowd-Control Weapons Against Protesters and Medics in Portland, Oregon', PHR, 8 October. Available online: https://phr.org/our-work/resources/now-they-just-seem-to-want-to-hurt-us-portland-oregon (accessed 10 July 2021).

Puar, J. (2008), 'Q & A with Jasbir Puar', [Interview] *darkmatter: In the Ruins of Imperial CulturePostcolonial Sexuality* [3]. Available online: http://jasbirkpuar.com/interviews (accessed 31 January 2022).

Scholars at Risk Network (2021), 'Academic Freedom Monitoring Project'. Available online: https://www.scholarsatrisk.org/report/2021-05-29-al-beroni-university (accessed 20 August 2021).

Small, C. (1998), *Musicking: The Meanings of Performing and Listening*, Hanover: University Press of New England.

Strouse, A. W. (2017), 'Transcending the Job Market', *The Chronicle of Higher Education*, 8 March. Available online: http://www.chronicle.com/article/Transcending-the-Job-Market/239407?cid=at&utm_source=at&utm_medium=en&elqTrackId=f57cf45b0a8c442297ef38fea480233c&elq=8f96c8019f9c4bcb8395de63825a9288&elqaid=12882&elqat=1&elqCampaignId=5305 (accessed 19 March 2022).

United States Census Bureau (2020), 'QuickFacts: Portland city, Oregon'. Available online: https://www.census.gov/quickfacts/fact/table/portlandcityoregon/AGE295219 (accessed 17 February 2021).

Wilson, C. (2021), 'DHS Sent More than 750 Federal Officers, Spent Millions Responding to Portland Protests', *OPB*, 21 April, updated 22 April. Available online: https://www.opb.org/article/2021/04/21/dhsreport-says-750-federal-officers-sent-to-2020-protests-in-portland (accessed 4 August 2021).

Winick, S. (2014), 'Ring around the Rosie: Metafolklore, Rhyme and Reason', Library of Congress, *Folklife Today*, 24 July. Available online: https://blogs.loc.gov/folklife/2014/07/ring-around-the-rosie-metafolklore-rhyme-and-reason (accessed 10 August 2021).

Index

abuse 17, 77, 87–91, 94, 95
activism 1, 2, 8, 41, 217
   anti-racist 8, 210
   curatorial 6
   feminist 42
   imperatives of 215
   online art music 6
   pedagogy of 120
   political 46
   student-led 120
activist 45, 47, 118, 213
   BLM 119
   movements 101
   scholar- 6, 108–10
antiracism 77, 104, 118, 121, 127, 147, 149, 209, 215, 218
   pedagogy of 6, 126
antiracist 7, 8, 77, 105, 107, 115, 116, 147, 153, 209
   activism 210
   curriculum policies 105
   pedagogy 28, 126
   praxis 143
   training 106
authority 88, 91–5, 102, 160, 166, 169
   gendered patterns of 90
   hierarchies of 46
   institutional 5, 89
   power and 5, 91, 92, 94–6

Black, Indigenous and People of Colour (BIPOC) 4, 6, 7, 79, 142, 144, 145, 148, 150–3
Black Lives Matter 1, 6, 76, 101, 105, 115, 116, 118, 119, 121, 122, 142, 145, 146, 153, 209, 213

career 4, 7, 16, 17, 20–2, 26, 27, 32–4, 50–60, 63, 65, 70–3, 76, 77, 79, 81, 83, 101, 104, 108, 161, 173–5, 178, 179, 181, 182, 185–95, 198, 200, 205
   bourgeois 14, 76
   DIY 8, 173, 174, 179–81
   pathways 1, 32, 34, 50, 53, 56, 57, 174
   portfolio 3
   protean 55
   trajectories 7, 66, 173, 180, 181
class 1, 5, 8, 14, 16, 33, 38, 42, 43, 67, 76, 78, 82, 88, 89, 91, 92, 103, 108, 109, 121, 130–3, 151, 161, 174, 182, 186, 189, 200, 209, 215, 216
colonialism 5, 34, 35, 102, 106, 151
   anti- 35
   colonial 102–4
   colonialist 6
   decolonial 7
   imperialism and 103
   post- 75, 110
competition 2, 26, 50, 92, 132, 138, 159, 160, 161, 170
   band 132
   concerts and 33
   culture of 44
   ensemble 132
   violin 28, 30
competitive 2, 4, 38, 40, 43–5, 103, 132, 133, 147, 160, 161, 168, 169, 177
curricula 2, 4, 5, 7, 18, 22, 28, 45, 64, 66, 75, 76, 78–83, 101, 104, 110, 130, 131, 160, 168
   anti-racist and inclusive 107
   Black Curriculum report 6, 106, 108, 109
   curriculum 4, 15, 65, 70, 72, 73, 102, 132, 134, 151, 152, 166, 212
   decolonization of the curriculum 46
   decolonized curriculum 47
   decolonizing curriculum 105
   design 1, 2

diversity 2, 7, 31, 32, 34, 35, 39, 42, 78, 80, 101, 106, 107, 116, 119, 120, 125, 130, 132, 133, 140, 142, 145–53, 159, 162, 165, 201, 206, 212
  initiative 6, 105, 142
  token 3
  work 6, 28, 142

employability 1, 3, 4, 7, 15, 18, 21, 32, 35, 50, 51, 55–7, 59–61, 93, 94, 132, 186, 192
  employable 3, 26, 34, 107
employment 3, 8, 18, 21, 33–5, 47, 52, 54, 60, 93, 111, 162, 164, 167, 169, 176, 177, 186, 187, 193, 203, 206
  alternative 205
  pathways 46
  precarious 177, 204, 212
  self- 7
  un- 7
entrepreneur 40, 41, 173, 174, 176–82
  of the self 7
entrepreneurial 8, 65, 67, 174, 201, 204, 212
  approach 58
  attitude 58
  career 3
  mindset 65
  position 178
  skills 32
  universities 2
entrepreneurialism 7, 44, 177, 198, 201, 202, 204–6
entrepreneurship 3, 4, 8, 46, 50, 52, 58–60, 78, 79, 161, 173, 174, 181, 182
ethnicity 1, 34, 35, 46, 130, 131, 133, 134
equality 46, 94, 135, 147, 149, 150, 159, 182, 215, 218
  Equality Act 88
  Equality, Diversity and Inclusion (EDI) 101, 106–8
equity 2, 7, 22, 101, 102, 109, 111, 136, 142, 144–7, 149, 150, 152, 202, 212

feminist 5–7, 42, 75, 79, 120, 178, 187, 188
  feminism 75

harassment 89, 93, 94
  gender 88
  rape and 77
  sexual 1, 5, 17, 87–9, 92, 95, 187

inclusion 4, 6, 7, 18, 42, 45, 46, 78, 81, 92, 94, 101, 116, 130, 132–4, 136–40, 151, 215
inequalities 1, 5, 14, 46, 88, 89, 108, 109, 149, 161, 187, 188
  inequality 4, 41, 122, 149, 174
injustice 118, 122–4, 127, 139, 143, 150

justice 111, 116, 117, 212
  creative 2
  racial 142, 144, 148, 150, 151–3
  social 6, 75, 82, 105, 109, 137, 138, 216

labour market 8, 17, 21, 28, 50, 51, 55, 58–60, 106, 132, 186
  music 1, 3, 7, 13, 33, 47, 72, 105

meritocracy 4, 75, 77–9, 83, 121, 123
  meritocratic 22, 42, 76
#MeToo 1, 77, 87, 187

neoliberal 1–4, 6–8, 13, 15, 20, 22, 26, 27, 32–4, 38–44, 46, 47, 50, 51, 54, 56, 59, 64–6, 71–3, 78, 79, 81, 82, 87, 88, 94–6, 105, 106, 131–3, 135, 138–40, 159, 161, 168–70, 173–5, 177–9, 185, 186, 189, 191, 193, 198, 203, 206, 209, 210–2
neoliberalism 1, 2, 4, 5, 7, 8, 26, 27, 39, 41–3, 64–6, 77, 82, 87, 88, 96, 129, 130, 131, 134, 135, 138, 139, 159, 173, 175–7, 182, 192, 203, 209, 211, 218
neoliberalization 75, 199
  neoliberalizing 200

pedagogies 1, 5–7, 28, 45, 47, 101, 109, 129, 131, 133, 136, 137
pedagogy 45–7, 102, 108, 131, 133, 135, 137, 159–63, 166–70
  3D 6, 109

community-based   127
of activism   120
of anti-racism   6, 126
of unlearning   121
power   1, 4, 5, 17, 28, 30, 33, 35, 78, 81, 82, 88–96, 109, 144, 149–51, 153, 160, 167, 178, 187, 210–2, 216, 217
precarious(ness)   3, 4, 7, 18, 33, 38, 40, 47, 50, 58, 60, 174, 176, 177, 179, 181, 182, 186, 189, 190, 193, 204, 205, 209, 210
precarity   7, 8, 17, 42, 59, 63, 78, 177, 197–200, 202–6, 209, 210, 215, 216

queer   5, 7, 120, 178, 180, 187, 188, 213, 217

race   1, 6, 28, 34, 35, 46, 67, 78, 105, 106, 108–10, 118–21, 130, 131, 133, 142–4, 146, 148, 209, 215, 216
critical race theory (CRT)   6, 118, 120, 121, 142, 143
racialized   3, 5, 28, 67, 89, 91, 92, 94, 106, 179, 210
racism   1, 3, 5, 7, 28, 42, 46, 76, 77, 82, 102, 106, 115–20, 122, 127, 132, 142–7, 149, 185, 209, 211, 216

violence   5, 88, 91, 95, 117–9, 120, 121, 127, 143, 210, 213, 214

whiteness   5, 26–30, 32, 34, 35, 76, 77, 104, 143, 147, 149, 151, 152
white supremacy   29, 123, 127, 143, 152, 209, 211, 216

www.ingramcontent.com/pod-product-compliance
Lightning Source LLC
Chambersburg PA
CBHW071831300426
44116CB00009B/1513